The Jossey-Bass Nonprofit Sector Series also includes:

Nonprofit Boards and Leadership

Nonprofit Boards and Leadership

Cases on Governance, Change, and Board-Staff Dynamics

Miriam M. Wood, Editor

JOSSEY-BASS
A Wiley Company
www.josseybass.com

Published by

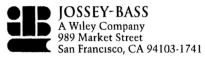 JOSSEY-BASS
A Wiley Company
989 Market Street
San Francisco, CA 94103-1741

www.josseybass.com

Jossey-Bass books and products are available through most bookstores. To contact
Jossey-Bass directly, call (888) 378-2537, fax to (800) 605-2665, or visit our website at
www.josseybass.com.

Substantial discounts on bulk quantities of Jossey-Bass books are available to
corporations, professional associations, and other organizations. For details and
discount information, contact the special sales department at Jossey-Bass.

We at Jossey-Bass strive to use the most environmentally sensitive paper stocks available to
us Our publications are printed on acid-free recycled stock whenever possible, and our
paper always meets or exceeds minimum GPO and EPA requirements.

Library of Congress Cataloging-in-Publication Data

Nonprofit boards and leadership : cases on governance, change, and
    board-staff dynamics / Miriam M. Wood, editor.
        p.   cm.—(The Jossey-Bass nonprofit sector series)
    Includes bibliographical references and index.
    ISBN 0-7879-0139-3
    1. Nonprofit organizations—Management.   2. Corporate governance.
3. Leadership. I. Wood, Miriam Mason. II. Series.
    HD62.6.N653   1996
    658'.048—dc20   95-24144

FIRST EDITION
HB Printing   10 9 8 7 6 5 4 3 2

The Jossey-Bass Nonprofit Sector Series

Contents

The Authors

Christy L. Beaudin is completing her doctoral studies in health services management and policy at the University of California, Los Angeles. A teaching assistant for three years in the areas of health care financing, organizational behavior, and delivery, Beaudin developed curricula for managed care courses taught through the Department of Health Services and UCLA Extension. She has also participated in research projects on health care and on nonprofit governance. After receiving her M.A. degree in social work from San Diego State University, Beaudin worked for fourteen years in the clinical, operations, and marketing areas of health care with Loma Linda Medical Center, Mercy Hospital in San Diego, Brotman Medical Center in Los Angeles, and National Medical Management Services in Washington, D.C. She provides health care consultation through C. L. Beaudin & Associates.

Henry Chauncey Jr., is lecturer and head of the Management Program in the Division of Health Policy and Administration, Department of Epidemiology and Public Health, Yale School of Medicine. Prior to joining the department, he was president of Gaylord Hospital in Wallingford, Connecticut; president of Science Park Development Corporation in New Haven; and secretary of Yale University. He received his B.A. degree (1957) from Yale College.

Ram A. Cnaan is an associate professor at the University of Pennsylvania School of Social Work. He received both his B.S.W. and M.S.W. from the Hebrew University in Jerusalem, Israel, and his Ph.D. in social work from the University of Pittsburgh. Cnaan's research focuses on volunteers in human services, voluntary action and organizations, community mental health, community organization from an international perspective, religiously based social service delivery, and policy practice. He has published numerous articles in these areas and serves on the editorial board of seven journals. Recently Cnaan was elected chair of the editorial board of *Nonprofit and Voluntary Sector Quarterly*. Currently he serves as a vice president for meetings of the Association of Researchers in Nonprofit Organizations and Voluntary Action.

Glenn Scott Davis is executive director of the New England Health Care Employees Union, District 1199, and the Connecticut Nursing Homes Training and Upgrading Fund. He received his B.A. degree (1981) in philosophy from the University of Bridgeport and his M.A. degree (1994) in liberal studies/social science from Wesleyan University. In 1992 he was a John D. Rockefeller III Fellow at the Program on Non-Profit Organizations, Institution for Social and Policy Studies, Yale University. His master's thesis was a history of the University of Bridgeport and he is currently working on a book about the University of Bridgeport and its affiliation with the Professors World Peace Academy.

Ronald C. Goodstein received his Ph.D. in business from the Fuqua School of Business at Duke University. He is assistant professor of marketing at the Anderson School of Management at UCLA. Goodstein has taught courses for the MBA, Fully Employed MBA, and Ph.D. programs on topics such as advertising, policy consumer behavior, elements of marketing, and management field study. He has published articles in *Advances in Consumer Research, Emotion in Advertising, Journal of Marketing Research, Journal of Consumer Research,* and *Journal of Marketing*. His work on Universal Pricing Code scanners has been cited by the National Institute of Standards and Measures as being among the definitive investigations in the field. He has received numerous teaching awards at UCLA and his teaching was recently recognized by the U.S. government, which awarded him an Academic Specialist Grant to teach his specialty at the University of Montevideo, Uruguay.

Bradford H. Gray received his Ph.D. (1973) from Yale University and is director of the Institution for Social and Policy Studies and the Program on Non-Profit Organizations at Yale, as well as professor (adjunct) of research in public health at Yale School of Medicine. He also holds an appointment in Yale's Department of Sociology.

He is author of *The Profit Motive and Patient Care: The Changing Accountability of Doctors and Hospitals* (Harvard University Press, 1991) and *Human Subjects in Medical Experimentation* (Wiley, 1975), and he is editor of *The New Health Care for Profit* (National Academy Press, 1983), *For-Profit Enterprise in Health Care* (National Academy Press, 1986), and *Controlling Costs and Changing Patient Care? The Role of Utilization Management* (with Marilyn J. Field, 1989). Gray has served as consultant to several governmental agencies, foundations, trade associations, and the National Academy of Sciences.

Peter Dobkin Hall is associate director and research scientist at the Program on Non-Profit Organizations, Yale University. Hall's published work includes *The Organization of American Culture, 1700–1900: Institutions, Elites, and the Origins of American Nationality* (1982); *Inventing the Nonprofit Sector and Other Essays on Philanthropy, Voluntarism and Nonprofit Organizations* (1992); and *Lives in Trust: The Fortunes of Dynastic Families in Late Twentieth Century America* (with George E. Marcus, 1992). Hall has served on the boards of churches, museums, and neighborhood organizations, and as a member of municipal planning, zoning, and historic district commissions.

John C. Lammers is assistant professor of organizational and health communication at the University of California at Santa Barbara and adjunct assistant professor of health services at the UCLA School of Public Health. He received his B.A. degree in psychology from Humboldt State College and his M.A. degree and Ph.D. in sociology from the University of California, Davis. He was a postdoctoral fellow in mental health systems and research at Stanford University and has served on the faculties of the University of Louisville, the University of California, Berkeley, and the University of Colorado. His current research and teaching interests include measuring quality improvement programs in veterans' hospitals, leadership in public health, and nonprofit sector governance.

Carl Milofsky is professor of sociology at Bucknell University. He is editor of *Nonprofit and Voluntary Sector Quarterly,* a scholarly journal sponsored by the Association for Research on Nonprofit Organizations and Voluntary Action and by the Program on Non-Profit Organizations at Yale University. He was editor of *Community*

Organizations: Studies in Resource Mobilization and Exchange (Oxford University Press, 1988), and has written extensively on the sociology of special education. He received his Ph.D. in sociology from the University of California, Berkeley.

Gwen Moore is associate professor of sociology at the State University of New York at Albany, where she is also director of the Institute for Research on Women. She received her A.B. degree (1966) in sociology and anthropology from Bucknell University and her M.A. (1971) and Ph.D. (1977) degrees in sociology from New York University. A former Fulbright scholar in Germany (1986–87), she is coeditor with J. Allen Whitt of the series of annual volumes *Research in Politics and Society* published by JAI Press.

Nancy E. Morrison received her B.A. degree (1993) in sociology and English from Bucknell University. She is currently a graduate student at Boston University School of Theology.

Lisa Silverman Pickard is a senior director in the Community Investments Division at the United Way of Massachusetts Bay. At this organization (1985-present) and formerly at the United Way of the National Capital Area in Washington, D.C. (1977–1985), she has held various positions, focusing her work on grantmaking, strategic planning, policy development, volunteer management, and agency/community relations. She received her B.S. degree (1974) in elementary education and her M.S.W. degree (1977) from Syracuse University. She served on the board of the Wellesley Community Children's Center from 1991–1995.

Judith R. Saidel is executive director of the Center for Women in Government, and research assistant professor in the Department of Public Administration and Policy, State University of New York at Albany. She teaches "Issues in Not-For-Profit Management" and "Nonprofits and Public Policy" in the Graduate School of Public Affairs. Her primary research interest is the relationship between government and the nonprofit sector. She is coauthor with Sharon S. Dawes of *The State and The Voluntary Sector, A Report of New York State Project 2000* (1988) and has published several book chapters. Her articles on nonprofit issues have appeared in *Nonprofit and Vol-*

untary Sector Quarterly, Public Administration Review, and *Nonprofit Management & Leadership.* She received her Ph.D. degree in public administration and her M.A. degree in American history from the State University of New York at Albany and her B.A. degree in political science from Wellesley College.

Mark Senak earned a J.D. degree (1981) at Brooklyn Law School, after receiving his undergraduate degree (1977) in rhetoric from the University of Illinois. He volunteered in 1982 with the Gay Men's Health Crisis as one of a small pool of lawyers who began doing pro bono work for people with AIDS. In 1985, he became the director of legal services for the Gay Men's Health Crisis and chair of the AIDS Resource Center in New York, and in 1988, he became director of client services for AIDS Project Los Angeles, the nation's second largest AIDS service organization. Since 1991, he has been a member of the AIDS Action Council Public Policy Committee, based in Washington, D.C., and is now director of strategic planning for AIDS Project Los Angeles. He has been a frequent author regarding various aspects of HIV, and his first book on AIDS and the law is being published by Plenum in the spring of 1996.

Melissa Middleton Stone is assistant professor of management policy at the Boston University School of Management, where she is also a core faculty member of the Program on Public and Nonprofit Management. She is a deputy editor of *Nonprofit and Voluntary Sector Quarterly* and an associate editor of *Nonprofit Management & Leadership.* She received her B.A. degree (1970) in political science from the University of Pennsylvania, and her M.A. degree in public and private management (1982) and Ph.D. degree (1989) in organizational behavior from Yale University. Prior to pursuing her graduate training, Stone founded and managed several nonprofit organizations in the social services field.

J. Allen Whitt is professor of sociology and urban affairs at the University of Louisville. He is also a research affiliate of the Program on Non-Profit Organizations at Yale University. Now actively pursuing research on networks among nonprofit organizations, he is coauthor with Joyce Rothschild of *The Cooperative Workplace* (1986), winner of the 1987 C. Wright Mills Award. With Gwen Moore, he is series editor of the annual *Research in Politics and Society* published by JAI Press. He received his B.A. (1964) from the University of Texas at Austin and his M.A. degree (1972) and Ph.D. degree (1975) from the University of California, Santa Barbara.

Candace Widmer is a teacher, researcher, and consultant to nonprofit organizations. She is currently professor of human services and sociology at Elmira College in Elmira, New York, where she is also director of the Human Services Program. She received her B.A. degree (1965) in biology from Gettysburg College, her M.A. degree (1969) in developmental biology and genetics from Temple University, and her Ph.D. degree (1984) in human service studies, organizational behavior, and public policy from Cornell University. She has worked as a consultant with a variety of grassroots and national nonprofit organizations, and has written on many aspects of nonprofit management, including the roles and responsibilities of nonprofit trustees, recruitment and retention of board members, role conflict, and the participation of those who are "minorities" within their organizations. She is a research affiliate of Yale's Program on Non-Profit Organizations and a Senior Fellow of the Cheswick Center.

Miriam M. Wood is an independent scholar and editor of the series Cases in Nonprofit Governance published by Yale University's Program on Non-Profit Organizations. Her research focuses on the leadership and management of charitable nonprofit organizations, on program evaluation, and on the application of research to practice. Author of *Trusteeship in the Private College* (Johns Hopkins University Press, 1985), she is also author or editor of various case studies and working papers, including *Short Takes on Nonprofit Governance* (Indiana University Center on Philanthropy, 1994). Her articles have appeared in *Harvard Business Review* and *Educational Record,* and she was recipient of the 1992–1993 Peter F. Drucker Prize for the best scholarly article in *Nonprofit Management & Leadership.* A graduate of Wellesley College with an M.A. degree from Stanford University, Wood received her Ed.D. from Harvard University. She has served on the governing boards of a child-care agency, hospital, liberal arts college, and library, among others.

Nonprofit Boards and Leadership

Governance and Leadership in Theory and Practice

Miriam M. Wood

This book contains thirteen teaching cases based on real-life issues in governance and leadership encountered by nonprofit board members, executive directors, presidents, and their consultants. Each case asks the reader to make a decision based on information supplied in the text and exhibits. All the cases focus on charitable nonprofits—those organizations qualifying as tax exempt under Section 501(c)(3) of the Internal Revenue Code.

Although college and university courses and formal programs that focus on nonprofit organizations are now well established, materials that examine the leadership nexus—the governing board and the chief administrator—usually consist of advice and exhortations to do better. This book takes a different approach, requiring the reader to develop a solution to the problem at hand.

To provide a rigorous intellectual challenge, questions for discussion and an annotated interdisciplinary bibliography are included at the end of each case. The bibliographies contain readings from the scholarly literature in nonprofit studies, sociology, business management, organizational behavior, social work administration, education, public health administration, political science, economics, history, and public policy, as well as the related "plain English" literature developed for board members and administrators. Among the readings are many of the scholarly touchstones in the study of nonprofits, as well as topical articles related to each case. Concepts and theories are not stated explicitly in the cases but are embedded in them as one of several analytic approaches that each case supports. For instructors, *Teaching Notes for Nonprofit Boards and Leadership* are available at no charge from Jossey-Bass.

The Audience

The cases are designed for graduate students, professors, and other professionals interested in problem solving and governance in charitable nonprofit organizations. The book may also interest readers seeking familiarity with a range of nonprofit organizations and issues in governance and leadership.

The cases can function as the core of a course syllabus on non-profit organizations, whether the course is taught in a school of management or business, social work administration, public health, education, or arts and sciences. They can also be used as examples of theory in action in courses in organizational behavior, sociology, social work administration, and public policy. In addition, an individual case used in a brief training session involving a variety of participants can provide a common medium for transcending differences in discussants' experiences and backgrounds.

Perspectives on Change, Governance, and Leadership

Organizational change, governance, and leadership are conceptual touchstones in all thirteen cases in this book.

Organizational Change

The familiar notion that reality is socially constructed (Berger and Luckman, 1967) is subsumed and reframed in these cases by the assumption that social reality is dynamic (Sztompka, 1994). Anyone who has worked in a charitable nonprofit organization or served on its governing board or studied its behavior knows that such organizations are never static: they change continually, influenced by the interaction of human volition and social structure. This constant activity is both individual and collective, and the social structures it generates may be formally constituted, as are organizations, or informally sustained, as are interpersonal networks.

Governance as an Evolving Concept

Governance rather than management is the focus of the cases. Management consists of decisions and actions linked to the performance of either an organizational subunit or the organization as a whole (Boyatzis, 1982, p. 17). Governance is a broader concept than management; it consists of decisions and actions linked to defining an organization's mission, to establishing its policies, and to determining the control mechanisms it will use to allocate power, establish decision-making processes, and set up procedures for performing specific tasks (Peterson and Mets, 1987, pp. 3–4). However, the realities of organizational life are far more problematic than this definition implies.

Contemporary conceptions of governance in charitable nonprofits (as distinguished from business corporations) have their antecedents in higher education in the 1960s. At that time, governance implied the so-called dual organization of faculty and administration. Within that structure, the faculty claimed authority to control the curriculum, and the administration was expected to "consult" with the faculty about any administrative policy or decision that impinged upon the educational program. From this precedent evolved the concept that governance implies willingness to confer with groups potentially affected by a decision.

Today governance entails consultation by administrators and/or governing boards with various "stakeholders," defined as "all those parties who either affect or are affected by an [organization's] actions, behavior, and policies" (Mitroff, 1983, p. 4; see also Neubauer and Demb, 1993, p. 202). Stakeholders external to a charitable nonprofit include public and private funders; elected and appointed government officials and their staffs at the city, state, and federal levels; families or other advocates of the recipients of charitable services; accrediting organizations; professional associations; any neighborhood, city, or other community of which an organization is perceived to be a part; and increasingly, the media. Internal stakeholders include service recipients such as students; employees; and the governing board itself. Stakeholders comprise those groups to which an organization perceives itself—or is perceived to be—accountable. In other words, one way to measure an organization's accountability is to assess its structures and processes of governance.

When higher education administrators in the 1960s could not resolve disagreements with faculty or students or other constituencies, the governing board of the institution, usually a board of trustees, had authority to step in as "the court of final appeal" (Nason, 1974, p. 23). From that precedent arose the concept that governance implies something more than administration or management or implementation; in practice, the word governance is usually reserved for decision making in which the governing board, situated at the apex of the organizational structure, plays a role. Two theoretical models of governance—the political and the paradoxical—are especially illuminating.

Governance as Politics: A Challenge to Leadership

The concept of governance-by-stakeholders is more compatible with the political model of decision making than with bureaucratic or consensual models (Baldridge, Curtis, Ecker, and Riley, 1977, pp. 13–19; Bacharach and Mitchell, 1987, pp. 405–17). In politicized settings, leadership behaviors that are likely to be effective include "getting people to clarify what matters most, in what balance, with what trade-offs" (Heifetz, 1994, p. 22). The effective leader of competing stakeholders is able to persuade the decision maker(s) for each stakeholder group to compromise somewhat on the commitments made to "home" interests (Heifetz, 1994, p. 119). This ideal is not exemplified, however, by the governing boards described in the cases in this book. Instead, in "Conflicting Managerial Cultures in a Museum" (Chapter Six), a few board members attempt to exert leadership by fiat; or in "The Governing Board Faces Rebellion in the Ranks" (Chapter Seven) and "Confronting Crisis" (Chapter Eight), the board finds itself in a reactive posture when unexpected personnel problems arise; or in "Mission Versus Revenue" (Chapter Twelve), a board is disempowered by corporate merger.

A milieu of differing stakeholder interests recalls Cohen and March's observation that "an organization is a collection of choices looking for problems, issues and feelings looking for decision situations in which they might be aired, solutions looking for issues to which they might be the answer, and decision makers looking for work" (1974, p. 81). At any time, as the cases illustrate, an array of topics is floating around an organization's environment, and the leaders of interest groups and coalitions formed within the organization or across its boundaries engage in negotiations—often unacknowledged and perhaps unconscious—that determine which topics are to be considered governance issues. The choice of issues varies over time at both the organizational and societal levels, but at present, topics widely recognized as appropriate for board attention include mission, strategy, organizational performance, and accountability.

The political model implies that governance performs three critical functions. First, it provides a consultative framework for airing and mediating differences of opinion among stakeholders whose right to participate in governance has been established. Second, the consultative framework offers organizational leaders precedents for conducting negotiations when a new individual or group seeks recognition as a party to governance. If the new group uses whatever techniques of power it can muster—picketing, the media, a letter-writing campaign—to establish its right to influence governance decisions, resolution usually occurs when the unrecognized stakeholder relinquishes power tactics in return for acceptance by the leadership as a participant in the governance process. Third, the ongoing practices of governance legitimate and institutionalize changes in relationships among stakeholders.

Of course, the view that a charitable nonprofit is a dynamic entity enmeshed in a changing environment populated by stakeholders to whom the organization is variously accountable is inconsistent with certain conventional interpretations of the role and significance of the nonprofit sector. For example, the interdependence of many charitable nonprofits and government units is incompatible with the assumption that the sector is "independent." Also, the dynamic qualities of charitable organizations and their environments are inconsistent with the notion that a certain set of behaviors constitutes "good" governing board practice. Most significantly, the issues played out in these cases cannot always be reconciled with the premise that charitable nonprofit organizations are indispensable instruments of the public interest in a civil society.

Governance as Paradox: A Challenge to Accountability

Nonprofit governance can also be modeled as a series of paradoxes arising from contradictions embedded in law. State statutes provide

that the board as a unit, not its individual members, has the authority to govern an organization. Yet once the governing board appoints an agent—the chief administrator, executive director, or
president—to be in charge of the organization's day-to-day affairs,
the conditions of paradox are met and are expressed through three
"structural tensions" (Demb and Neubauer, 1992, pp. 5–7).

The first tension arises because, although the board is legally
responsible for the organization, the staff has the knowledge,
human resources, and time required to fulfill that responsibility.
Social scientists refer to this paradox as the principal-agent problem, in which the principal (for example, the governing board)
appoints an agent (the chief administrator) to act in the principal's place but cannot fully control what the agent does. A second
paradox concerns the board's capacity to add value to an organization. Convention holds that a board can fulfill this expectation
through the exercise of dispassionate judgment. However, accumulating the knowledge required for perceptive critique requires
reliance on the administrative staff, thus undercutting the board's
independence. A third structural tension emerges when a board is
made up of outstanding individual performers. The paradox is that
an individualistic orientation is inconsistent with the group orientation implicit in board membership.

Numerous books and articles have been written defending the
proposition that a part-time, absentee governing board, whether
overseeing a charity or a business, can address substantive issues in
an accountable fashion in an environment both political and paradoxical. Boards of charitable nonprofits are urged to become
"more involved" and to concern themselves with "what human
needs are satisfied, for whom, and at what cost" (Carver, 1990,
pp. 193, 35). In the for-profit sector, where stakeholder insurgency
(especially on the part of institutional investors) coexists with "fundamental problems" of governance resulting from "subtle failures
in the decision-making process," boards are urged to "foster effective decisions and reverse failed policies" (Pound, 1995, pp. 90–
91, 93).

In contrast, the cases in this book do not suggest prescriptive
solutions. Instead, the reader is invited to participate in a political
environment in which the governing board is constrained by structural paradoxes and by other dimensions of governance, especially

mission, industry, and strategy; history and culture; organizational form; networks; and funding arenas.

Mission, Industry, and Strategy. Charitable nonprofits with similar missions naturally find themselves dealing with the same public and private entities, and the result of these relationships is an organizational field or "industry" (DiMaggio and Powell, 1983), the dynamics of which are illustrated in "Planning in Interdependent Environments" (Chapter Two) and "The Evolving Board-Executive Relationship at a Women's Shelter" (Chapter Five). An organizational field develops its own distinct agenda of governance issues, as suggested by "The Public Interest and Tax Exemptions for Nonprofit Hospitals" (Chapter One), because all of the individual organizations are responding to the same pattern of external stimuli, such as state regulations, funders' requirements, professional associations, and the activities of organizations perceived as "leaders" in the organizational field.

Notwithstanding differences among industries, at any point in time certain governance issues may be prominent throughout the entire charitable universe. Currently, for example, resource development and accountability are key governance issues in virtually all fields, as demonstrated in "The Evolving Board-Executive Relationship at a Women's Shelter" (Chapter Five), "Dissolution or Survival" (Chapter Eleven), and "Mission Versus Revenue" (Chapter Twelve).

An organization's plans for implementing its mission in the context of its particular organizational field are usually referred to as *strategy*. Effective strategy has been defined as the outcome of trade-offs between four elements: (1) the strengths of the organization, (2) the opportunities in the environment, (3) what organizational participants want to do, and (4) what is legal, moral, and ethical (Andrews, 1980, p. 30). The products of strategic planning—including mission statements, vision statements, strategies, and goals—are attempts to make the past meaningful and to inspire collective action in the future, as illustrated by "Planning in Interdependent Environments" (Chapter Two), and "Strategic Planning at AIDS Project Los Angeles" (Chapter Thirteen). Recently, a useful distinction has been proposed between strategic planning and strategic thinking. Strategic planning is "about analysis—about breaking down a goal or set of intentions into steps," while strategic thinking is "about synthesis" and "an integrative perspective on the enterprise" (Mintzberg, 1994, p. 108).

Organizational History and Culture. The interwoven strands of an organization's history and culture constitute another dimension affecting governance and leadership. Although the existence of an organizational field fosters conformity among organizations, the details of an organization's history and the characteristics of its culture remain a critical variable in understanding why a particular governance decision is up for action at a particular time. In practice, a history of shared experience is the source of an organization's culture; culture is the "pattern of basic assumptions," largely unconscious, developed to cope with the problems of integrating internal activities and adapting to the environment (Schein, 1985, p. 9). The constraints of history and culture are prominent in "Planning in Interdependent Environments" (Chapter Two), "The Evolving Board-Executive Relationship at a Women's Shelter" (Chapter Five), "Conflicting Managerial Cultures in a Museum" (Chapter Six), "Confronting Crisis" (Chapter Eight), "Mission Versus Revenue" (Chapter Twelve), and "Strategic Planning at AIDS Project Los Angeles" (Chapter Thirteen).

Organizational Form. The influence of organizational form on governance and leadership is clarified by a typology developed by Mintzberg (Mintzberg, 1979, pp. 305–480). The *simple structure* is the "one-man or one-woman band," often a grassroots organization like those in "The Grantmaker" (Chapter Three). Such organizations have little or no administrative structure, a loose division of labor among volunteer participants, and a chief administrator who may be the only paid worker. A second organizational form is the *professional bureaucracy,* as appears in "Dissolution or Survival" (Chapter Eleven) and "Mission Versus Revenue" (Chapter Twelve). In this model, specialists and professionals work relatively independently of one another but closely with the clients they serve, and performance standards are strongly influenced by professional associations, state regulators, and other external agents. A third model is the *divisionalized form.* It consists of quasi-autonomous entities coupled more or less tightly by a central administration.

Examples include nonprofits with franchises (Oster, 1992), such as United Way of America and hospital chains with subsidiaries. These franchises are the subjects, respectively, of "Investing Donor Dollars at the United Way" (Chapter Four) and "Mission Versus Revenue" (Chapter Twelve).

Networks. The relationships of authority that formally define governance and leadership are overlaid with or supplemented by informal networks based on relationships of generalized mutual exchange and benefit enacted through conversation, advice, and friendship (Nohria, 1992). Many political transactions are conducted through these informal networks, some of which cross organizational or even sectoral boundaries. In "The Public Interest and Tax Exemptions for Nonprofit Hospitals" (Chapter One), a senator's chief donors are also trustees of hospitals that will be affected by the senator's vote on a bill abolishing tax exemptions. In other instances, an informal network may provide links within a single organization, as in "The Governing Board Faces Rebellion in the Ranks" (Chapter Seven), in which an employee of the agency talks to his mother-in-law, who is a board member, about the shortcomings of the executive director.

Through their network ties, members of a governing board span the boundary between the organization and its environment (Middleton, 1987, p. 141) and provide information from a variety of sources. How a governing board can systematically go about establishing itself in a central position in a community's organizational network—and therefore be in an improved position to capitalize on flows of information and resources—is the subject of "Using Community Networks to Diversify a Board" (Chapter Ten). A more typical approach to the same goal—drastically changing the composition of the governing board and creating an advisory committee—is illustrated in "Outgrowing the Governing Board" (Chapter Nine).

Funding Arenas. Although funders do not always exercise their potential clout, they are perceived as important stakeholders by boards and administrators and therefore influence governance and leadership. Funders may be aggregated into seven arenas: federal government, state government, local government, businesses, foundations, religious organizations, and autonomous fundraising activities (Milofsky, 1988). Of particular interest are government arenas because government grants, contracts, and reimbursements account for more than 30 percent of the revenues of charitable nonprofits (Salamon, 1992, p. 26). Although one recent study finds that individual board members sometimes play a role in "facilitat[ing] and maintain[ing]" the government-organization relationship (Saidel, 1993, p. 48), most studies say that reliance on government funds results in greater control by the executive director and staff and a lessened leadership role for the board (Grønbjerg, 1993, pp. 271–272; Kramer, 1984, p. 195). The illustrative cases are "Planning in Interdependent Environments" (Chapter Two), "The Evolving Board-Executive Relationship at a Women's Shelter" (Chapter Five), "Confronting Crisis" (Chapter Eight), and "Outgrowing the Governing Board" (Chapter Nine).

Overview of the Cases

The thirteen cases are divided into three sections. Part One, "The Role of External Stakeholders in Governance," examines charitable nonprofits as they appear from the vantage point of external stakeholders. The first case, "The Public Interest and Tax Exemptions for Nonprofit Hospitals" by Bradford H. Gray, Henry Chauncey Jr., and Miriam M. Wood, illustrates the problematic character of charitable status by asking the reader to play the role of a U.S. senator and to vote yea or nay on continuing tax-exempt status for nonprofit hospitals. Melissa Middleton Stone's "Planning in Interdependent Environments: The Local Association for Retarded Citizens" describes what happens when the state agency on which the focal organization is financially dependent considers strategic planning to be the state's role and not the role of its nonprofit contractors. In Wood's "The Grantmaker," the reader-as-program-officer must accommodate her personal philosophy of philanthropy with her foundation's priorities in evaluating the proposals of applicant agencies. The section concludes with Lisa Silverman Pickard and Melissa Middleton Stone's role-playing exercise, "Investing Donor Dollars at the United Way," which illustrates the influence of interpersonal dynamics on group decision making when community volunteers allocate monies to local agencies.

Part Two, "Complexities in the Board-Staff Relationship," examines decision making at the nexus of organizational leadership. In Carl Milofsky and Nancy E. Morrison's "The Evolving Board-Executive Relationship at a Women's Shelter," the agency is threatened by ongoing friction among various coalitions in the agency and community over the proper interpretation of the organization's feminist mission. Peter Dobkin Hall's case about a history museum focuses on disagreement between the executive director and the board chair about the board's ethics, role, and decision making, which are shown to be a function of conflicting managerial cultures. In "The Governing Board Faces Rebellion in the Ranks," Candace Widmer describes an agency for the developmentally disabled in which staff members threaten to resign because of their objections to the executive director. In Ram A. Cnaan's "Confronting Crisis: When Should the Board Step In?" the elite, hands-off board of a large, multisite housing and social services agency suddenly learns that millions of dollars of debt threaten the organization's survival. Issues of board member competence are raised in Judith R. Saidel's "Outgrowing the Governing Board: A Conundrum" when dependence on government funding prompts the executive director to suggest appointing an advisory committee or reducing the number of clients' parents who serve on the board. In J. Allen Whitt and Gwen Moore's "Using Community Networks to Diversify the Board," a nominating committee discusses who among potential board members would contribute most to the organization's welfare.

Part Three, "Interpreting Mission and Accountability," examines the potential and limitations of the governing board in accommodating differing stakeholder views while also fulfilling its role as guardian of the public interest. In Glenn Scott Davis's "Dissolution or Survival: The University of Bridgeport and the Unification Church," unresolved conflicts among constituencies coupled with financial exigencies muddy the waters of governing board accountability. In John C. Lammers and Christy L. Beaudin's "Mission Versus Revenue: The California Hospital Medical Center," the community-oriented mission identified by the board clashes with the revenue-generating policies of the hospital's corporate parent. The section concludes with "Strategic Planning at AIDS Project Los Angeles," in which Beaudin, Mark Senak, and Ronald C. Goodstein illustrate how an expanding client base, a growing organization, and proliferating constituencies make designing a planning process an intellectual and moral task of the first order.

The Data

All cases, except for the first one, are based on actual events. Some authors promised anonymity to the board members, administrators, and other staff who spoke with them about the problems and challenges of governance and leadership, and in these cases the accompanying exhibits are disguised, although based on real data. Undisguised organizations include the United Way of Massachusetts Bay, the California Hospital Medical Center, and AIDS Project Los Angeles. Two other organizations, the University of Bridgeport and the Unification Church, are undisguised, but the case in which they appear is built around a fictional character.

Acknowledgments

The Program on Non-Profit Organizations at Yale University provided auspices for developing the cases in this book through the Project on the Changing Dimensions of Trusteeship, directed by Peter Dobkin Hall. Funding for the project was provided by the Lilly Endowment, Inc. Undertakings such as this book, which integrates issues from the worlds of research and practice, have been encouraged by Craig Dykstra, D. Susan Wisely, and other members of the Endowment's Leadership Education Committee. For the committee's sustained intellectual and financial support, Peter Dobkin Hall joins me in expressing gratitude.

I am indebted to Melissa Middleton Stone of Boston University for her insightful and faithful colleagueship throughout the development of this book; to Rikki Abzug of New York University for a felicitous offer of assistance; and to Shirley S. Howard, whose secretarial and administrative skills made possible the timely completion of a manuscript involving eighteen authors.

Chambersburg, Pennsylvania   Miriam M. Wood
August 1995

References

Andrews, K. R. "Directors' Responsibility for Corporate Strategy." *Harvard Business Review,* 1980, *58*(6), 30–35.

Bacharach, S. B., and Mitchell, S. M. "The Generation of Practical Theory: Schools as Political Organizations." In J. W. Lorsch (ed.), *Handbook of Organizational Behavior.* Englewood Cliffs, N.J.: Prentice Hall, 1987.

Baldridge, J. V., Curtis, D. V., Ecker, G. P., and Riley, G. L. "Alternative Models of Governance in Higher Education." In J. V. Baldridge and G. L. Riley (eds.), *Governing Academic Organizations: New Problems, New Perspectives.* Berkeley: McCutchan, 1977.

Boyatzis, R. E. *The Competent Manager: A Model for Effective Governance.* New York: Wiley, 1982.

Berger, P., and Luckman, T. *The Social Construction of Reality: A Treatise in the Sociology of Knowledge.* Garden City, N.Y.: Anchor Doubleday, 1967.

Calder, B. J. "An Attribution Theory of Leadership." In B. M. Staw and G. R. Salancik (eds.), *New Directions in Organizational Behavior.* Chicago: St. Clair, 1977.

Carver, J. *Boards That Make a Difference: A New Design for Leadership in Nonprofit and Public Organizations.* San Francisco: Jossey-Bass, 1990.

Cohen, M. D., and March, J. G. *Leadership and Ambiguity: The American College President.* New York: McGraw-Hill, 1974.

Demb, A., and Neubauer, F. F. *The Corporate Board: Confronting the Paradoxes.* New York: Oxford University Press, 1992.

DiMaggio, P., and Powell, W. W. "The Iron Cage Revisited: Institutional Isomorphism and Collective Rationality in Organizational Fields." *American Sociological Review,* April 1983, pp. 147–60.

Grønbjerg, K. A. *Understanding Nonprofit Funding: Managing Revenues in Social Services and Community Development Organizations.* San Francisco: Jossey-Bass, 1993.

Heifetz, R. A. *Leadership Without Easy Answers.* Cambridge, Mass.: Harvard University Press, 1994.

Kramer, R. M. "A Framework for the Analysis of Board-Executive Relationships in Voluntary Agencies." In F. S. Schwartz (ed.), *Voluntarism and Social Work Practice.* New York: University Press of America, 1984.

Middleton, M. "Nonprofit Boards of Directors: Beyond the Governance Function." In W. W. Powell (ed.), *The Nonprofit Sector: A Research Handbook.* New Haven, Conn.: Yale University Press, 1987.

Milofsky, C. "The Structure of Funding Arenas for Neighborhood Based Organizations." In C. Milofsky (ed.), *Community Organizations: Studies in Resource Mobilization and Exchange.* New York: Oxford University Press, 1988.

Mintzberg, H. *The Structuring of Organizations.* Englewood Cliffs, N.J.: Prentice Hall, 1979.

Mintzberg, H. "The Fall and Rise of Strategic Planning." *Harvard Business Review,* 1994, *72*(1), 107–114.

Mitroff, I. I. *Stakeholders of the Organizational Mind.* San Francisco: Jossey-Bass, 1983.

Nason, J. W. *The Future of Trusteeship.* Washington, D.C.: Association of Governing Boards of Universities and Colleges, 1974.

Neubauer, F. F., and Demb, A. "Corporate Governance: A Burning Issue." In B. Sutton (ed.), *The Legitimate Corporation: Essential Readings in Business Ethics and Corporate Governance.* Cambridge, Mass.: Basil Blackwell, 1993.

Nohria, N. "Is the Network Perspective a Useful Way of Studying Organizations?" In N. Nohria and R. G. Eccles (eds.), *Networks and Organizations.* Boston, Mass.: Harvard Business School, 1992.

Oster, S. M. "Nonprofit Organizations as Franchise Operations." *Nonprofit Management & Leadership,* 1992, *2*(3), 223–238.

Peterson, M., and Mets, L. *Key Resources on Higher Education Governance, Management, and Leadership.* San Francisco, Calif.: Jossey-Bass, 1987.

Pound, J. "The Promise of the Governed Corporation." *Harvard Business Review,* 1995, *73*(2), 89–98.

Saidel, J. R. "The Board Role in Relation to Government." In D. R. Young and others (eds.), *Governing, Leading, and Managing Nonprofit Organizations.* San Francisco: Jossey-Bass, 1993.

Salamon, L. M. *America's Nonprofit Sector: A Primer.* New York: The Foundation Center, 1992.

Schein, E. H. *Organizational Culture and Leadership.* San Francisco: Jossey-Bass, 1985.

Sztompka, P. *The Sociology of Social Change.* Cambridge, Mass.: Basil Blackwell, 1994.

The Role of External Stakeholders in Governance

Embedded in the four cases in Part One is the dynamic of resource dependence, whereby organizations accommodate to some extent the preferences of funders. For example, hospitals generate community service reports to substantiate their contribution to the public welfare; neighborhood organizations conform to the "priorities of the moment" of their funders; and virtually all agencies "play games with funders" by adjusting programs and proposals to fit criteria issued by government agencies, private foundations, and federated funders like United Way. As sociologist W. Richard Scott observes (1987, p. 111), "No organization is self-sufficient; all must engage in exchanges with the environment as a condition of their survival. The need to acquire resources creates dependencies between organizations and outside units. . . . Economic dependencies give rise to political problems and may succumb to political solutions."

In recent years, political consequences have followed from changes in the scale and economic behavior of certain larger nonprofits, notably hospitals, and doubts about their "charitable" functions have been raised. Are hospitals actually commercial enterprises masquerading as charities and reaping a windfall at taxpayers' expense? In the first case in Part One, "The Public Interest and Tax Exemptions for Nonprofit Hospitals," by Gray, Chauncey, and Wood, this question is translated into an issue of public policy.

The case, fictional in its particulars, suggests that the 501(c)(3) designation is conditional for nonprofit hospitals and, by implication, for the entire charitable nonprofit sector. The case demonstrates that moral and ethical issues of accountability are being played out in public policy arenas, including state courts, and that charitable status is a political agreement subject to the pulls and tugs of powerful external stakeholders.

External stakeholders also exert enormous control over the funding streams of charitable nonprofits. Government funding in particular is accompanied by control mechanisms that sometimes reduce an organization's capacity to pursue its mission on its own terms and increase its risk of being "coopted into the political agenda" of the funding agency (Grønbjerg, 1993, pp. 193, 185). In Stone's "Planning in Interdependent Environments: The Local Association for Retarded Citizens," a membership organization depends heavily on a single state agency for funding. What kind of planning, this case asks, is "strategic" in such an environment? The planning process is complicated by differences of opinion within an important stakeholder group—the parents of clients—about what the agency's mission ought to be.

Dependence on external stakeholders for resources is as acute in grassroots enterprises as in more developed charitable nonprofits. Sometimes, grassroots founders are volunteers who exhaust themselves trying to implement an organization's mission before seeking funds to pay someone else to do the work. When the first proposal is submitted, the "emerging" organization finds itself competing with other grassroots organizations that are slightly more developed and are engaged in their second or third year of solicitations. In Wood's "The Grantmaker: Inner City Organizations Compete for Funds," four neighborhood-based organizations are seeking grants from the city's community foundation. The organizations represent distinct, if overlapping, groups of stakeholders, and the grantmaking officer must decide which organizations are most likely to achieve results that advance the foundation's priorities. Implicit in this case is the problematic role of a funder in a grantee organization's governance structure.

An external stakeholder important to many charitable nonprofits is the local chapter of United Way of America. In Pickard and Stone's "Investing Donor Dollars at the United Way: A Role-

Playing Exercise," participants evaluate the demands implicit in United Way recipient status and review materials indicating that an organization may chafe at those demands. The exercise provides an opportunity to compare the constraints on decision making experienced by the paid program officer in "The Grantmaker" with those that develop when volunteers work in groups to divide monies among competing community organizations. Analyzing the decision-making processes of the role-playing groups also offers insights into other settings where public or private funds are allocated through a similar process of group decision making.

References

Grønbjerg, K. A. *Understanding Nonprofit Funding: Managing Revenues in Social Services and Community Development Organizations.* San Francisco: Jossey-Bass, 1993.

Scott, W. R. *Organizations: Rational, Natural, and Open Systems.* Englewood Cliffs, N.J.: Prentice Hall, 1987.

Chapter One

The Public Interest and Tax Exemptions for Nonprofit Hospitals

Bradford H. Gray
Henry Chauncey Jr.
Miriam M. Wood

Senator Irwin "Muletrain" Borax dropped heavily into the uphol-stered chair in his windowless hideaway office deep in the recesses of the Capitol. It was Friday evening, and he had only two more days to prepare for his appearance on "Meet the Press." A junior senator elected less than two years before, he had lobbied for an opportunity to appear on the prestigious Sunday morning televi-sion program, only to be ambushed by happenstance: S. 6903, a bill to require the IRS to withdraw tax-exempt status from hospi-tals, had become the health care news story of the week just a few hours ago. As a relatively new member of the Senate Finance Com-mittee, he had not expected his views to be in the spotlight. But one of the staffers for "Meet the Press" was from his state and undoubtedly knew something of the Borax-for-Senate campaign, in which Borax's theme, "Health Care the Way You Like to Receive It," had been featured prominently in the media.

Two years ago it had seemed self-evident to Borax that no changes should be made in tax-exempt status for hospitals. Now he was not so sure. The arguments of experts who had appeared before a subcommittee had influenced his thinking, no doubt about it, and tax assessors in Metro City, the largest city in his state,

were trying to increase property tax rolls by adding the holdings
of many nonprofits, beginning with the city's hospitals. But he
could not forget that four of his key supporters were on the boards
of hospitals in his home county—two were trustees of the major
teaching hospital in the state, University Hospital, and another
chaired the board of the 250-bed Community Hospital where he
himself had once been a trustee. Moreover, the Political Action
Committee of the state's hospital association was his third largest
campaign contributor.

Voting for withdrawal or reduction of tax exemptions for hospitals had the potential to make Borax a one-term senator. However, he thought ruefully, he was still idealistic enough to want to
make a decision based on the merits of the issue. So he had asked
one of his aides to write a memo setting out the arguments in favor
of continuing tax exemptions for hospitals and another to write a
memo setting out the arguments against. He specified that the
memos should cover three issues: (1) the pros/cons as reflected
in his constituent mail and in the press of his state; (2) the
pros/cons as presented by his state's hospital association; and (3)
the pros/cons of a more technical nature as reported in testimony
before the subcommittee.

Borax rose from his chair, walked over to his desk, and pulling
open the middle drawer, lifted out the two memos. One was
headed "Reasons to Repeal Tax Exemptions for Nonprofit Hospitals"; the other was titled "Reasons to Continue Tax Exemptions
for Nonprofit Hospitals." As usual, his assistants had attached a
few illustrative documents for him to look at. He would read
through the materials as if he were once again a hospital trustee,
he thought. That would help him bring the merits of the issue
together with the perspective of his core supporters, each of
whom he planned to telephone tomorrow in advance of his
appearance on "Meet the Press." He was already pacing as he
began to read.

To: Senator Borax
From: Ray Z. Funds, Legislative Assistant, Tax Issues
Re: Reasons To Repeal Tax Exemptions For
           Nonprofit Hospitals

Lee and I agreed to divide up a bit of background on this issue. Therefore, I will explain what is at stake, and Lee will provide some history.

Background: What Is at Stake

There are three broad reasons for ending or substantially narrowing the tax exemptions for hospitals.

One reason is the eroding tax base of the nation and its localities. The number of tax-exempt nonprofits has grown from less than three hundred thousand in 1962 to more than one million today, and the consequent decrease in the tax base must be of concern to any responsible policy maker. Addressing the hospital case might lead to a more thorough examination of the justification for tax exemption for all nonprofits that raise revenues through the sale of services.

The revenue foregone as a result of hospitals' exemptions is very substantial. One published estimate a few years ago found the value of exemptions for nonprofit hospitals to be $1.6 billion from the exemption from federal income tax, $1.7 billion from the ability to issue tax-exempt debt to raise capital, $1.2 billion from donors' deductions of charitable contributions to hospitals from their federal income tax, $2.8 billion from the exemption from state income and excise taxes, and $1.2 billion from the exemption from local property taxes, for a total of $8.5 billion in exemptions. Though state and local governments set exemption policies for taxes at their levels, they usually follow federal exemptions. A federal decision to withdraw 501(c)(3) status for hospitals could raise a great deal of tax revenue at all levels of government.[1]

As an example, a letter signed by more than half the city council in Metro City asks your support for legislation making it easier for the city to tax two of its 501(c)(3) hospitals. The resulting income would help to maintain or lower the city's tax rate, thus

---

1. These estimates appear in John Copeland and Gabriel Rudney, "Federal Tax Subsidies for Nonprofit Hospitals." *Tax Notes,* 1990, *46*(26), 1565. Although some questions have been raised about these figures, they constitute the only comprehensive account by neutral parties of the value of foregone revenue.

relieving local taxpayers, many of whom are elderly, living on a fixed income, and unable to bear the property tax increases required to support basic city services. If the city council's attempt to tax nonprofit hospitals lands in court, federal legislation would presumably bolster their case.

Fairness is a second rationale for ending nonprofit hospitals' exemptions. About 15 percent of the nation's hospitals are tax-paying, for-profit organizations that complain that nonprofits' exemptions create unfair competition. We have also received letters from several family-owned pharmacies in Metro City saying that University Hospital's new pharmacy is taking business from them; they want to know why they have to pay income and real estate taxes when University Hospital does not.

However, the most important reason for ending nonprofit hospitals' tax exemptions is that their performance does not justify preferential treatment. Though exempted as "charities," the revenues of most hospitals today come almost exclusively from the sale of services. Many nonprofits seem to have lost their sense of mission. When service to people who are unable to pay has been examined by the General Accounting Office (GAO) and by authorities in several states and cities, it has been apparent that many hospitals are providing very little free care to poor people. No good reason exists to continue subsidizing "charitable" organizations that are primarily commercial entities and neither receive nor dispense much charity.

Constituents and the Media

We have not logged in much constituent mail on this issue, and the major newspapers have been split. Judging from what the newspapers have written, several would support a decision by you to oppose continued blanket tax exemptions for nonprofit hospitals. Editorials have pointed out that most patients now have insurance, vastly reducing the hospitals' charitable role of earlier years. The *Chronicle* has calculated the value of Community Hospital's tax exemptions and expressed great skepticism that city residents are receiving adequate benefits to compensate for the revenue loss.

The increasingly commercial behavior of hospitals in the state has also elicited press commentary. Advertising by nonprofit hospitals has, of course, become pervasive, but their commercial activity goes far beyond that. Many hospitals in the state now have for-profit subsidiaries and have entered into a variety of joint ventures with for-profit organizations. For example, in addition to its pharmacy, University Hospital rents out space on the first floor of its big garage to retail stores, operates a home care company as a for-profit subsidiary of the hospital, and has purchased the practices of several primary care physicians in the city to assure itself a continuing source of patients. University Hospital also has a joint venture (for-profit, I think) with Rehabilitation Hospital for outpatient physical therapy. St. Joe's runs a for-profit "Wellness" program and physical fitness center, operates a for-profit dialysis program at another location, and provides sports medicine in four towns through a major for-profit subsidiary.

In supporting a change in exemption policy for nonprofit hospitals, you can argue that these institutions have outlived the need for tax exemptions. The exemptions were established at a time when the elderly and poor could not afford to pay for care and hospitals needed subsidies to be able to serve them. Medicare and Medicaid vastly reduced the number of people who lack health insurance. Although the number of uninsured people has been increasing for more than a decade, most of them are from working families, and we can argue that this problem should be dealt with directly through health care reform, not indirectly by continuing tax exemptions for nonprofit hospitals.

Expert Opinion

An important source of expert opinion on this topic is economists, who generally believe that direct governmental subsidies are more efficient than indirect subsidies. That is, they argue that rather than government giving up x million dollars in foregone tax revenues to subsidize institutions caring for the poor, it would be more efficient to abandon tax exemptions and to use tax revenues to purchase care for those who cannot afford it.

On the other hand, experts retained by the hospital associations' lobby contend that taxes would be a new cost that hospitals cannot afford to absorb. There is some political danger here. Most unbiased health care experts say we have too many hospitals in this country; the fact that occupancy rates average about 60 percent supports this point. Some hospitals—probably smaller ones—will close in the next few years, whether or not tax exemption policy is changed. If you support an exemption change resulting in tax bills for hospitals, you may be blamed for closures that would have occurred anyway.

However, many hospitals are doing well financially and will not go out of business, even if they have to pay some new taxes. These hospitals are widely seen as fat and removed from many of the state's most important health care problems. You can correctly argue that they can afford to pay taxes and should do so out of fairness because exemptions have become too costly to taxpaying citizens.

At the very minimum, you could argue for the need to scrutinize closely the activities of hospitals not only in our state but in many parts of the country. To what extent are they actually providing community benefits beyond the services for which they are paid? Several national associations of nonprofit hospitals have developed guidelines for identifying such benefits, but voluntary efforts may be window dressing designed to forestall meaningful regulatory requirements (Exhibit 1.1). If you want to look further into the issue of community benefits, I would be glad to help you think through the kinds of questions we should ask in such an inquiry.

To: Senator Borax
From: Lee V. Malone, Legislative Assistant, Health
Re: Reasons To Continue Tax Exemptions For
          Nonprofit Hospitals

In this memo I discuss (1) the history of hospitals' tax exemptions, (2) constituency mail and the press, (3) activities of the state hospital association, and (4) the views of "experts."

Background: History of Hospitals' Tax Exemptions

Removing hospitals' tax exemptions would change a practice established when the first federal income tax law was passed in 1913. Interestingly, Section 501(c)(3) of the IRS Code does not explicitly mention provision of health services in its list of purposes that qualify an organization for exemption (Exhibit 1.2). Instead, hospitals have always been exempt as "charitable" organizations, although teaching hospitals may have additional grounds for exemption because of the educational and scientific purposes they serve.

At one time, hospitals largely served the poor and were major recipients of charitable donations. In 1969, after passage of Medicare and Medicaid, the IRS adopted the position that provision of health services for the community-at-large is itself a charitable purpose (Exhibit 1.3). Since then, hospitals have not had to demonstrate that they are either recipients or dispensers of charity to meet the federal requirements for exemption.

Some of your colleagues, however, have questioned the status quo, and the GAO report requested by Representative Roybal (*Nonprofit Hospitals: Better Standards for Tax Exemptions Needed,* 1990) indicated that the amount of free services provided by many hospitals is substantially less than the value of the tax benefits they receive through the exemption. Whether these hospitals provide community benefits that are not easily measured and were thus overlooked in the GAO study is not known.

To date, the leading proposals to change the federal tax law would not end hospitals' exemptions in a blanket fashion but would establish more rigorous criteria than now exist. One proposal, for example, would require that hospitals provide free services up to the value of the tax exemption. In addition, the courts and legislatures in many states have taken up the question of exemptions from state and local taxes (for example, the property tax), and some hospitals in several states, including Pennsylvania and Utah, have lost their exemptions. In effect, such states have adopted more rigorous standards than the federal government requires (Exhibit 1.4).

On "Meet the Press," you may be asked about the blanket removal of nonprofit hospitals' tax exemptions (as happened with Blue Cross insurance plans in 1986). Blanket removal is easy to reject since some hospitals, most notably urban teaching hospitals, provide very significant amounts of charity care. You can score points by asking why we would remove the exemption of a charitable organization just because it happens to be providing health services, rather than, say, social, religious, or cultural services or education.

You will undoubtedly be questioned about proposed legislation to tighten the federal tax rules to require hospitals to take concrete steps to justify their exemptions (Exhibit 1.5). A solid basis exists for opposing changes in the tax rules, and as you requested, I will discuss the issue from three standpoints.

Constituency Mail and the Press

We have received no letters supporting the status quo on tax exemptions for hospitals, except from hospitals themselves, which are lobbying hard. Constituent letters and the press suggest, however, that some hospitals have a considerable reservoir of support—St. Joe's gets rave reviews, and we hear about extraordinary services performed on major medical problems at University Hospital. I believe these hospitals could generate considerable constituent opposition for you if you were to suggest that you might favor ending exemptions.

The issue is beginning to receive press attention. Although three papers have floated editorials questioning exemptions for nonprofit hospitals (including university hospitals) and suggesting payments in lieu of taxes, two have published persuasive editorials supporting the continuation of exemptions. They point to emergency rooms as a source of primary care for the poor and the failure of Medicare or Medicaid to pay hospitals fully for the costs of that care. Moreover, many hospitals support significant outreach programs to the poor. For example, St. Joe's has a van that roams the poorer sections of Metro City, giving mammograms, dispensing wellness information, and providing health advice. University Hospital has significant AIDS outreach programs conducted in conjunction with the medical school and the school of public health. Nobody really knows the extent of unfunded community services provided to those unable to pay, but it would be safer for you to presume that hospitals can make the case that they do provide substantial unfunded services than to assume the opposite.

In response to the proposal that hospitals document the community benefits they provide, you can argue, as hospitals do, that the costs of such demonstration will only take away from the services themselves. Furthermore, if documentation of specific services (such as free care for the indigent) were to be required as a condition of continued exemption, hospitals might change their community benefit activities in ways that do not necessarily serve the community best. You can mention that the 1990 legislative proposal requiring hospitals to provide charity care up to the value of their tax exemptions was poorly conceived because of its focus on only one aspect of hospitals' community benefit mission. If hospitals had to report only on charity care, they might stop their other beneficial activities in order to finance it. In addition, the very existence of requirements would imply that Congress or the IRS knows better than the governing board of a local hospital which services are appropriate for that hospital to provide.

The state hospital association has urged improved performance (or better public relations) on member hospitals. To the charge that hospitals have become too commercial, the association aggressively promotes the counterargument that a hospital must charge for its services to survive, and the surpluses generated by some services are used to subsidize services that don't break even. Many hospitals have been showing a surplus in recent years, but the hospital association says that this situation could change rapidly as managed care spreads and further cuts occur in the amount paid to hospitals for services rendered. University Hospital, for example, already has a problem resulting from cuts in federal subsidies for training health professionals. The bottom line is, you can say, that taxes on hospitals that today would reduce a surplus could later cause job elimination and financial deficits.

What is at stake for hospitals? The value of exemptions has been estimated at 6 to 8 percent of the revenues of the average nonprofit hospital. The imposition of new costs of that magnitude would have an effect. The hospital association will point out that hospitals would have to choose between cutting costs, which might reduce quality, or raising charges. No one wants to see quality diminished, and staff reductions would exacerbate the state's serious unemployment problem, especially in the inner cities, where hospitals are a major employer. Moreover, you can point out that cost increases to make up for the revenue lost to taxes would affect everyone—consumers, insurers, and the federal government, whose Medicare program is the largest single purchaser of hospital services.

Hospitals have been urged to be more responsive to community needs by several national associations, including the American Hospital Association, the Catholic Health Association, and Voluntary Hospitals of America. Whether stimulated by the increasing commercialization of the field or by the growing restiveness of tax authorities, they call on their member institutions to define their responsibilities to their communities, include community benefit activities in their budgets, and document their services to the community. On the basis of these efforts, you can take the position that questioning the rationale for hospitals' tax exemptions has already benefited our communities, while repeal of exemptions might result in loss of desirable services.

Views of Experts

The subcommittee hearings provided several reasons for you to favor continuing hospital exemptions. First, no one advanced a principled reason for singling out nonprofit hospitals while leaving alone nonprofit organizations that are exempt from tax under Section 501(c)(3). Nonprofits such as colleges, museums, symphonies, and the like are not expected to justify their exemptions on grounds such as service to the poor. It is presumed that by their basic functioning, under the control of a volunteer board of trustees, these organizations benefit the community. Is this not also true of hospitals?

Second, regarding arguments about fairness to competing for-profit organizations, it is certainly true that for-profit corporations are liable for income taxes from which nonprofit corporations are exempt. However, the taxes on for-profit corporations are essentially taxes on increases in the wealth of corporate owners. Because nonprofit organizations do not have owners and are required to use their surpluses for their tax-exempt purpose, taxes would only serve to reduce these organizations' ability to carry out their mission. In this regard, it is important to understand that hospitals' surpluses are essential to their ability to accumulate capital. Because of the cost of new technologies, hospitals are very capital-intensive institutions. If federal taxes were imposed on nonprofit hospitals' surpluses, those surpluses might disappear. That is, once surpluses were taxed, hospitals might decide to expend all excess revenues on current expenses (no incentive for efficiency there) instead of accumulating the capital needed to stay abreast of the latest technological developments. Taxation might fail to produce much revenue for government while also discouraging hospitals from remaining state of the art.

Third, removal of nonprofit hospitals' tax benefits could also stimulate a wholesale conversion of hospitals to for-profit ownership, and this development could be very bad for the nation. Organizations guided by the profit motive may be more willing to exploit the vulnerabilities of patients and of third-party payers. They also tend to be more expensive, to provide less uncompensated care, and to be less stable (the amount of buying and selling among for-profit hospitals is quite amazing). I have documentation of these points from a neutral source, the Institute of Medicine's 1986 report, *For Profit Enterprise in Health Care.*

Finally, bear in mind that nonprofit hospitals rarely pick up and move when economic times get tough. Instead, they search for new sources of revenue and try to maintain the mission for which they are chartered. The lack of nimbleness that comes with governance by a voluntary board can be a source of stability; facilities owned by large for-profit firms are much more likely to be sold, closed, moved, or converted to other purposes. I do not think that you want to sponsor a proposal that could result in the loss of local control of nonprofit hospitals, whose boards include leading citizens, in favor of control by hospital chains headquartered in other states.

Based on these arguments, I think you should favor the status quo and view hospitals, like our colleges, universities, social service agencies, art museums, and religious institutions, as positive contributors to the welfare of our communities. Benefits may be achieved by urging that hospitals give greater attention to the health needs of the poor, but there is little federal tax revenue to be gained—and much benefit to be lost—if hospitals' tax exemptions are ended.

Questions for Discussion

1. Identify the various stakeholders in the issue of hospital tax exemptions. In what respects do "the merits of the issue" differ among them?
2. Should tax exemptions for nonprofit organizations—health care or others—rest on their meeting performance criteria as opposed to a general presumption of public benefit? If so, what do you think the criteria for health care organizations should be?

3. If you were Senator Borax, what position on tax exemptions for nonprofit hospitals would you take and why? Write a statement for your semiannual newsletter to constituents that justifies your position.
4. As a private citizen, assume that you disagree with Senator Borax's position above. Write him a letter giving specific reasons for your own position and conclude it by explaining how the position you favor advances the public interest.
5. Should there be limits to the sorts of public policy goals for which tax exemption policy might be used by legislatures or courts?

Exhibit 1.1.   Excerpts from Inventory of Community Programs, Services, and Activities (American Hospital Association, 1988).

Clearly one of the most tangible ways in which a hospital can attest to the fact that it provides community benefit and that it is deserving of its tax-exempt status is the actual community services and programs it provides. Too often, in challenges to hospital tax exemption, the focus on providing community benefit rests solely on the amount of charity care provided by a hospital. There is a tendency, even by hospitals, to overlook the variety of community-oriented activities, services, and programs that they provide. As a result, the total amount of benefit that the voluntary, not-for-profit hospital sector provides goes unnoticed or, at best, is underestimated. Recently, however, hospitals whose tax exemption has been challenged have taken a more careful inventory of their community activities and services. In the process, not only have they discovered that they were overlooking many community benefit programs and services that they provide but they also began to question whether they would be able to continue to provide the level and array of such services should they lose their tax-exempt status. . . .

The best way to demonstrate that your hospital deserves its tax-exempt status is to highlight the hospital's programs and services that provide high-quality health care and that, in general, promote the overall level of health within the community. It is the services and programs that courts and governmental authorities will focus on in their determination of whether the hospital can be characterized as "a charitable organization that provides benefit to the entire community."

Like most of the other aspects of a hospital that are scrutinized in determining whether its tax status is justified, there is no prescribed set of services or programs that a hospital must provide to receive or maintain tax exemption. The key concern is whether the hospital has made a concerted effort to design programs and services that meet the health needs of its community, particularly the health needs of the disadvantaged and medically indigent. To the extent that your hospital has accomplished this, it is likely that it will be viewed favorably in any challenge to its tax-exempt status. Moreover, demonstrating the link between the hospital's community services and programs and its community-oriented mission and policies and procedures will build an even stronger case for the hospital.

Although only conjecture, predicting in a thoughtful and unexaggerated manner whether your hospital would be able to maintain its capacity to provide particular community services, or would be forced to reduce or eliminate such services should the hospital lose its tax-exempt status, can help put the issue in perspective in any challenge to the hospital's tax-exempt status. Going through this self-examination process can help illustrate some of the benefit that the community receives by virtue of the hospital's tax exemption as well as some of the potential ramifications should the hospital lose this exemption. In a challenge to the hospital's tax-exempt status, these potential effects, if presented in a straightforward manner, could significantly influence the courts or other officials in assessing the value of maintaining the hospital's tax exemption. Recently, for example, one hospital attributed part of its success in defending its tax-exempt status to the submission of information that outlined long-term implications if the hospital lost its tax exemption, including how such a loss would hamper its ability to provide the full range and diversity of services that it now provides. . . .

Identifying those services and programs operated at a loss or break-even also can be helpful in showing the value in maintaining the tax-exempt status of your hospital. Under no circumstances, however, does this mean that the only value or even the primary value in maintaining tax exemption is for those services or programs that are offered at a loss or break-even; a "charitable" organization is not synonymous with an organization that loses money. Ultimately, the value of a particular service or program is determined by your community. Whether your hospital generates a positive or negative margin on a particular service is irrelevant in determining the benefit of that service to your community. Nevertheless, that your hospital continues to offer valuable community services at a loss or break-even can be effective in demonstrating the value your hospital places on providing community benefit over purely financial considerations.

It can be assumed that the ability of your hospital to continue offering services and programs that it currently provides at a loss or break-even may make it particularly vulnerable if your hospital loses its tax exemption. By highlighting this vulnerability, you can clearly articulate to those who challenge the tax-exempt status of your hospital the potential problems that can be anticipated in terms of the community's access to such services. . . .

Source: Community Benefit and Tax-Exempt Status: A Self-Assessment Guide for Hospitals. Chicago: American Hospital Association, 1988. Used by permission of the publisher.

Exhibit 1.2. Existing Internal Revenue Code Criteria for Section 501(c)(3).

IRC Section 501(c)(3) exempts from federal income tax: corporations, and any community chest, fund, or foundation, organized and operated exclusively for religious, charitable, scientific, testing for public safety, literary, or educational purposes, or to foster national or international amateur sports competition (but only if no part of its activities involve the provision of athletic facilities or equipment), or for the prevention of cruelty to children or animals, no part of the net earnings of which inures to the benefit of any private shareholder or individual, no substantial part of the activities of which is carrying on propaganda, or otherwise attempting to influence legislation (except as otherwise provided in subsection (i), and which does not participate in, or intervene in (including the publishing or distributing of statements), any political campaign on behalf of any candidate for public office.

Source: Exempt Organizations Handbook, Internal Revenue Service, Department of the Treasury 311, July 1988, p. 7751–27.

Exhibit 1.3. Existing Internal Revenue Code Criteria for Hospitals.

Since 1969, the Internal Revenue Code criteria for tax exemption for nonprofit hospitals have defined "charitable" broadly in terms of providing community benefit rather than in terms of the relief of poverty. As applied by the IRS, "community benefit" has meant

1. Operation of an emergency room open to all persons
2. Provision of hospital care in nonemergency situations for everyone able to pay the cost thereof, either themselves or through third-party reimbursement
3. Having a governing board drawn from the community and an open medical staff (that is, open to all physicians who meet the hospital's credentialing requirements)
4. Treating people whose bills are paid by public programs such as Medicare and Medicaid
5. Applying any surplus receipts to improving facilities, equipment, patient care, medical training, and research and education (that is, not giving surpluses to parties such as owners)

Source: Exempt Organizations Handbook, Internal Revenue Service, Department of the Treasury 311, July 1988, p. 7751–5616.

Exhibit 1.4. State Criteria for Hospital Tax Exemptions.

The courts and/or legislatures in several states have developed more detailed and demanding criteria than are used by the Internal Revenue Service. Two examples appear below.

Pennsylvania

In a case that did not involve a hospital, a 1984 decision by the Pennsylvania Supreme Court included the following interpretation that has subsequently been applied in some hospital cases in Pennsylvania:

An entity qualifies as a purely public charity if it possesses the following characteristics:

1. Advances a charitable purpose
2. Donates or renders gratuitously a substantial portion of its services

3. Benefits a substantial and indefinite class of persons who are legitimate subjects of charity
4. Relieves the government of some of its burden
5. Operates entirely free from private profit motive.

The word "charitable," in a legal sense, includes every gift for a general public purpose, to be applied, consistent with existing laws, for the benefit of an indefinite number of persons, and designed to benefit them from an educational, religious, moral, physical or social standpoint. In its broadest meaning it is understood to refer to something done or given for the benefit of our fellows or the public. . . .

Whether or not the portion donated or rendered gratuitously is "substantial" is a determination to be made on the totality of circumstances surrounding the organization. The word *substantial* does not imply a magical percentage. It must appear from the facts that the organization makes a bona fide effort to serve primarily those who cannot afford the usual fee. [*Hospital Utilization Project* v. *Commonwealth.* 507 Pa. I, 487 A.2d 1306 (1985)]

Utah

A 1985 Utah Supreme Court decision, reaffirmed in 1994, established six criteria for determining whether a hospital qualifies for a charitable exemption:

1. Whether the stated purpose of the entity is to provide a significant service to others without immediate expectation of material reward
2. Whether the entity is supported, and to what extent, by donations and gifts
3. Whether the recipients of the "charity" are required to pay for the assistance received, in whole or in part
4. Whether the income received from all sources (gifts, donations, and payment from recipients) produces a "profit" to the entity in the sense that the income exceeds operating and long-term maintenance expenses
5. Whether the beneficiaries of the "charity" are restricted or unrestricted and, if restricted, whether the restriction bears a reasonable relationship to the entity's charitable objectives
6. Whether dividends or some other form of financial benefit, or

assets upon dissolution, are available to private interests, or whether the entity is organized and operated so that any commercial activities are subordinate to or incidental to charitable ones (*Utah County by County Bd. of Equalization* v. *Intermountain Health Care.* 709 P.2d 265, Utah 1985).

Note: Pennsylvania's concern with an "indefinite" number of persons and Utah's concern with "unrestricted" beneficiaries both go to the point of distinguishing a charity from a private trust (which a wealthy person might establish for grandchildren) or a mutual benefit organization (such as a cooperative).

Exhibit 1.5. Proposed New Federal Criteria for Hospital Tax Exemptions.

Although health reform legislation failed in 1994, several of the proposals contained revised exemption criteria for hospitals and other health care organizations. Two examples appear below:

Tax-Exemption Standards for Hospitals as Proposed in President Clinton's Health Security Act (S. 1757, Nov. 1993). Sec. 7601. Treatment of Nonprofit Health Care Organizations.

(a) Treatment of Hospitals and Other Entities Providing Health Care Services. Section 501 (relating to exemption from tax on corporations, certain trusts, etc.) is amended by redesignating subsection (n) as subsection (o) and by inserting after subsection (m) the following new subsection:

(n) Qualification of Organizations Providing Health Care Services as Charitable Organizations. For purposes of subsection (c)(3), the provision of health care services shall not be treated as an activity that accomplishes a charitable purpose unless the organization providing such services, on a periodic basis (no less frequently than annually), and with the participation of community representatives

(1) assesses the health care needs of its community, and

(2) develops a plan to meet those needs.

In the case of a health maintenance organization, the provision of health care services shall not be treated as an activity that accomplishes a charitable purpose for purposes of subsection (c)(3) unless, in addition to meeting the requirement of the preceding sentence, such services are provided as described in subsection (m)(6)(B)(i).

Exemption Provisions from the Health Security Act as passed by the Senate Finance Committee, August 1994.

This bill (S2351) added the following to the existing "community benefit" requirements to be interpreted and applied by the Internal Revenue Service.

An organization whose predominant activity is the provision of health services would be tax exempt only if it meets community benefit standards and

(a) If it (with "participation of community representatives") annually assesses its community's needs for health care services and outreach services, and prepares a written plan to meet those needs;
(b) if it provides "significant qualified outreach services" pursuant to this plan;
(c) if it does not discriminate against individuals on the basis of their participation in a government-sponsored health plan; and
(d) if it does not discriminate against individuals in the provision of emergency health care services on the basis of ability to pay.

The bill then defined "qualified outreach services" to mean health care services (or preventive care, educational, or social services related thereto) in a medically underserved area, at below cost to individuals who could not afford such services, or in emergency facilities that provide "specialty services" and that "normally operate at a loss."

Suggested Readings

Gray, B. H. *The Profit Motive and Patient Care: The Changing Accountability of Doctors and Hospitals.* Cambridge, Mass.: Harvard University Press, 1991. Analysis of evolution of health care in America since the 1960s. Shows how care has been affected by changes in control of health care organizations and among professionals who make health care decisions. See especially Chapter Four.

Gray, B. H. "Why Nonprofits? Hospitals and the Future of American Health Care." *Frontiers of Health Services Management,* 1992, *8*(4), 3–33. Discussion of nonprofit hospitals, their evolving relationship to for-profits and government, and the problem of their tax exemption.

Hansmann, H. "Economic Theories of Nonprofit Organization." In W. W. Powell (ed.), *The Nonprofit Sector: A Research Handbook.* New Haven, Conn.: Yale University Press, 1987. Discussion of economic theories in the nonprofit sector in the context of the role of nonprofits and the behavior of nonprofits.

Marmor, T. R., Schlessinger, M., and Smithey, R. W. "Nonprofit Organizations and Health Care." In W. W. Powell (ed.), *The Nonprofit Sector: A Research Handbook.* New Haven, Conn.: Yale University Press, 1987. An overview of the historic role of the nonprofit in health care and the emerging for-profit health care sector.

Simon, J. G. "The Tax Treatment of Nonprofit Organizations: A Review of Federal and State Policies." In W. W. Powell (ed.), *The Nonprofit Sector: A Research Handbook.* New Haven, Conn.: Yale University Press, 1987. Reviews tax issues relating to nonprofits and analyzes proposed changes.

Young, D. R. "Beyond Tax Exemption: A Focus on Organizational Performance Versus Legal Status." In V. A. Hodgkinson and R. W. Lyman (eds.), *The Future of the Nonprofit Sector.* San Francisco: Jossey-Bass, 1989. Argues that the nonprofit sector is "the original medium" for all organizations. Proposes special benefits be accorded to organizations in any sector that provide services to the needy and open their books to public scrutiny.

Chapter Two

Planning in Interdependent Environments

The Local Association for Retarded Citizens

Melissa Middleton Stone

It was mid January of 1988, and Julie Chertow was quite satisfied with the progress that her agency, the Local Association for Retarded Citizens (LARC), had made in the two and a half years she had been there. The board of directors had just approved a new three-year plan that Chertow felt gave her and her two top managers a much clearer sense of direction for the LARC. During the month-long planning process, she had found by chance a new facility to house their growing administrative staff and space next door for a storefront bakery and luncheonette in which their clients could work. She felt that the board was really pulling together for the first time. Its six newly recruited members were enthusiastic and supported fully her efforts to professionalize the agency. She had almost entirely replaced the thirteen-member staff she had inherited with people who were formally trained in working with the handicapped. Chertow felt particularly proud of the accountant she had located and hired to handle the fiscal requirements of the Department of Mental Retardation's (DMR's) new fiscal accounting system.

She was concerned however about the readiness of the staff and board for the rapid growth that would take place as a result of the three-year plan and the move to new facilities. Some of the "holdovers" from previous years were expressing overt and covert resentment of how quickly she was making changes. Chertow also wondered whether the LARC was becoming too dependent on DMR for future funding. Contracts from the department made up over 70 percent of the LARC's budget, not an unusually high percentage for most nonprofit contractors with the state but one that certainly tied the LARC's fate to that of DMR.

History of the LARC and the ARC Movement in Connecticut

Like many other chapters of the Association for Retarded Citizens (ARC), the LARC was founded in the early 1950s by a local group of concerned parents of mentally retarded children. The parents wanted to share common concerns and needed a place from which they could collectively advocate for services, particularly educational opportunities for their children. In the words of a longstanding LARC member and parent, "We needed to know what to do with our sons and daughters. . . . We had to fight for everything."

During its first two decades, the LARC was recognized in Connecticut as a strong chapter. Its membership numbered close to three hundred, and it successfully organized parents to fight for the development of a state-run regional center to provide locally based residential and skills training for mentally retarded adults. In 1978, it joined with the other local chapters of the Connecticut Association for Retarded Citizens in filing a class action suit against DMR. The suit alleged that the care received by the DMR's clients in the state training school violated the U.S. Constitution, and it essentially sought to close down the training school and to deinstitutionalize all residents.

In the mid 1970s, the board president (and parent of a mentally retarded child) took over as executive director of the LARC. The agency remained focused on advocacy, despite the fact that new members, who were young parents, expressed a desire for less advocacy and more direct service provision by the LARC. The agency not only chose to advocate for certain issues about which younger and older parents disagreed, but some of its positions on issues alienated other agencies working with the mentally retarded, including the state DMR. An organized group of younger parents severed their affiliation with the LARC. The general membership languished and, after a series of executive directors, the agency appeared stuck in an internal debate over whether it was primarily an advocacy or service delivery agency. (These two directions were considered incompatible because advocacy in the mental retardation field often involves critiquing the quality of service provision; hence, to provide both within one agency is considered to be a conflict of interest.) This tension between direct services and advocacy was being felt throughout the ARC movement because some members felt that the ARCs were losing much of their constituent-based power by providing services almost totally funded by the state.

LARC's Long-Range Plan for 1984–1988

The LARC's first long-range plan signaled the end of its stagnant period. In 1984, the organization began to look at itself and plan how it was going to help mentally retarded individuals. The "Long-Range Plan, 1984–1988" was developed by the board and staff through a series of special meetings and an all-day retreat. A consultant from a local firm specializing in strategic planning facilitated the process.

The plan was fifty pages long and contained seven statements of mission and ten goals (Exhibit 2.1). An appendix specified the goals and objectives for which the board, its committees, and the staff were responsible. Board committees were responsible for implementing eight of the ten goals including securing accreditation by the national accrediting body, expanding employment opportunities for all mentally retarded adults in the city, determining all advocacy positions and participating in advocacy efforts, and planning and developing a residential services component. Staff, on the other hand, were to serve as information conduits for board committees, run the client and family support services, and supervise volunteers.

In what appears to have been an attempt to balance the direct services versus advocacy dilemma, the plan stipulated that the Employment and Work Activities Committee of the board would "serve as a 'human rights' review panel for the LARC by regularly reviewing care plans for clients and ensure that the LARC can ethically provide both advocacy and direct service programs at the same time without conflict of interest." The board therefore not only had considerable responsibility for planning and implementing specific agency programs but in this instance was to act as the agency's quality assurance arm, evaluating on a case-by-case basis the work of the staff.

The 1984–1988 planning document attempted to solve the myriad of problems that the LARC faced, including the need to be accredited to qualify for state monies in the future. In reality, however, fifteen board members and thirteen staff could not possibly begin to implement the fifty pages of strategies. In the meantime, the organizational membership was beginning to change. Six new board members were recruited, and several did not agree with the contents of the 1984–1988 plan.

LARC's Efforts to Professionalize

By 1986, the board was frustrated with the lack of progress the agency was making in meeting many of the goals in the 1984–1988 long-range plan. Shortly after the new members joined the board, a new executive director was hired. She was the LARC's first professionally trained and experienced manager.

Julie Chertow had a university degree in special education and had worked in the field for ten years, first as principal of a school for the handicapped and later as director of services for a county department dealing with handicapped clients. She described her management philosophy as basing all organizational decisions on providing "quality services to *clients*," firmly believing in full community integration of all mentally retarded individuals regardless of the severity of their handicap. She spoke with frustration about finding one coordinator at the LARC who would not allow any clients with behavior problems on her unit. Chertow believed in "management by walking around" and a highly participative decision-making process. She found after her first six months at the LARC, however, that the staff were not certain they could trust her or her service philosophy.

The agency she inherited had twenty-seven mentally retarded clients participating in a Work Activity Center that in reality was a sheltered workshop, in which clients were protected from some of the demands of the typical workplace. The sheltered workshop consisted of a bakery and a crafts and woodworking room. Clients were brought there every day from group homes or from their parents' homes. Staff helped them learn basic social and personal hygiene skills in addition to cooking, sewing, and woodworking. No clients worked away from the center, which was located in an abandoned and rundown school several miles from the center of town.

The LARC's budget was under half a million dollars, 76 percent of which came from DMR to pay for these day activities for DMR clients. The other 24 percent came from the United Way, the sale of products made in the Work Activity Center, a thrift shop, and small volunteer fundraising efforts such as bake sales.

There were thirteen full-time and two part-time staff. The fifteen-member board of directors included three parents, a couple of teachers, a college professor, a few business people, and two directors of social service agencies. The membership, which was inactive, stood at two hundred.

LARC's Eighteen-Month Plan

In the first few months on the job, Chertow met with the planning committee of the board. She wanted to hold a planning retreat that would include the board, staff, and membership, and she wanted a new plan, one that was more realistic than the 1984–1988 plan, given the LARC's resources and current capabilities. Several committee members were reluctant to give up the old plan, and one particularly influential trustee resigned from the board. Chertow pushed ahead with the planning retreat idea and with the need for a planning document that would give the LARC a clearer sense of direction. "I needed a planning document, period. I need the accountability and structure of a planning document. You can't lead an agency somewhere unless there is a consensus on where you want to go. There are a number of directions I could take this agency and would probably succeed in some and fail in others. The LARC is at a crossroads—either expand or go out of business. DMR has had it with us."

The planning retreat was held five months after Chertow began her job and was facilitated by the director of another agency for the mentally retarded who had a great deal of planning experience. The retreat involved about thirty people—the board, staff, and some of the membership. A DMR representative had been invited but was unable to attend. The day-long retreat used a "nominal group process" where participants brainstormed lists of goals for the agency, combined these into broader categories of goals, and then voted on their priority order. The final document was a mere two pages long, covered an eighteen-month time period, and listed goals for eight general areas (Exhibit 2.2). The board's planning committee was then charged with making the plan more specific, adding objectives and timetables for implementation.

Most important to Chertow was that she believed the plan and the planning process had begun to move the agency toward direct service provision and toward a clear philosophy of community integration.

> That's the difference—we now have a group of board members who really believe in the new philosophy and a small group of old board members who believe in control and protection of clients. . . . It will be an evaluation tool for me with staff. I can tie performance into job descriptions and job evaluations. And, people don't mind being rated on performance when they know what the goals are, especially when they had a chance to set them. . . . I don't think there will be a meeting that passes that I don't reference the plan. The staff meeting I had the week after the retreat, it made my life a lot easier because, all of a sudden, some of these crazy changes that the new director wanted to put in were part of the planning retreat and they were things I was talking about beforehand, but now staff owned the changes. . . . It is also a tool I can use when I am trying to make a proposal to the board to do something. It will be helpful to me if I get calls from board members who have some crazy ideas. And, I assume, it can also be used against me—if I come up with a great idea that is not in the eighteen-month plan. That's okay, too.

The LARC's planning process was similar to the one used at that time in the state by many nonprofits serving the mentally retarded. Executive directors described the short time horizon, eighteen months, as being most appropriate, given the rapid changes taking place within DMR. Chertow echoed other executive directors in contrasting operational planning with longer-range strategic planning: "I view strategic planning as more

long-term planning, five years down the road. What I have seen
happen when that comes into effect in small agencies is the same
thing that happened with our five-year plan—it's put on the shelf.
It's too overwhelming, the time periods are too long. It's so hard
to predict human services compared to selling a product. If we
were selling widgets, we would kind of have a pulse on what is
going on and where it is going to be in ten years. There are so
many outside factors now, with what is going on in DMR, that we
just cannot predict."

There were, in fact, significant changes taking shape within
DMR.

Activities at the Department of
Mental Retardation, 1984–1988

After five years of litigation, the court accepted a decree plan developed by the state, the Connecticut Association for Retarded Citizens (CARC), and other nonprofit organizations to resolve the class
action suit. The state was to deinstitutionalize all but 123 of the
1,340 mentally retarded adults in its training school by June 1989.
To meet those requirements, the plan spelled out a service delivery
system that would substantially rely on private nonprofit providers.

In 1985, a young administrator from Arizona was hired as commissioner of DMR. He was the candidate favored by CARC and
considered nationally to be progressive in his views toward services
for the mentally retarded. The new commissioner wasted no time
operationalizing his philosophy of normalization, a process that
insists upon the mentally retarded person being integrated as fully
as possible into regular community life. Within his first year, he
developed and widely disseminated a DMR mission statement, the
central tenets of which were "presence, participation, competence,
choices, relationships, dignity, and respect" for all persons with
mental retardation. He also secured large budget increases for several new program initiatives, such as competitive and supported
employment (jobs for mentally retarded adults in the normal workplace rather than in isolated, sheltered workshops) and the development of small group homes and supervised apartments. He
wanted nonprofit providers to develop these programs quickly in
order to begin taking clients from the state training school.

While most nonprofit contractors shared the progressive philosophy of DMR, it was not without controversy. Some parents feared that their adult sons and daughters would not be able to cope with life outside the institution and would suffer major setbacks if placed too quickly in community settings. They were concerned that their children would be ridiculed and taken advantage of. Staff at some agencies also were concerned about how clients would make the transition and worried that they themselves could not handle the new and rigorous job requirements of helping clients move from sheltered workshops to competitive employment. The first clients that came to nonprofit agencies from the state institution were much like the clients with which these agencies had experience: they were moderately retarded young or middle-aged adults. Soon, however, DMR was asking agencies, as a condition of their contracts, to serve a different type of individual—profoundly retarded, medically fragile, and elderly.

Early in his tenure, the commissioner reorganized DMR, consolidating twelve regional offices into six and more clearly separating central office functions from those at the regional level. The central office was now responsible for fiscal and administrative matters, including licensing and program reviews, developing major program initiatives, conducting statewide long-range planning, and monitoring compliance with the court order to deinstitutionalize. Regional offices would decide upon all contracts with private providers in their regions, would develop annual plans that were in line with DMR's long-range plan, and would have their own budgets and citizen advisory councils. With these changes, relationships between regional offices and nonprofit contractors became far more important than in the past, and in the LARC's region, a particularly testy relationship developed between agency contractors and the regional office.

Regional staff perceived local providers as recalcitrant and, feeling the pressure to meet DMR's goals for services to the deinstitutionalized population, the regions began to consolidate their positions elsewhere. For example, frustrated by the slow response of local nonprofits, the regions turned to large, out-of-state providers to establish and manage group homes. Regional staff were quite clear about the advantages of using these types of providers. They described the out-of-state providers as large entities similar to business corporations (although they were, in fact, nonprofits) that were well managed and innovative. They could hire quality staff to run residential programs because they paid higher salaries than most local providers.

A particular advantage cited by regional staff in using out-of-state providers was not having to deal with local boards of directors. According to regional staff, the trustees of the out-of-state providers had "expectations different from those of local ARCs; ARC boards are fine but not what we need right now." Regional staff felt that ARCs wanted to be the major DMR service providers but were not always willing to take the kinds of clients DMR sent them. Out-of-state organizations, however, saw a great deal of opportunity in states that were deinstitutionalizing because such mandated activities guaranteed a flow of clients and funds. Their staff were experienced negotiators with state agencies and their boards welcomed expansion. They were also less contentious than local groups, having no history of or interest in advocacy.

Many providers in the LARC's region were openly resentful of increasing state control over their programs. For example, one local provider said: "How do we maintain our identity when they come down with everything? They want to make us an arm of the state. . . . I foresee that many local providers will merge and become satellite agencies of DMR. It used to be that parents would get together to organize. Now the state says what clients you can take. I find DMR annoying to work with. If the department only believed that they needed us, they'd be nicer to us. Instead, it's a constant hassle. They tend to be nasty in this region."

In addition to the lack of goodwill between local providers and the regional office, there was little communication among providers themselves. Most saw the region as being highly competitive and splintered.

LARC's Evaluation of Progress

During the year following the planning retreat in 1986, Chertow moved quickly to further consolidate the consensus within the board and staff concerning the direction of the agency. Seven staff resigned (three direct-care workers, one program manager, two supervisors, and a bookkeeper), several because they disagreed with the new LARC direction. They were replaced by staff committed to normalization and community integration. Five new board members were also recruited to replace those who had resigned. The LARC's 1988–1989 budget was more than double the budget when Chertow had arrived.

Amid these changes, the executive director and the planning committee of the board sat down to evaluate progress on the eight goals in the eighteen-month plan. According to Chertow, the agency had accomplished two of the eight goals—to develop a value-based philosophy and to begin to expand vocational services—but the other six were too vague to evaluate. She wanted even more focus and direction from a plan, especially regarding provision of jobs in the community for clients. As the new program manager commented, "It was clear to everyone that in order to stay viable, because of the competition in this region, we would have to change our way of doing things. It has been hard to boost the enrollment in our vocational program. This program is one of the least community-integrated programs I have ever seen."

The planning committee agreed, and at the board's next meeting, it voted to have the executive director, together with her financial and program managers, develop a three-year plan specifically targeted at major expansion of vocational services. The board gave the three-person team six weeks in which to develop the plan and its financial projections.

LARC's Three-Year Plan

The three planners sequestered themselves for several days during the next month. During that period, they met with the board planning committee, staff, the young parents' support group, and DMR representatives to gather reactions to their emerging plan.

A serendipitous event accelerated the momentum surrounding the proposed expansion of vocational services. In the middle of the planning process, the executive director heard of a newly renovated downtown property that was well suited to a storefront bakery and luncheonette. Next door was space for the administrative offices. This property gave concrete expression to much of the plan and could ensure rapid implementation.

The full board did not see the results of the planning effort until the team mailed out the document and supporting financial projections. The final three-year plan included a mission statement; six goals (Exhibit 2.3) supplemented by measurable objectives and implementation strategies; and client and financial projections. The board approved this plan at its next meeting, at which time the staff reported on the availability of a new property. At the following board meeting, an eight-year lease agreement for the new facility was approved.

The three-year plan stated that the LARC would grow from serving twenty-seven clients to nearly one hundred clients by 1991. The financial projections used in the plan rested on assumptions made by the executive director and her new financial manager that program growth would give rise to new revenues from DMR. The financial manager agreed that the successful implementation of the plan depended in large measure on funding from the state and those revenues were still "a big question mark" because legislative appropriations to DMR were never certain. Both the financial and the program managers also worried about the lack of any middle management layer to cope with the rapid expansion. They already felt stretched thin with their responsibilities.

In general, board members and staff were enthusiastic about the direction in which the LARC was headed and approved of the direct service rather than advocacy focus for the agency. Nine of the fifteen board members and ten of the thirteen staff, including the three senior managers (the executive director, the financial manager, and the program director) had been with the LARC three years or less. They in particular felt that the LARC was now being run in a more businesslike manner because of its planning activities. Of the nine new board members, four had careers in either banking or finance, and a fifth was currently with a consulting firm after having spent several years as a bank manager. Another was a lawyer and the other three were professionals working with handicapped people. None were parents of mentally retarded people, although three were family members.

While broad agreement existed within the LARC, there were also serious differences of opinion between older and newer board members and staff. For example, a new board member said, "Some people on the board are no longer interested in the direction of the LARC. . . . It's not their agency anymore. You lose that intimacy.

This is also a result of professional management. We won't have the luxury of having the executive director hold hands with parents or clients. Now, if someone wants to talk money, they'll have to talk with the financial manager; if they want to talk program, talk with the program manager. It's a trade-off. . . . We cannot provide all the support. . . . New programs will be easier to implement than dismantling old ones. Older staff are real sweet, dedicated people but not the kind you need to lead a risky venture into corporate America."

A staffperson with the agency for several years presented a different attitude toward these changes: "We've had a very family-type feeling here. We'll lose the closeness, lose the time to put into relationships with clients. It becomes more like a business. I don't know if anyone has proved that's more effective for clients. . . . We are becoming more like the DMR Regional Center, having clients separate nuts and bolts. They were running sewing machines, baking pie crusts. Now they are cleaning toilets. Where is the sense of pride?" According to the LARC's managers, however, staff felt the loss of a family atmosphere partly because managers were beginning to evaluate staff job performance and were asking staff to take on more challenging responsibilities with clients.

What parents could expect from the LARC was also changing, a circumstance that at least a few board members found detrimental. A longstanding member of the organization, a former board member and also a parent, was incensed at the planning process with its limited scope and limited participation. In a lengthy letter to the board president and executive director, he aired his strong views that the lack of participation by laypersons, parents, and family members in the planning process damaged the credibility of the plan's focus.

Newer members however did not feel strongly that parents should be directly involved in planning; they felt that the LARC's top-level managers should be the ones most involved in setting the future direction for the agency. The three top managers did not want to expand the role of parents, although they made important distinctions between older and younger parents and between parents and other family members. These distinctions related principally to parental attitudes concerning the role of professionals and the active involvement of mentally retarded individuals in determining their own futures. When parents attending a statewide conference of the Association for Retarded Citizens criticized professional domination of local ARCs, an exasperated Julie Chertow stood up and said to the group that she, as a professional, was sick and tired of being "kicked around by parents." She would rather listen to the mentally retarded persons themselves.

attitude

There were also important differences in attitude about the ways in which the LARC related to DMR. Older members were wary of increasing the LARC's dependence on DMR. They remembered well the long court battle with the state over the deinstitutionalization issue. Some felt that the LARC was becoming an arm of the state and was only "jumping on the supported employment" bandwagon because that was where the money was. Newer board members and managers however felt that the three-year plan represented the desired direction for the LARC and certainly increased the probability of substantial increases in contract monies from the state.

Meanwhile, as Chertow contemplated the LARC's recent planning effort and the tasks that lay ahead to get ready for the relocation downtown, the DMR was publishing its first strategic plan.

DMR's Five-Year Strategic Plan

The impetus to develop DMR's long-range plan came from the commissioner, who liked the notion of a five-year plan that would tell the legislature, nonprofit providers, the governor's Office of Policy and Management, and the citizens of the state what DMR intended to do in the future. With this information, he hoped that no one would be surprised by DMR's annual budget requests. DMR's chief planner felt that it was DMR's responsibility to develop a strategic plan for the state and that DMR's planning was distinct from that done by providers whom the planner doubted were able to see the "big picture."

DMR's "Strategic Plan for the Future, 1988–1992" (Exhibit 2.4) presented the overall philosophy of service delivery as well as goals and targets for placement, first for the population needing to be deinstitutionalized and second for those clients outside of institutional settings. Within these guidelines, it was then the responsibility of each region to develop an annual operating plan using information on client needs from its case managers and from local advisory councils of parents and concerned citizens. These plans formed the basis for regional budget requests that were reviewed by the central office staff and consolidated into an overall budget request made to the governor. Following completion of the legislative session, a base budget and any new program resources would be allocated to the regions, which then negotiated contracts with providers.

At the time the DMR plan was released, Connecticut newspapers were full of predictions about a major state deficit, the first in many years, and substantial cutbacks in the state's budget being prepared by the governor's Office of Policy and Management. DMR's chief planner worried that if DMR experienced two years of no budget increases, much in the plan could not be completed. She also worried about whether DMR was creating a "monster" with all of these nonprofit providers, some of which had budgets that were 97 percent dependent on DMR for funding.

Questions for Discussion

1. What have been the most important decisions or actions taken by the LARC in the last few years? With what results? Overall, how would you assess the changes?
2. What role did the three planning processes play in these changes? Evaluate each plan's process and content. To what degree, if at all, is each plan "strategic"? How have changes in the LARC's external environment been reflected in these plans?
3. Does the LARC have an overall strategy? Is it sustainable? What advice would you give Julie Chertow and the board about the future?

Exhibit 2.1. Excerpts from the LARC Long-Range Plan, 1984–1988.

Introduction

This document outlines a structured plan of growth and development for the Local Association for Retarded Citizens (LARC). It is intended to provide a blueprint for the directors and staff of the

LARC to use in planning their activities during the next five-year period and to provide a means of measuring progress against specific goals.

The plan is intended to be flexible enough to permit revision after periodic review by the board of directors, yet specific enough to allow the LARC to focus its activities on those areas that the board and staff have determined to be of highest priority. Proposals for the use of funds and other resources can be evaluated in light of their contribution to accomplishing the goals of the organization.

This plan has been designed by the board of directors and staff of the LARC through a series of special group meetings, including an all-day retreat. These discussions provided a format for the exchange of ideas on organizational purposes, dreams, priorities, needs, strengths, weaknesses, and opportunities for the future. The plan reflects all of this exchange and is designed especially to capitalize on the LARC's strengths as an organization.

Ten primary areas for future development were identified during the planning process, and individual goals and objectives have been designed in those ten areas. They should be thought of, however, as a unified plan. It would be impossible to accomplish program expansion and development goals, for example, without also achieving financial goals.

The LARC's program for the future is designed to be accomplished over five years, with benchmark evaluation points for specific accomplishments at one, three, and five years. The plan itself contains five basic parts: (1) the foundation and guiding principles of the LARC including the mission, a statement of philosophy on the LARC's responsibilities for both advocacy and direct services, and a review of organizational strengths and weaknesses; (2) goals and objectives, and strategies for accomplishing them; (3) an activity management chart for each goal illustrating the timetable for completion; (4) roles and responsibilities for accomplishing goals and objectives; and (5) benchmarks for measuring results.

Mission

- To promote the general welfare of all mentally retarded individuals wherever they may be—at home, in institutions, or in

public or private schools—toward the greatest possible normalization of the retarded individual

- To actively engage in community organization for the development of services from public, private, and professional agencies toward the solution of the problems of all mentally
  retarded and their families
- To develop public understanding of mentally retarded
  individuals
- To encourage training and education in the field of mental
  retardation
- To advise and aid parents of mentally retarded individuals in
  the solution of problems, and to coordinate their efforts and
  activities
- To serve as a clearinghouse for gathering and disseminating
  information regarding mental retardation and service provision to mentally retarded individuals and their families
- To provide programs when needed on a pilot or ongoing basis

Summary of the LARC Goals 1984–1988

1. To have the LARC accredited by the Council on Accreditation
   of Rehabilitation Facilities (CARF) by the end of 1985
2. To advocate on behalf of all mentally retarded individuals living in the area, or who are from the area but are living in an
   institutional setting, to promote their general welfare as individuals or as a group toward the greatest possible normalization of the individual
3. To inform and educate the general public, but especially parents of the retarded, about mental retardation; and generally
   to promote a positive image of mentally retarded persons
4. To increase opportunities for adult mentally retarded individuals living in this city to work or receive training at the level
   and location most appropriate to their individual needs during the next five-year period
5. To develop four residential group homes serving twenty-four
   to thirty-two mentally retarded adults by the end of 1988
6. To provide support services to mentally retarded citizens and
   their families that will enable them to successfully remain in

the community; and to vary the kinds of support services that are provided based on documentation of needs

7. To work toward consolidation of the local chapter structure and build the regional focus of the association gradually during 1984–1985
8. To increase the membership of the LARC from 350 to 700 over the next five-year period
9. To develop a comprehensive plan for fundraising, from both private and public sources, that will ensure the future financial stability of the LARC over the next five-year period and beyond
10. To develop and support the human resources—board members, staff and volunteers—needed for the successful implementation of the organization's goals and objectives

Exhibit 2.2. The Local Association for Retarded Citizens Eighteen-Month Plan for Period 1/87–6/88 Presented to the Board of Directors on December 10, 1986.

Vocational Services

- Expand present vocational services and create a new array of vocational services.
- Increase supported/competitive employment opportunities.
- Increase job placement opportunities.
- Work to remove disincentives in order for individuals to succeed in the workplace.
- Move the Rainbow Bakery to a storefront location.

Community Awareness of the LARC

- Increase community awareness of the LARC.
- Increase community involvement and public awareness. Public relations should include self-advocacy.
- Individuals with mental retardation will have increased involvement on committees and an active role on the board of directors.
- Increase the visibility of the LARC in the community.

Independent Living

- The LARC will be a catalyst for fostering independent living.
- The LARC will advocate integration in school/work and the community.
- The LARC will become more involved in community residential programs (apartments, group homes, and so on).
- The LARC will increase independence by increasing access to the community.

Membership

- The LARC will increase the involvement of the general membership in activities.
- The LARC will assess the needs of the membership and the community.
- The LARC will increase membership involvement in developing and implementing programs.
- The LARC will provide more information to members from the state in a timely fashion.

Service Provision

- The LARC will increase their involvement in direct service provision.
- The LARC will develop a quality respite care service.
- The LARC will provide in-home aid as a direct service.
- The LARC will promote through training an integrated day care for infants/children and for after-school/work.
- The LARC will provide direct care in an integrated after-school/work day care program.

Support Services

- The LARC will provide support groups for parents, siblings, and clients as well as other support services.
- The LARC will work legislatively to ensure funding for community support services.
- The LARC will increase comprehensive services to the minority community.

Policy Participation

- The LARC will become a participant in the DMR process of policy formulation.
- The LARC will improve relationships and communications with other agencies including DMR, SS, and other service providers.
- The LARC will speak out and monitor policies of DMR and the Regional Center.

Value-Based Philosophy

- The LARC will determine a value-based philosophy and mission statement.
- The LARC is committed to self-determination of life choices.
- The LARC will be mindful that we send messages to the public that people with disabilities have abilities and competencies.

Exhibit 2.3. Excerpts from the LARC 1988–1991 Plan.

Introduction

This planning document focuses on the development of a strong vocational program that will grow from its current size of 28 individuals to a maximum of 100 individuals by 1991. The program will change its focus from an activity center to a community-integrated supported employment program. Vocational programs offered will provide a clear array of services to allow choice and appropriate programming and employment for individuals with mental retardation regardless of functioning level.

In recent years, the Local Association for Retarded Citizens has not been a successful service provider or advocacy agency. Past programming attempts have failed due to the lack of a cohesive attitude and environment and a lack of resources, both professional and financial. The LARC has been a victim of "trying to be all things to all people" and suffering from paralysis of tangible achievement as a result. In the last year and a half, the professional staff and the volunteers have pulled together to create an atmosphere of change and achievement. The most recent history of the LARC represents the building of a strong foundation from which to grow.

The decision to focus on vocational services is based primarily on the fact that the LARC currently serves twenty-nine individuals in a day program. This program has changed dramatically in the last year. Currently, ten individuals are working out of house in supported employment sites. The improvements are not enough. It is appropriate that the LARC focus on its existing programs to build a strong agency.

This decision is not to be viewed as one that means the board or staff is unaware of the importance and need of other programs and services. Rather it is meant to be a starting point for the development of a strong multifaceted organization that within ten years will be offering a full range of programs and services for individuals with mental retardation in the area.

Summary of the LARC Goals 1988–1991

1. To develop a complete array of vocational services for individuals with mental retardation located in an integrated environment
2. To develop and implement a comprehensive client and family services program
3. To develop and implement a self-supporting accounting services program
4. To complete all necessary preliminary work for residential development to implement in 1992
5. To develop and implement a formalized program of public relations and fundraising
6. To develop and implement the involvement of individuals with mental retardation on the board of directors and in planning and evaluation

Exhibit 2.4. DMR Strategic Plan for the Future, 1988–1992.

Office of the Commissioner
State of Connecticut
Department of Mental Retardation

Planning is one of the most important responsibilities of the Department of Mental Retardation. Planning is also a cornerstone of good management. A well-developed and thoughtful plan sets a solid direction for the organization; a plan can also form the basis for program development and a framework for legislative appropriations. I am both pleased and excited to present this DMR five-year plan.

The distribution of this first five-year plan document begins a planning process designed to be responsive to local advice for its further refinement. Each region and training school will host local planning meetings at specific times throughout the year in order to gather and document your suggestions and advice for improving the plan. Statewide organizations can provide their advice directly to DMR during that same period. The five-year plan will then be updated, extended an additional year, amended to reflect actual levels of resources, expanded to include more specific information, and made to reflect new or changing directions. By July 1 of each year, an updated and revised plan will be completed which will form the basis for our budget development and legislative program for the next legislative session. Priorities must be set. The plan will be implemented only if we stay within the world of the realistic and practical.

Much of what this department does is driven by the residential needs of the people we serve. The development and operation of residential services takes up the largest portion of our energy and financial resources. Therefore, the five-year plan first addresses our resource allocation strategy for residential development by describing our department's mandates, obligations, and responsibilities. Our goal is to reduce mandatory placements and increase discretionary residential placements as quickly as possible so we can more equitably distribute our limited resources.

At the same time that we are working to meet and reduce our mandates and obligations, we are working to increase and strengthen the variety and availability of family support services, programs for young children with special developmental needs, and daytime alternatives for adults. Our vision is that children and adults with mental retardation be provided with services which are dignified, respectful, and as much a part of our local communities as possible.

You can see that we need your help in making this plan the best it can be for Connecticut. We also need your support, advocacy, and encouragement so that the direction set by this plan and the timetables for reaching our goals can be realized. The accomplishment of this five-year plan must become a priority of our state government. Only you—the parents, advocates, providers, staff, and persons concerned about our citizens with mental retardation—can make it a priority. We must have intensive, broad-based, and unified support if we hope to succeed.

Brian R. Lensink, Commissioner
State Department of Mental Retardation

Mission Statement and Goals

DMR's mission statement, adopted in 1986, set the direction for Connecticut's mental retardation services system: The mission of the Department of Mental Retardation is to join with others to create the conditions under which all people with mental retardation experience:

- *Presence* and *participation* in Connecticut town life
- Opportunities to develop and exercise *competence*
- Opportunities to make *choices* in the pursuit of a personal future
- Good *relationships* with family members and friends
- *Respect* and *dignity*

Goals

Focus on these eight goals will align the mental retardation system with DMR's mission and operating principles and allow us to meet our development requirements.

Goal 1. Increase the availability of a broad array of community living arrangements.

Goal 2. Provide a variety of flexible support services to promote good relations between a person with mental retardation and his or her family.

Goal 3. Reduce reliance on segregated programs or services and improve the quality of life of people receiving services in those settings.

Goal 4. Increase the participation of people with mental retardation in Connecticut's labor market.

Goal 5. Promote access to educational opportunities available to all children and adults in Connecticut for people with mental retardation.

Goal 6. Expand opportunities for people with mental retardation to participate in integrated health, social, and recreational activities.

Goal 7. Increase and improve the administration and management systems that support existing and new services.

Goal 8. Strengthen services through training, program development, and quality assurance to enable them to be more consistent with the mission.

Suggested Readings

Bryson, J. *Strategic Planning for Public and Nonprofit Organizations.* San Francisco: Jossey-Bass, 1988. Presents in Chapter Three a model of planning that takes into account particular characteristics of nonprofit organizations, such as politically contested goals and external constraints. Also makes an important distinction between strategic planning and strategic thinking.

Lipsky, M., and Smith, S. R. "Nonprofit Organizations, Government and the Welfare State." *Political Science Quarterly,* 1989–1990, *104*(5), 625–648. Examines relationships between nonprofit organizations and public agencies under social service contracting regimes. Discusses fundamental differences between these two kinds of organizations.

Saidel, J. R. "The Dynamics of Interdependence between Public Agencies and Nonprofit Organizations." In J. Perry (ed.), *Research in Public Administration.* Vol. 3. Greenwich, Conn.: JAI Press, 1994. Explores three key sources of interdependence between state government agencies and nonprofit organizations, including resource dependence, bureaucratic and interest group politics, and the institutional environment.

Stone, M. M. "Planning as Strategy in Nonprofit Organizations: An Exploratory Study." *Nonprofit and Voluntary Sector Quarterly,* 1989, *18*(4), 297–315. Empirical study of the adoption of formal planning processes by social service and performing arts nonprofits. Focuses on differences in planning behaviors driven by particular internal and external variables such as the funding environment.

Young, D. R. "Executive Leadership in Nonprofit Organizations." In W. W. Powell (ed.), *The Nonprofit Sector: A Research Handbook.* New Haven, Conn.: Yale University Press, 1987. Makes a persuasive argument that executives of nonprofit organizations must possess a dual set of skills, operating both as businesspeople and as politicians.

Chapter Three

The Grantmaker
Inner City Organizations Compete for Funds
Miriam M. Wood

Victoria Angelini, program officer at the Community Foundation of the City (CFC), was deciding how to allocate $225,000 over three years to organizations in the inner city neighborhood of Round Hill. The funds would become available in three equal installments—now, in twelve months, and in twenty-four months—and Angelini was free to recommend that grants be made to as few or as many agencies as she chose so long as each installment was disbursed by the foundation by the subsequent December 31. For each recipient agency, she had to fill out a board of directors' Proposal Review Summary (Exhibit 3.1).

The foundation's mission emphasized "opportunities where grant support can make a significant difference in our community" (Exhibit 3.2). Within those constraints, she could make decisions according to her personal philanthropic principles, namely: the program must have a very long vision; the beneficiaries should be treated as part of the family, not guests; and when a program served young people, it must relate them to the larger community.

In a city known for the distinctiveness of its neighborhoods, Round Hill was usually referred to by the press and other outsiders as "Precinct 12," the identification used by the city police depart-

---

Note: Carolyn Brown and Marlene L. Bryant assisted in the research upon which this case is based.

ment. It was actually a twenty-six-square-block area left over after the more prominent neighborhoods of Plymouth Square and Chamberlain Heights had been taken into account. The entire neighborhood consisted of rundown two- and three-story single and multiple family dwellings situated on dilapidated streets controlled by drug dealers from late night through the small hours of the morning. The neighborhood had the highest homicide rate in the city. The average age of its residents was twenty-one and the average family income, at $17,000, was below the poverty line.

Proposals from four grassroots organizations had been submitted to the foundation, each incomplete in some respects and probably written by a volunteer or perhaps after hours by a staff member. To complement the written material, Angelini had invited each organization's contact person to her office for informal conversation. Round Hill was a predominantly African American neighborhood, and Angelini, an Italian-American sensitive to racial and ethnic issues, wanted to become personally acquainted with the contact person from each organization before she made a decision about funding. These meetings had revealed that the four applicant agencies, in spite of certain commonalities, offered distinct choices in focus and style. Thumbing through her worksheets for each organization, Angelini recalled the conversations one by one.

Reverend Lewis and the FreeYouth Project (Exhibit 3.3)

Reverend Leroy Lewis was an activist who ministered to the small, exclusively black 312 Pentecostal Church, which was composed of graduates of elite colleges and universities who were committed to living in Round Hill. Now in their twenties and thirties, church members viewed themselves as a model for black middle-class involvement with the urban poor, especially poor youth. The FreeYouth Project was the separately incorporated social action mission of the church.

Reverend Lewis focused much of his activity on the district courthouse that had jurisdiction over Round Hill and other neighborhoods in the northwest quadrant of the city. He provided bail for young men from Round Hill, made himself known to probation officers and judges, and otherwise tried to position himself and his congregation as a quasi-family network of support for Round Hill's young men. His goal was "to build intimate relationships of trust and respect with black males aged sixteen to twenty-two and to have them view me as essentially a respected father figure, and to turn the direction of their lives around so they can be participants in society. . . . The ones who're off the rails don't interact with me because of my lifestyle, which renders a verdict on them. Take Little Al, he's seventeen and just committed a heinous crime, a homicide where he shot two other black kids. He keeps a distance from me. When they're really off the rails, they don't interact. The ones I interact with want to get on the rails."

Lewis said of his congregation, "We're in it for the long haul, but we had no vision of how our lives would have to change as our families changed." Now in their prime child-rearing years, church members wanted to focus on the integrity of their own families, in part to compensate for the poor schools and ever-present violence in their immediate surroundings. As pastor, Lewis wanted to provide them with the necessary religious and social supports. Not that the members were slacking off by normal standards, Lewis assured Angelini; in contrast to most organizations, "where 20 percent do 80 percent of the work," the 312 congregation had achieved something "amazing" because seven out of the twenty adult members participated in the social action mission on a "no-joke-seven-days-a-week" basis.

Initially, Lewis's ministry had been met with hostility. Young men on the street had viewed him as a "snitch" (an informer to the police). Meanwhile, the police suspected him of being a drug dealer. At the courthouse, white probation officers had been highly skeptical of a fast-talking black man who was a relative newcomer to the city. Now, even the probation officers trusted him, Lewis said, and Angelini remembered an article in the *Morning News,* the city's major newspaper, in which the chief probation officer had remarked, "Reverend Lewis is in this courthouse more than any other minister as an advocate for kids in trouble."

Lewis was known to have been an effective leader in persuading the city's black ministers to adopt a common activist agenda to attack street crime. However, at a luncheon with grantmakers from other local foundations, Angelini had heard that in Lewis's own bailiwick, he was a "loner" and "competitor" who "doesn't like to work with anybody." Recently, an agency executive from an adjacent neighborhood had remarked that Lewis and Reverend Elliot of the Round Hill Baptist Church Community Center should just say to one another, "Okay, you work with those forty kids, we'll work with these forty, and let's not try to think one is better than the other."

Angelini reckoned Lewis to be an intuitive genius in handling the media. He and the 312 Pentecostal congregation had been featured locally on television and radio, in newspapers, nationally on the network television show "Street Stories," on a CNN news magazine show, and on National Public Radio. A recent front-page story in the *Morning News* had described Lewis's "unconventional ministry" as a "holy war." No doubt about it, Angelini thought, Reverend Lewis had become a personage in the city.

Reverend Elliot and the Round Hill Community Center (Exhibit 3.4)

Shortly after Reverend John Elliot seated himself at Angelini's small conference table, he observed that as a white person coordinating the community center of a predominantly black church in an predominantly black neighborhood, his presence conflicted with the Afrocentric orientation of a well-known outreach worker in the neighborhood, Reverend Leroy Lewis. Because of this implicit conflict, Elliot had determined to maintain a low-profile leadership style, remaining in the background and avoiding credit or attention. Instead, he had taken on the role of empowering others.

His strategy was to invite needy community groups to share on a rent-free basis the space occupied by the Community Center in the basement of the Round Hill Baptist Church. Elliot hoped that proximity among staff and volunteers from various neighborhood agencies, reinforced by meetings he would set up, would result a more cohesive sense of community in Round Hill.

Elliot said, "We spend a lot of time together just figuring out what our priorities are for next year, goal setting, and we'll set up maybe four or five community meetings a year and then we'll set up maybe four or five focused-type meetings on particular issues a year. We found that if the staff people don't have time to get together, you can't do much to try to get the programs together.

And most programs traditionally don't get together—most programs do run separately. What I try to do—when we do have meetings—is to make sure we cosponsor. We don't need to push our own thing; we need to work together."

Elliot's words unintentionally suggested a larger scope than existed in reality. He later explained that the paid staff of the Community Center consisted of himself and a divinity school student who worked a few hours a week. Elliot also indicated that foremost among organizational ties were those among himself, Charlene Hunter (the paid coordinator of the Round Hill Neighborhood Safety Coalition), and Don Bowles (a volunteer serving simultaneously as chair of the board of the Neighborhood Council, chair of the board of the neighborhood's Business Association, and cochair of the board of the Neighborhood Safety Coalition).

Elliot's attempts at community empowerment had not prevented the demise of a number of programs for which the Community Center had provided space. As Elliot described these defunct groups, Angelini reflected that technical assistance was at least as important as free office space to start-up neighborhood organizations. As it was, however, the center was not able to offer technical expertise. By default, the survival of the agencies it housed depended not on their usefulness to Round Hill residents but on the managerial and fundraising skills of their existing paid or volunteer staff.

Elliot spoke of the success of the Youth Development Program, which met weekly during the school year. The program had evolved out of an earlier effort to assist older black male teenagers who had been arrested and were already in the court system. The difficulty of supervising these young men had prompted Elliot to focus on younger boys who had not been arrested for criminal activity but were "at risk" for various reasons. In this fashion, he was trying to spend time with that segment of youth most likely to respond positively to the center's efforts:

> So we mainly work with educational issues with seventh through twelfth graders. Every week we say, "How're you doing in school?" They might say, "Oh, I got three D's, but I got a B." We affirm their honesty to tell us that they got three D's by celebrating that they're making it. And then the ones that come in and say, "I'm on the

honor roll again," we try to play them down so they don't embarrass the others, but we also celebrate the fact that they're still on it
and make sure that they stay at that level of commitment. So mainly
we talk about just anything they have to celebrate. Getting them to
share their feelings about somebody getting shot, or if somebody
lost a job or something, is hard, so we're building up pretty much
like a family. We call it the "family circle": they get together at family circle time and we all hold hands in the beginning and share
some thoughts and plans for the night. Then we hold hands at the
end in a circle, planning for the next time and highlighting anything that happened within those few hours."

Don Bowles and the Round Hill
Neighborhood Council (Exhibit 3.5)

Don Bowles, originally from Trinidad, walked into Angelini's office
with his grizzled head cocked and a smile on his face. He recalled
that when he had moved into Round Hill twenty-four years before,
it had been "a very thriving neighborhood." Later, he and other
black residents had remained when "blockbusting" resulted in
white flight to the suburbs. Now most of the original business estab-
lishments were gone, and no money had been invested in the
neighborhood for at least fifteen years.

Bowles had founded the Round Hill Neighborhood Council
two and a half years ago, after a teenager was shot to death in front
of the dry cleaners that Bowles owned and operated. "We decided
that we had to do something because nobody else would listen or
do anything. Our neighborhood council is the first one in the city,
as I know it, that gave birth to itself. The others are regarded in
some aspects as a political wing of the mayor, who has put them in
place so he can have people to talk to from time to time. But we
gave birth to ours because we thought there was a need to do
something. After we were formed, the mayor came around and
gave it his blessing." Other neighborhood councils had received
funding from the city for paid staff, but the Round Hill Neighborhood Council had not.

Bowles explained that the proposal to the foundation requested funds for a paid executive director for the neighborhood
council because "there is so much to do." Morale in the neighborhood was improving "because of the little things we're doing,

and people are beginning to feel a sense of belonging." Real progress however depended upon making city officials "take notice." "By that I mean we have to go out there and vote because nobody listens unless you do. And too often we say, 'Why vote? Nothing will change!' But we can look and see the examples around us. Those areas where they vote in high numbers, high percentages, they get things done. And in those areas where numbers are low, nothing happens." The outcome of making the city acknowledge Round Hill would be commercial development, the second goal of the neighborhood council:

> The City Facilities Department started working in Plymouth Square. About two years ago we asked them, "Well, what's happening here in Round Hill?" We had been talking to them constantly, asking why they weren't doing something here. I attended a meeting where the city said that they would be doing things in this area and so on—that they were picking out some areas in which to work and so on, and to put some money in and things like that. But they told us that the areas they wanted to do were Chamberlain Heights, Plymouth Square, and a couple of other places. We asked at that time, "Why are we not included?" And it was said eventually—by the people from the City Facilities Department—that to be included we should become a part of Plymouth Square. Okay, they agreed to link us with Plymouth Square, and we were part of the language but we were not part of the plan because nothing was concretely done to put us in. So much so that in a display of the areas they were covering—the display that went up with all the photographs and so on—they only went up to Calumet Street: they left us out completely! So we went up and said, "What's going on here?" They went back down and extended the map to include us, but that's all the inclusion we have gotten so far.

Bowles was clearly frustrated by his inability to get residents to attend meetings and remarked that in other neighborhoods "everybody comes out" for meetings. But Angelini knew from Reverend Elliot, who several years before had worked in Plymouth Square, that of the sixty merchants there—the prime beneficiaries of city development dollars—eight would typically show up for a meeting.

Charlene Hunter and Round Hill
Comprehensive Services (Exhibit 3.6)

Round Hill Comprehensive Services was an offshoot of the Round Hill Neighborhood Safety Coalition, which had been part of a two-year, four-site grant from another foundation. Charlene Hunter, the coalition's coordinator, had owned a home in Round Hill for ten years, but as consultant to a national community organizing association, she had traveled widely and trained dozens of other black women to be managers in low-income housing projects in Los Angeles, Atlanta, Chicago, and Cleveland. She had taken the poorly paid position with the coalition in order to remain at home full time with her eleven-year-old son. Also, she was "between jobs" and "intrigued" that Round Hill volunteers had succeeded in persuading representatives of thirty-two organizations to form a cooperating neighborhood safety group that included the police and other municipal departments and agencies as well as neighborhood churches, social service agencies, schools, and business owners. However, the coalition did not function as its new coordinator expected: "Since the coalition happened, many people have spun off and written proposals for the exact same thing we're doing. Which to me is kind of weird—why would they write something about public safety when we're doing something about public safety in this community already? But they know it's something people will fund." Now, after eighteen months, the coalition was falling apart because it was "agency driven," and each agency had its own agenda to attend to.

As a result, Hunter and several other Round Hill activists had founded Round Hill Comprehensive Services. It would be "community driven"; that is, neighborhood residents would participate on a purely voluntary basis and *their* interests would shape the new organization's goals and activities. Community driven is "the only way" to organize communities, Hunter said, "because if the community doesn't want it, it's not going to fly anyhow." Another factor prompting the incorporation of a new organization was the imminent closure of the coalition's fiscal agent, the local office of Citywide Housing Services. "So they're no longer a viable partner for the coalition as a parent organization. The Community Center at the Baptist Church I think is in the same— It's not in the same shape but close to the same shape of not having a lot of funding to really survive. So we are talking about sometime later merging the Community Center with Comprehensive Services and letting them be their own separate little thing together. But for now, Comprehensive Services is seeking its own 501(c)(3), which we are actively doing right now."

Angelini was startled. Reverend Elliot had said nothing about a merger. Then Hunter explained that the plan had crystallized just two weeks before, several days after Elliot had been at the foundation offices. Comprehensive Services would continue to organize residents to promote public safety. However, it would also use networking techniques to enable Round Hill residents to access services Hunter and other founders of the new agency had become familiar with through the coalition. In particular, a mutually beneficial relationship with Plymouth Square Health Center was envisioned:

> Now, if I go into someone's home here in Round Hill because I'm formalizing a street block watch, and one of the residents I happen to see is having tremendous health problems and doesn't know that a health center is within their reach at Plymouth Square and that it's on a sliding scale of payment, I'm able to send a whole new family to the Health Center to be treated. Another family might need something totally different. So I'm in a position the Plymouth Square Health Center is not always in to be knocking on a particular door and actually getting to know people on a more intimate level than they have. So Comprehensive Services will be like more of a resource bank, a referral system, and it'll change how people feel about other agencies that they may not know about.

A third activity would be the Summer Youth Camp, which had resulted from meetings between Hunter and residents of the wealthy suburb of Stoneview who had wanted to support an inner city activity. For two summers the camp program had been funded by Stoneview residents' donations supplemented by city funds that paid college students to work as camp counselors.

And believe it or not, even though the LA riot was far away, it affected us directly in this community. You noticed a lot of animosity, a lot of anger amongst our young people. And we could see it happening, and I said, "This is going to be a horrible summer." So in the middle of just trying to get the coalition built and meeting all the coalition partners, I realized there were no services for youth in our area. Well, I had been on the job, I had come in April, and by July, I had started a summer camp program for two hundred kids. That was nowhere in the coalition proposal, nowhere written, nowhere part of what we were doing.

The Recommendation

Angelini made her decision. She must now complete the paperwork for the foundation's board of directors (Exhibit 3.1).

Questions for Discussion

1. Describe the governance structure of each applicant organization. Would you argue that the Community Foundation of the City is, or is not, a part of the governance structure of an agency it funds? Why?
2. Describe the differences in approach to neighborhood problems among applicant agencies. To whom does each of the four contact persons appear to feel his/her agency is accountable?
3. To what extent, if any, is nonprofit entrepreneurship at the grassroots level inconsistent with oversight by a governing board?
4. Formulate a grantmaking decision in which Angelini would maximize the foundation's impact on the governance of each of the applicant agencies. Formulate a second decision designed to minimize the foundation's impact on agency governance.
5. If you were Angelini, how would you allocate the grant monies? What are your criteria? On the basis of these criteria, to whom/ what is Angelini accountable?

Exhibit 3.1. Board of Directors' Proposal Review Summary.

Organization requesting funds:

Grant period:

Amount requested:

Amount we are considering:

Proposed CFC payment schedule to grantee:

Schedule of grantee reports to CFC:

Grantee budget(s):

CFC program officer:

Background Information

A. *Grant purpose:* Describe as clearly and completely as possible the purpose of the proposed grant:

B. *Grant activities:* What activities have been proposed to achieve this purpose?

C. *Grant results:* What does the grantee expect the program to accomplish? Do you agree with these expectations?

D. *Geographic scope* of the project

E. *Evaluation:* How does the grantee propose to evaluate this project?

F. *Qualifications of sponsoring organization:* Who are the key people for this project?

G. *Sources of support:* Do you foresee that this effort will require CFC support beyond the proposed grant? Are there current sources of funding for this effort?

Exhibit 3.2. Foundation Mission and Guidelines.

The mission of the Community Foundation of the City is to exercise leadership in local philanthropy by making grants, loans, and awards to meet changing community needs. The CFC encourages philanthropic giving by providing a common source for contributions to charity and other local concerns.

Guidelines and Application Procedures

Four times a year, the CFC awards grants from its Unrestricted and Field of Interest Endowments to a wide range of tax-exempt organizations whose programs benefit health and human services, education, youth, arts and culture, civic affairs, environmental conservation, and historic preservation.

To be eligible, organizations must be nonprofit tax-exempt "public charities" as defined in Section 501(c)(3) of the Internal Revenue Code and must be providing services within Metropolitan City.

The foundation seeks opportunities where grant support can make a significant difference in our community. In addition to proposals from established organizations, the CFC welcomes proposals to provide start-up or short-term funding for innovative, potentially replicable projects that meet new needs or demonstrate new solutions for old ones.

In the evaluation of proposals, careful attention is given to the following:

- The potential impact of the request and the number of people who will benefit
- The degree to which the applicant works with or complements other organizations
- The commitment and composition of the organization's board of directors
- The extent of volunteer involvement and support for the project
- The organization's fiscal responsibility and management qualifications
- The possibility of using the grant as seed money for matching grants from other sources
- The ability of the organization to obtain additional funding to implement the project
- The assurance from the organization of its ability to provide ongoing funding

Exhibit 3.3. FreeYouth Project.

Mission: FreeYouth is the social action ministry of the 312 Pentecostal Church, which was founded by a handful of black Christian activists and intellectuals from Harvard, Metropolitan University, and Northwestern. The church is a base Christian community with a grassroots ministry to live among and serve the poor of African descent in the heart of the ghetto in northwest Metropolitan City.

Project to be funded: The FreeYouth Project is a multifaceted effort to combat the material and spiritual sources of poverty and dependency.

Amount requested: $75,000, 1 year.

Contact person: Reverend Leroy Lewis, Executive Director; Lewis is pastor of the 312 Pentecostal Church.

Description of the project: The nucleus of the project has existed for several years but only in the last two years has funding been secured to employ Lewis full time to pursue his street ministry. The project focuses on the estimated 7,500 to 8,000 black people in Round Hill, especially youth, whose lives are rarely if ever touched by social agencies. The project has no office but through its work on the streets, implemented primarily by Lewis, it advocates for youth in the municipal courts; offers temporary shelter and meals in 312 Church members' homes; and provides clothing, tutoring, jobs, training and, on occasion, bail for youth whom the members consider de facto orphans. The project operates the four programs described below.

Youth Advocacy Project (YAP): This program involves individualized work with street youth. Over the past year, Lewis has appeared in district court on behalf of approximately forty-five young men. He reports to the court three or four days per week, visits that can take anywhere from one hour to most of the day. Lewis has taken fifty-six young men to the Urban League for readiness training and job referral, and twenty have become employed.

Community Youth and Technical Exchange Program (CYTE): This program is run by a couple from the 312 Church out of their home. Its goals are (1) local youth-centered economic development and (2) technical education. Youth in CYTE learn to fix basic electrical appliances and thereby offer useful services within their own neighborhoods. CYTE also provides a computer literacy program. Last summer, CYTE worked with twenty-three young men and women between the ages of sixteen and twenty. If funding permits, this program will be expanded to spring and fall.

Women's Training Program: This program is a new initiative that will offer young single mothers an environment where they can interact with positive role models in the persons of 312 Church women. A primary goal will be to help these young mothers become self-sufficient by developing their own businesses in the neighborhood. The pilot program will offer approximately ten women, primarily between the ages of eighteen and twenty-five, computer training as well as teaching and discussion in the following areas: budgeting, nutrition, childrearing, health, job readiness skills, sex education, and violence prevention.

FreeYouth Youth Council: The council will be comprised of participants in the various FreeYouth programs who exhibit leadership abilities.

Governance: Although the church is a 501(c)(3), FreeYouth has been constituted as a separate 501(c)(3) with its own four-member governing board consisting of Reverend and Mrs. Lewis and two of the church's elders. The board meets quarterly. An advisory committee of seven meets two or three times per year. Five of its seven members are white and directly or indirectly associated with funding sources; one is a black woman from the

Budget Summary

	Current Year	Next Year
Expenses		
Personnel		154,940[a]
Program Expenses		48,380[b]
		203,320
Revenues		
Hummingbird Foundation	25,000	
First Church, downtown	15,000	15,000 est.
City Youth Services Commission	10,000[c]	
Valpark Trust	39,500	
Miscellaneous Gifts	12,296	14,000 est.

[a]Executive director $60,000; program coordinator $35,000; 5 part-time $32,000; Social Security and other benefits $27,940.

[b]Equipment, activities, transportation, books and materials, youth stipends of $30,800; intern instructor stipends of $2,000; child care.

[c]Stipends from the city to cover some wages of part-time help.

Round Hill neighborhood whose son has been involved in Free-Youth activities; the seventh member is an African American minister from a two hundred–member church in an adjacent neighborhood.

Exhibit 3.4. Round Hill Community Center (Baptist Church).

Mission: The Round Hill Baptist Church is an imposing eighty-year-old stone building serving the Round Hill neighborhood as well as parishioners who have moved elsewhere in the city. The church sponsors a Community Center, which is the project to be funded. The center is housed in the church basement.

Project to be funded: The Community Center (1) works with "at-risk" youth through the Youth Enrichment Program; and (2) assists emerging neighborhood-based organizations by providing them with free space for office or program activities.

Amount requested: $58,000, 1 year.

Contact person: Reverend John Elliot.

Description of the project:

Youth Development Program: This centerpiece program operates when school is in session. It provides a family-like support network for boys who otherwise turn to gang membership for personal support. Academic achievement is encouraged and rewarded, as is vocational goal setting. Peer role models provide the informal mechanism by which these objectives are accomplished. The decision to work with younger boys before they get involved in gangs and the court system was partially based on the idea that young men who successfully graduate from high school and the program will become positive role models for younger neighborhood teens. Preventing gang activity in one youth cohort will presumably diminish the likelihood that the upcoming cohort will become gang-involved.

Other programs offered by the Community Center include:

Youth Drama Program: A program run by volunteers from Cityside Community College to expose local youth to the performing arts. Operates two months in autumn and two months in spring.

Budget Summary

	Current Year	Next Year
Expenses		
Salaries, wages[a]	56,000	59,000
Facilities[b]	—	—
Office supplies	250	250
Phones	500	500
Refreshments, Youth Events	4,800	4,800
Loan Fund[c]	—	1,000
Computer, printer, software	—	5,200
	61,550	69,750
Revenues		
Church offering	1,200	1,300
Jonel Fdn.[d]	50,000	—
City Youth Program	10,000	10,000

[a]Includes FICA, Workers' Compensation, Unemployment Compensation for 1 full time at $48,500 plus 1 part time at $10.50/hour.

[b]Provided by Baptist Church.

[c]One-time expense for short-term fund for youth; they will be required to repay.

[d]One-year nonrenewable grant.

Educational Instruction: Offered in computer literacy and creative writing and run by suburban volunteers. Offered as needed.

Cable Television and Video Training: Offered cooperatively with a local cable company twice yearly for two weeks after school.

Arts and Crafts Instruction: Offerings depend upon availability of skilled volunteers from the church or neighborhood. One course in knitting has been very successful in making a positive change in the self-esteem of the instructor.

Programs based at the Community Center include:

Round Hill Neighborhood Safety Coalition: A network of neighborhood agencies organized around safety issues.

The CityNorth Alcohol and Drug Abuse Prevention Project: A substance abuse education and referral program serving the larger community.

The Round Hill Neighborhood Council: A neighborhood improvement association made up of concerned residents.

Narcotics Anonymous: A twelve-step program for drug addicts.

ESL Classes: For native Haitian-Creole speakers who wish to learn English. Taught by volunteers from the Baptist Church congregation.

Governance: The governing body of the church is equivalent to a board of directors; Reverend Elliot directs the Community Center under the supervision of the church minister.

Exhibit 3.5. Round Hill Neighborhood Council.

Mission: The Round Hill Neighborhood Council seeks to make the Round Hill area more livable for the people who spend their nights there, the people who come to do business there, and the youth who are growing up there.

Project to be funded: Having been run by volunteers in the past, the Neighborhood Council is now seeking funds to underwrite the salary of an executive director. Office space will be provided at no cost by the Baptist Church Community Center.

Amount requested: $42,000, 1 year.

Contact person: Don Bowles, chair of the Board of Directors.

Description of the project: Initially the organization will have two main objectives: (1) voter awareness and (2) coordination with and among other neighborhood groups, especially the Business Association, the Neighborhood Safety Coalition, and the Baptist Church Community Center. Without a paid staff member, it is impossible to go door-to-door to attract the interest of neighborhood residents. At present, the volunteer board chair distributes flyers to announce meetings, but this technique has not been successful. In terms of voter awareness, the goal is to instill in community residents the desire to become more involved in civic processes, especially voting. Bowles wants residents to understand that high voter turnout translates into adequate garbage removal and quick response by the police to 911 calls. Bowles has been unsuccessful to date in persuading city officials to invest in Round Hill although heavy investments by the city continue to be made

Budget Summary

	Current Year	Next Year
Expenses		
Personnel	—	42,000
Miscellaneous	482.50	1,800
	482.50	43,800

in the adjacent neighborhoods of Plymouth Square and Chamberlain Hill. There are only six or eight businesses remaining, and at meetings of the Round Hill Business Association, of which Bowles is also chair, often only he will show up.

Negative attitudes in the neighborhood are a concern. Residents tend to feel helpless about changing the atmosphere. For example, in the past few years Round Hill has lost two chain groceries, chiefly because of pilferage. If residents saw an adult or child stealing, they looked the other way. Youth growing up know no other way of life, and the Neighborhood Council will work closely with the Neighborhood Safety Coalition, which runs a summer camp in the suburbs for neighborhood youth. There the youth can observe that not all walls have graffiti and not everyone uses obscene words to express what they want to say.

The Neighborhood Council also wants to secure more consistent coverage from the Plymouth Square and Chamberlain Hill health services to compensate for the absence of health services in Round Hill. Through the Council's efforts, an agreement was reached that two outreach workers from Plymouth Square Health Service would spend part time in Round Hill, but so far they have not shown up. The presence of a full-time executive director would allow for the continual follow-up necessary to secure health services and to implement the other activities described above.

Governance: The five-member board of directors includes two Round Hill businessmen in addition to Bowles, Reverend Elliot of the Baptist Church Community Center, and Charlene Hunter of the Neighborhood Safety Coalition. The council was founded and incorporated eighteen months ago and recently received its tax-exempt ruling letter from the IRS.

Exhibit 3.6. Round Hill Comprehensive Services.

Mission: The mission consists of (1) public safety, (2) economic development, (3) resource and information network referral, (4) youth services, (5) family support and violence prevention, and (6) education/cultural service programs.

Project to be funded: This start-up organization is an offshoot of the Round Hill Neighborhood Safety Coalition funded by the Kalmet Trust. The new organization is incorporated and expects to receive its ruling letter from the IRS in a few weeks. The founders believe that the new organization, with its expanded service focus, will better address the underlying causes of violence and crime in Round Hill.

Amount requested: $41,500, 1 year.

Contact person: Charlene Hunter, prospective executive director.

Description of the project: The underlying philosophy is to build goals and activities around what neighborhood residents say they want rather than around what service providers say the residents need. The following five programs are planned:

Networking and Referral: An important asset in implementing the comprehensive approach will be an information base and network of contacts resulting from Hunter's and the board's association with people inside and outside the immediate neighborhood. Providing referrals to neighborhood residents is a concrete service that will show results to the community and get people involved.

Economic Development: Comprehensive Services will work closely with the Business Association, which has no staff. Currently, Round Hill has six to eight businesses, each with one or two employees. The concept of "The New Round Hill" will be promoted through community meetings focusing on how to secure job training, get a job, or become a franchisee. The prospective executive director has learned through experience that residents will turn out to discuss economic possibilities but not public safety.

Youth Development: Comprehensive Services will operate the summer camp formerly run by the Round Hill Neighborhood

Budget Summary

	Current Year[a]	Next Year
Expenses		
Personnel	32,300[b]	45,000
Program (camp)	17,700	20,000
	50,000	65,000
Revenues		
Kalmet Trust	25,000	—
Fundraising, Stoneview	15,500	16,000
City Youth Corps	4,500	7,500

[a]Current year budget is for Neighborhood Safety Coalition.

[b]Executive director $22,300; youth mentor $10,000.

Safety Coalition. Presumably the camp will continue to be funded by private contributions from supporters in the wealthy suburb of Stoneview. Some funds are provided by the city. Activities include a one-week overnight camp in the suburbs and two in-city day camp programs, also one week in duration.

Health Development: Comprehensive Services will work closely with Plymouth Square Health Services.

Safety Development: Comprehensive Services will organize community residents, children as well as parents, to maintain "a watchful eye." Volunteer organizers will be trained to go door-to-door to set up block watches.

Governance: The board of directors includes the minister of the Round Hill Baptist Church; Don Bowles, president of the all-volunteer Neighborhood Council and the all-volunteer Business Association; Angelo Colangelo, Stoneview lawyer, white, providing pro bono legal services to the organization; and Eugene Washington, professor of African American Studies at Cityside Community College.

Suggested Readings

Bielefeld, W. "What Affects Nonprofit Survival?" *Nonprofit Management & Leadership,* 1994, 5(1), 19–36. Informative elaboration of the ecological theory that younger and smaller organizations are at risk for survival. In comparison to surviving nonprofits, nonsurvivors focused more on retrenching than on seeking new sources of funding.

Gould, S. J. "The Two Great Problems of the Burgess Shale." In S. J. Gould, *Wonderful Life: The Burgess Shale and the Nature of History.* New York: W. W. Norton, 1989. Argues that survival of the fittest is a tautology and that apparent adaptive superiority of living forms does not necessarily result in survival. Intriguing analogy to ecological theory of organizational survival (which the author does not discuss).

Hunter, A., and Staggenborg, S. "Local Communities and Organized Action." In C. Milofsky (ed.), *Community Organizations: Studies in Resource and Mobilization Exchange.* New York: Oxford University Press, 1988. Reviews some of the significant scholarship related to neighborhood organizations. Discusses importance of local community characteristics to welfare of small organizations.

Milofsky, C., and Romo, F. "The Structure of Funding Arenas for Neighborhood Based Organizations." In C. Milofsky (ed.), *Community Organizations: Studies in Resource and Mobilization Exchange.* New York: Oxford University Press, 1988. Holds that development of a neighborhood-based organization is more dependent on its participants than on structural factors such as organizational age, size, and sources of funding.

Young, D. R. *If Not for Profit, for What?: A Behavioral Theory of the Nonprofit Sector Based on Entrepreneurship.* Lexington, Mass.: Heath, 1983. Argues that the nonprofit sector encompasses a broad spectrum of entrepreneurial activity and motivation. See especially Chapter 5, "Models of Entrepreneurs."

Chapter Four

Investing Donor Dollars at the United Way

A Role-Playing Exercise

Lisa Silverman Pickard
Melissa Middleton Stone

At the United Way of Massachusetts Bay (UWMB), as at other local United Way agencies, volunteers make decisions about which applicant agencies will receive grants and the amount of funding each will receive. In this role-playing exercise, participants act as "fiduciaries" for other people's philanthropic dollars. Participants make specific resource allocation decisions in a setting where resources are limited and applicant agencies are needy.

Prior to class discussion, each participant assesses applicant agencies in relation to UWMB's review criteria and develops a personal opinion about how the available funds ought to be divided (Exhibits 4.1 to 4.7; Table 4.1). The participants then meet as a group to conduct the role play.

A two-hour role play and discussion session is recommended, as follows:

Introduction	10 minutes
Dividing participants into small groups	5 minutes
Making allocation decisions in small groups	40 minutes
Reconvening in large groups for small group reports	25 minutes
Comments by observers on small group process	15 minutes
Debriefing with large group	20 minutes
Summary	5 minutes

Small groups of six to eight participants are optimal. A presenter/reporter and timekeeper for each group should be assigned. It is also helpful to assign one participant as an observer who remains silent throughout the group's deliberations but records how the decision-making process unfolds.

Once the participants have reconvened in the large group, each reporter gives a five-minute summary of her or his group's decisions and identifies the review criteria that seemed to emerge as most important. If time permits, participants from the large group can ask questions and share similarities or differences in approach. After the small group reports are completed, each observer makes a three- or four-minute report.

Questions for Discussion

The exercise closes with discussion by the larger group of questions such as the following:

1. What was the experience like?
2. Which behaviors facilitated decision making? Which made decision making harder? How did the group deal with logjams?
3. Who did participants feel they were representing during the exercise?
4. Did participants' individual decisions change as a result of the group's deliberations? Did the participants feel that the group made the "right" decisions?
5. What is the value of the allocations process to donors? To the United Way? To the agencies themselves?
6. In what sense, if any, is a United Way allocations committee a stakeholder in its recipient agencies? In what sense, if any, is a local United Way a part of the governance structure of its recipient agencies?

Exhibit 4.1. Setting the Stage.

United Way of Massachusetts Bay volunteers are fiduciaries for donors' investments. As one of 250 volunteers, it is your responsibility to provide the quality control that United Way donors expect. Your goal is to allocate funds to effective agencies that document significant impact and show financial need.

During the ten-month allocations process, your committee has been assessing the effectiveness of several agencies. You have visited sites and observed agency programs. You have talked to agency board and staff about goals and results. You have reviewed detailed budget information and the audit. During meetings with the agency, you have discussed issues or concerns and have asked questions about the funding request.

This year's campaign raised enough to allocate $380,000 to these five agencies, a 16.5 percent decrease ($75,000 less) in total funding from last year. Your committee will distribute this amount to its five agencies.

Exhibit 4.2. Review Criteria.

- *Excellence: Management and Governance* (demonstrates skilled governance, fiscal stability, and the management capacity to implement effective programs; responds to UWMB concerns)
- *Capacity-Building/Prevention* (focuses on self-sufficiency and self-development, builds capacity of individuals/communities to prevent problems, values diversity, builds leadership, supports children and their families)
- *Results/Outcomes* (documents significant impact and improvement in the well-being of children and their families, promotes long-term systemic change)
- *Greatest Needs* (documents community need, focuses on populations with limited access demonstrating financial need)
- *United Way Campaign Support* (conducts a UWMB workplace campaign, participates in speakers bureau, takes every opportunity to identify UWMB affiliation)
- *Volunteer Involvement* (leverages involvement of volunteers for cost effectiveness and as a community-building strategy)
- *Relative Financial Need* (demonstrates financial need and lacks access to other resources)

Table 4.1. Comparative Financial Analysis.

	Current UWMB Allocation	Agency Request	Requested % Change	Individual Preliminary Recommendation	% Change	Group Final Recommendation	% Change
Safe Haven	$30,000	$60,000	100.0%				
Children's Place	$150,000	$200,000	33.3%				
Multi-Service Center	$200,000	$200,000	0.0%				
Kids' Clubhouse	$40,000	$45,000	12.5%				
Boston Advocates	$35,000	$45,000	28.6%				
TOTAL	$455,000	$550,000	20.9%	$380,000	-16.5%	$380,000	-16.5%

Exhibit 4.3. Safe Haven.

Safe Haven, a Chelsea shelter for battered women and their children, has strived since 1990 to put an end to the violence committed against women and their children. 1994 budget is $400,000.

The eight staff members assisted over 2,500 women and 1,500 children through a number of programs that include safe homes, counseling, information and referral, legal and housing advocacy, and Southeast Asian outreach. Women served are 75 percent Latina, 15 percent Asian, and 10 percent white. Agency has eighty volunteers providing child care, mentoring, and violence prevention training in schools.

Community need: Domestic violence is the leading cause of injury to women, greater than automobile accidents, rape, and muggings combined. In 1989, a woman was murdered as a result of domestic violence every twenty-two days in Massachusetts. In the first half of 1993, a woman was murdered every fourteen days.

Chelsea is the poorest city in Massachusetts by many standards. Fifty percent of the population receives some form of public assistance. Twenty-four percent of total population (43 percent of Latinos) live in poverty.

Agency funding: Fifty-five percent government, 30 percent foundations/contributions, 7 percent special events, 8 percent UWMB.

Unrestricted fund balance: $60,000 (two months' operating budget).

Current UWMB allocation: $30,000.

Requested UWMB allocation: $60,000 (includes $15,000 to open a transitional living house).

Previous panel comments:

- Board is small (seven members). Agency needs to increase its board size and recruit persons with expertise in areas such as financial management and fundraising. Board development training is recommended.
- Staff is dedicated and effective; many are former clients.
- Agency receives in-kind support from churches, community groups, and individuals.

- Results and impact are well documented. Program promotes self-empowerment and enhances capacity of women to advocate for themselves.
- Community and participant need is well documented.
- Agency does no UWMB campaign speeches, citing limited available staff time. A UWMB workplace campaign was conducted only after much prodding.

Major discussion issues:

- Lack of UWMB campaign support.
- Significant impact on target population and documented community need.
- UWMB funds help leverage many other resources including in-kind and volunteer.
- In a time of decreased funds available, should UWMB be funding new programs?

Exhibit 4.4. Children's Place.

The Children's Place, founded in 1967, is a day-care center in Roxbury serving children three months to six years old, 85 percent African American and 15 percent Latino. Most children (90 percent) are from low-income, single-parent families. Parents are involved in parenting skills workshops, discussion groups, curriculum development and planning, and board committees. 1994 budget is $1,000,000.

Forty-five staff members (twenty additional summer positions) serve a total of 450 children.

Community need: In Roxbury, nearly a third of African Americans and almost half of Latinos live below the poverty line. Forty-one percent of Hispanic families in Boston are headed by single parents of which four out of five are living in poverty.

Approximately 270,000 or 60 percent of children under six years old in Massachusetts live in families where a single parent or both parents work outside the home. However, less than half the three-to-five-year-olds in Massachusetts attend preschool programs, with children from low-income families the least likely to be in preschool.

Agency funding: Seventy percent government, 5 percent self-pay, 10 percent contributions, 15 percent UWMB.

Unrestricted fund balance: ($15,000); audit shows $70,000 operating deficit for past year.

Current UWMB allocation: $150,000.

Requested UWMB allocation: $200,000.

Previous review panel comments:

- Agency serves a target population and geographic area of great need with few resources.
- Program builds leadership among parents, promotes self-development, and involves parents in decision making.
- Serious concerns exist regarding current organizational and fiscal capacity, including turnover in executive directors (four in four years); tax liabilities, weak financial status, late audits; and insufficient board capacity to address these challenges.
- UWMB allocation was escrowed due to lack of response to concerns. Agency had not contacted Management Consulting Service and Boardbank for board development, fundraising, and financial systems assistance.
- Recently hired interim executive director has aggressively addressed financial problems by reducing and/or eliminating programs with insufficient financial support. Improvement is noted but continued progress is critical.
- Agency does not involve volunteers.
- UWMB campaign support is good.

Major discussion issues:

- Major organizational problems: ongoing financial and management issues.
- No other agency is providing these services in this neighborhood.
- Agency meets prevention/capacity-building model.
- Need for UWMB funds is high.

Exhibit 4.5. Multi-Service Center.

The Multi-Service Center, founded in 1866, serves the entire Greater Boston area through three offices (Natick, Boston, Dorchester). Program offerings are home health aide, elderly services, AIDS education/awareness, family counseling, and substance abuse counseling. Target population is low-income, frail elders and families in crisis. 1994 budget is $1,000,000.

Agency staff is seventy-five. Agency reports serving 1,500 in elderly services, 750 in family counseling, 250 in substance abuse counseling, 250 in home health aide program, and 100 in newly formed AIDS education/awareness program. A centralized volunteer program places forty volunteers throughout the agency. Majority of services focus on a professional counseling relationship with clients. Agency is beginning to initiate self-help groups.

Community need: In Boston, more than a hundred thousand persons or 19 percent of the population live in poverty, including almost 15 percent of the elderly. Research has indicated that families living in poverty are at higher risk of substance abuse, single parenthood, and domestic violence.

In Massachusetts, an estimated 290,000 persons abuse alcohol and another 122,000 are addicted to other drugs. As of June 1993, nearly seven thousand people have been diagnosed with AIDS in the Commonwealth. Intravenous drug use has become the leading mode of transmission, representing 39 percent of all AIDS diagnoses.

Agency funding: Forty-five percent government, 3 percent foundation/contributions, 2 percent special events, 15 percent program service fees, 15 percent investment income, 20 percent UWMB.

Unrestricted fund balance: Agency has a $500,000 endowment and $100,000 unrestricted fund balance. Last year, the agency used $30,000 of their reserves to begin the AIDS program.

Current UWMB Allocation: $200,000.
Requested UWMB Allocation: $200,000.
Previous panel comments:

- Although board is "well connected," with many corporate members, average attendance is only 40 percent. Panel sug-

gests increased board involvement, more strategic leadership, and greater diversity to be reflective of communities served.
- Relative financial need is not as compelling as other agencies.
- Agency staff is professional and impressive but does not collaborate with other providers.
- Agency is an active supporter of the UWMB campaign, giving many speeches, tours, and conducting a trailblazer campaign.

Major discussion issues:

- Relative financial need is not compelling.
- Active supporter of UWMB campaign.
- Politically connected board; reductions could have impact on UWMB campaign.
- Prevention/capacity-building activities are minimal, although agency wants to move in this direction.
- Documents significant need among target populations.
- Agency does not collaborate with other community agencies.

Exhibit 4.6. Kids' Clubhouse.

The Kids' Clubhouse, founded in 1952, provides after-school recreation, cultural enrichment, homework support, and summer day camp for children six to seventeen years old in Newton. 1994 budget is $160,000.

A staff of ten (and nine summer positions) works with six hundred kids. Many kids participate in more than one agency program. There are 150 children in the summer day camp, 525 in "drop-in" recreation programs, 210 in the homework club, and 50 children are matched with volunteer adult mentors. Children served are 80 percent white, primarily from working-class families.

Community need: Students who have unstructured, unsupervised time to fill on their own after school are at twice the risk of drug and alcohol abuse than those who are supervised.

In Newton, 93 percent of residents are white and 3.3 percent of families with children live in poverty.

Agency funding: Twenty percent foundation/contributions, 15 percent special events, 5 percent government, 35 percent membership fees, 25 percent UWMB.

Unrestricted fund balance: $12,000 (one month's operating budget).
Current UWMB allocation: $40,000.
Requested UWMB allocation: $45,000.
Previous panel comments:

- Board is active, diverse, and representative of community.
- Staff is effective and committed. Agency has a strong, effective volunteer program.
- Agency has excellent community relations.
- Recreation programs, although "drop-in" style, are used by many working parents as after-school day care.
- Panel asks for better documentation of target population needs and program impact.
- Agency is supportive of UWMB campaign.

Major discussion issues:

- Relative need of target population and geographic area is less compelling.
- UWMB funds represent a large percent of the agency's budget relative to other funded agencies.
- Program is cost effective (serves many with a small budget) and involves volunteers.
- Agency needs to show clearer results and impact of programs.

Exhibit 4.7. Boston Advocates.

Boston Advocates was founded in 1985. Its mission is to advocate at the state level for positive policy change and resources to reduce infant mortality and provide adequate prenatal health care for pregnant women. Special focus is on teen mothers. Agency works as a consortium of fifty-three human service agencies from across the state (85 percent are Boston based). 1994 budget is $350,000.

Agency has four staff members. Statistics show about one hundred thousand persons served indirectly by benefiting from policy change. Volunteers (250 from staffs of member agencies and other individuals) assist at community organization and advocacy events/activities.

Community need: From 1980 to 1990, the birth rate among Massachusetts teenagers increased 19 percent. Infants of teen mothers are twice as likely to be born with low birth weight and twice as likely to die before their first birthday. In addition, 50 percent of teens giving birth before age eighteen never receive a high school diploma.

Agency funding: Eighty-five percent foundation/contributions, 5 percent membership dues, 10 percent UWMB. Agency does not seek state funding since they are strong advocates for change in state government.

Unrestricted fund balance: $30,000 (one month's operating budget).

Current UWMB allocation: $35,000.

Requested UWMB allocation: $45,000.

Previous panel comments:

- Board is diverse, representative of community, and very active.
- Agency recently completed a comprehensive strategic plan.
- Advocacy at the State House leverages funds to support many direct service agencies. Better documentation of actual impact and results versus process would help to assess effectiveness.
- Agency initiates collaborative activities with other organizations.
- Staff is well respected in the field.
- Agency conducts a UWMB campaign. They have been reminded many times to include UWMB identification at events, on newsletters, and in agency mailings. They reluctantly participate in UWMB speakers bureau.

Major discussion issues:

- Agency impact: advocacy versus direct services.
- Board and staff is highly competent and respected.
- Need for UWMB funds is high.
- Agency needs to better document program results and impact.
- Campaign support is minimal.

Suggested Readings

Alderfer, C. P. "The Invisible Director on Corporate Boards." *Harvard Business Review,* 1986, *64*(6), 38–52. Explores group dynamics of for-profit boards, including roles board members may play and the development of inner circles and factions.

Brilliant, E. L. *The United Way: Dilemmas of Organized Charity.* New York: Columbia University Press, 1990. Useful background in Chapter 4, "From Allocations to Alternative Funds," on challenges to the United Way's allocation process and the formation of alternative federated fundraising groups.

Eddy, W. B. *The Manager and the Working Group.* New York: Praeger, 1985. Basic information on the dynamics of working groups in organizations, including phases of group development, roles group members often play, and problem-solving approaches in Chapter Four, "Understanding How Groups Work," and Chapter 7, "Problem-Solving Groups."

Polivy, D. K. "The United Way: Understanding How It Works is the First Step to Effecting Change." In C. Milofsky (ed.), *Community Organizations: Studies in Resource Mobilization and Exchange.* New York: Oxford University Press, 1988. Empirical study of the admissions policies and practices of United Ways in eight cities, paying particular attention to the constraints embodied in the United Way's federated structure.

Complexities in the Board-Staff Relationship

Part Two examines the interplay between governing board oversight and administrative management. Theoretically, the board "makes policy" while the chief administrator and staff implement it. However, determining which issues are policy issues can be difficult because the views of stakeholders, as well as the passage of time and changes in circumstance, have a decisive effect on perceptions (Wood, 1983; Chait and Taylor, 1989). By today's standards, however, the central issue in each case in this section is clearly a "board issue." Each issue also qualifies as a "classic" of governance: a situation that frequently occurs across the universe of charitable nonprofits and, over a period of years, may recur within a single organization.

The familiar dynamic of creeping bureaucratization as charitable organizations age and/or increase in size (Wood, 1992) is illustrated in "The Evolving Board-Executive Relationship at a Women's Shelter." In this two-part case, Milofsky and Morrison show that when a grassroots organization becomes more bureaucratic, the resulting tensions are expressed in relationships among stakeholders, especially between the governing board and the chief administrator. In "Conflicting Managerial Cultures in a Museum," Hall describes powerful board member stakeholders whose use of business practices typical of for-profit corporations alienates the executive director and threatens to undermine the organization's mission. This case recalls Chapter One, "The Public Interest and Tax Exemptions for Nonprofit Hospitals," by suggesting that the emphasis on becoming more businesslike can transform the character of a tax-exempt organization in ways presumably not intended by promoters of sound management practice.

"The Governing Board Faces Rebellion in the Ranks," by Widmer, illustrates how little a governing board normally knows about staff members' opinions of the chief administrator. Structurally, the chief administrator is the single link between the board on the one hand and the staff on the other. A staff member who talks to a board member about the chief administrator may be viewed as a "tattletale." To the extent that a board tolerates these unofficial messages, it undermines the authority of its agent by establishing an informal network for the flow of information. To the extent that a board ignores these messages, or refuses to act on them, it may be imperiling the organization's welfare. Widmer's case implies that any tactic for handling staff discontent with the chief administrator has its downside.

A "rubber stamp" board that ratifies the chief administrator's recommendations and otherwise simply goes through the motions of oversight is an anathema in the exhortatory literature that urges governing boards to be "involved." In "Confronting Crisis: When Should the Board Step In?" Cnaan's history of New Frontiers Inc. enables the reader to judge when and on what basis a hands-off board might have been more vigilant. Embedded in the story of New Frontiers Inc. is the question of whether an absentee board that is inexpert in nonprofit finance—although prominent in banking, law, and commerce—can be expected to identify problems that can eventually lead to a crisis of survival. A related issue of board member competence is raised in Saidel's "Outgrowing the Governing Board: A Conundrum." In this case, the executive director of Windham Programs seeks the support of knowledgeable outsiders to avoid the kind of crisis experienced by New Frontiers Inc. To achieve that end, he will have to change the membership of a board composed of parents dedicated to Windham and its mission but ill equipped, in the executive director's view, to deal with the impact of government-funded programs on organizational values. Ironically, the executive director's plan to change the composition of the board, or to supplement it with an advisory committee, would bring to Windham Programs the types of people who serve on the board of New Frontiers Inc.

At Windham Programs, the executive director's father is a prominent person who, through his personal networks, can recruit other prominent individuals to the advisory committee for his son's agency. Other methods are employed by the part-time executive director of Montrose City Community Theater, as described by Whitt and Moore in "Using Community Networks to Diversify the Board." The case is written as a playlet. It presents the nominating committee's reaction when the executive director proposes candidates whose membership on other boards will secure a more central position for the theater in a citywide network of charitable and for-profit organizations. The resulting potential resources, human and financial, would be greater than those offered by the nominating committee's candidate, who is wealthy but does not move in circles populated by the city's "movers and shakers."

References

Chait, R. P., and Taylor, B. E. "Charting the Territory of Nonprofit Boards." *Harvard Business Review,* 1989, *67*(1), 44–54.

Wood, M. M. "What Role for College Trustees?" *Harvard Business Review,* 1983, *61*(3), 52–62.

Wood, M. M. "Is Governing Board Behavior Cyclical?" *Nonprofit Management and Leadership,* 1992, *3*(2), 139–163.

Chapter Five

The Evolving Board-Executive Relationship at a Women's Shelter

Carl Milofsky
Nancy E. Morrison

After five years of steadily increasing funds and expanding programs, Wild River Women for Change (WRWC), a women's shelter, was at a crossroads. Although the organization had grown from a largely volunteer operation into a respected and important social service agency in the town of Wild River, staff members felt overworked and underpaid. A new executive director, determined to attack the agency's chronic funding problem, underestimated the continuing influence of the agency's history and set off a chain reaction that prompted WRWC program staff and traditional supporters in the community to challenge her initiatives. Responding to these pressures, the governing board dismissed the executive director and must now decide on a course of action.

Part A: The Seeds of Crisis

In 1976, a group of women and a few men who realized that domestic violence was becoming an increasingly important problem organized a network of "safe houses" wherein they offered their own homes as a safe place for battered women to escape domestic violence. They obtained a small grant to rent an office and pay part-time workers to spend time there. After one year, the original funding ran out and the group and its safe-house network dissolved as some of the original activists moved out of the area.

Barbara Armonk was one of the original women who remained and decided with another group of women to resurrect the idea in 1979. They organized another meeting to talk about the battering problem and to try to start a local movement against domestic violence and rape, and they decided to create a formal organization. Some of the women agreed to be on a board of directors, and the fledgling organization, the Wild River Women for Change, began to look for funding.

In January of 1980, the women gathered to decide when to put their plans into action. They did not have enough money to run a hotline for an entire year, but they decided to go a month at a time and see if they could make it through a year. They took the small amount of money they had been able to raise, rented an office on Main Street, and installed a hotline phone. The women went around town leaving the hotline number in the bathrooms of bars and taped to public telephones.

Armonk was a divorced, single parent at the time the hotline began. She quit her job and went on welfare so she could devote all of her time to writing proposals to seek funding for WRWC. Six months later, these efforts proved successful and Armonk became the first paid staff and the executive director by default.

The Collective

Once the grant was in place, WRWC decided to run volunteer training sessions about three times a year. These first training sessions were run by a board member, Carrie Troup. She and the other board members were extremely active in the organization. They not only ran the volunteer training sessions but also answered the hotline on weekends. Although Barbara Armonk was paid and was tacitly recognized as executive director, all of the women worked together collectively to keep the place running.

The training groups Troup ran were determinedly democratic and sought to lower any barriers of class or personal history that might separate staff or volunteers from women who sought help. Training sessions conveyed information about the extent and dangers of domestic violence, and WRWC also ran self-examination groups in which all members were asked to think about and discuss their relationships with men. These groups often included student volunteers from the local college and middle-class women. Battered women were also members of these groups. They provided a service to the others by sharing personal experiences that helped women not in crisis to examine their lives and to discover how they also had been disempowered. In this way, the organization rejected the model of professional service provision in which social workers or other experts minister to needy clients.

At this point, the organizational structure was an assemblage of overlapping groups from the community, including committed feminists, women who identified themselves as victims of abuse, and concerned citizens. Although WRWC had five paid staff, the organization as a whole was collectivist. Formal division of labor was minimal and, while some were leaders, any division of labor had very little to do with a formal organizational title, and everyone participated in decision making. This style of organization is often described as more "feminine" than the bureaucratic style. Whether or not that observation is true, the people involved in this intense, egalitarian period in the life of WRWC remained devoted to the organization, to the values of the women's movement it was carrying out, and to the goals they shared. Long after they stopped playing an active role in WRWC, they and an ongoing collection of active volunteers formed a sort of "Greek chorus" in the town of Wild River that watched the organization, supported it when needed, cheered its successes, and loudly challenged its deviations from founding values.

Rather than having a hierarchical approach to decision making, the women worked out conflicts through group discussion until there was consensus. Democracy was exercised in two ways. First, Barbara Armonk led the meetings, but she made few independent decisions. As a result, board meetings were very long, often over four hours, but active members knew intimately about every issue that affected WRWC. Second, each member did all of the organization's jobs. Everyone provided counseling, accompanied women to court, or carried the hotline pager at different times. As a result, particular individuals were prevented from acquiring high status because they were responsible for more attractive or powerful jobs. "Role switching" also meant that every

WRWC service provider knew and had close relationships with the women who were receiving services. Services were provided through egalitarian discussion groups, and consequently, even those receiving services were not placed on a lower level than staff.

Despite the democratic ethos of the organization, Barbara Armonk played a crucial role. First, she had a lot of power in the organization because she had earned the respect of the other workers. Not only did she do the work well, but more than any other member she devoted her whole life to the organization, putting all of herself into making WRWC function and grow. Furthermore, she was the only woman who had been there from the beginning, which made her the founding mother.

Armonk also used her authority. She might have quietly coordinated the work of others and stayed in the background, but she did not. A staunch feminist who believed in consensual decision making, she shared her authority with the staff but was frequently the source of ideas and the person whose seal of approval was required for action to be taken. Armonk's assertive presence meant that the organization had a strong sense of direction and that she was closely in touch with the staff and the organization's activities. By performing direct services like everyone else, she never became isolated by the arduous work of grantwriting; the executive director and the staff were a unified group.

In 1982, the women decided that the hotline was not providing sufficient protection to battered women in the area who needed to leave their abusive husbands and had nowhere to go. They therefore recreated the safe-house network and took battered women into their homes to hide and protect them. This sheltering effort laid the foundation for creation of a permanent shelter in 1984.

New Director, Big Changes

The year 1986 saw many changes at WRWC. Most importantly, Barbara Armonk, feeling burned out after seven years, quit as executive director and left the area. She was replaced by Megan Ford. Ford had the daunting task of taking over for the charismatic founder who knew every person and every issue intimately.

Beyond the challenge of replacing a dynamic leader, Ford also had to work with the strong feminist legacy that Armonk and the other founders had built into the organization. Foremost was the notion that only a collectivist organization could be truly feminist. Ford disagreed. With a background in direct provision of social services, she saw in WRWC an organization that ran inefficiently, did not serve many of the people who needed it, and desperately required resources.

values

These deficiencies could best be attacked by making the organization more professional and centralized. She wanted staff members with skills and experience in relevant fields who could take over specific jobs and do them well. She wanted to separate the board and the staff, recruiting to the board people with skills and contacts that would help put the organization on a more secure footing. Most importantly, she wanted to craft a niche for herself and a few other administrators where they could effectively play a managerial role. She wanted to bring planning, grantwriting, supervision, and accountability together so that a few people would be responsible for the whole organization and so that all decisions would have to pass through and include them.

*Professionali-
sm
&
Centralism*

These changes amounted to making the organization dramatically more "bureaucratic" in just the sense that feminists opposed. Ford's goal was to build a strong executive group that would be the most powerful force in the organization and would stand between—and control—the board and the staff. Her strategy was to build a stable, strong executive niche by claiming some essential organizational functions and making the roles of the board and the staff contingent on the help and supervision of the executive. However, the changes she initiated amounted to forcing the creation of three new stakeholder groups in the agency where previously there had been only one.

contrasts the "values"

When Megan Ford arrived at WRWC, the staff included five full-time members. Turnover during her first year included the introduction of new staff members and the loss of one of the founders, Carrie Troup. After an initial contraction, however, WRWC began to grow rapidly as it moved into a new shelter and added staff whose philosophies of service were more professional and less oriented to the earlier model in which the organization was seamlessly integrated with the broader community of women. The transition to a new style of organization was made easier

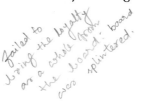

failed to living by the loyalty from a while board: board the board splintered. once

focus was on to make it bigger; rather than its self-sufficiency & sustainability

because Megan Ford was a newcomer to Wild River. Her lack of social ties and loyalties helped her to look objectively at the organization and to institute necessary changes. She had experience doing direct service work and was familiar with the problems involved in running a shelter. WRWC as Ford initially encountered it was very much a grassroots organization, committed to remaining that way. However, the national movement on family violence had grown and developed enormously in the seven years that WRWC had existed. Ford wanted to organize and professionalize WRWC because she did not think it could last much longer if it continued to run on such a touch-and-go basis. She began formalizing staff relationships and organizational procedures, believing that such changes would make WRWC more manageable.

A loss of ideology flowed from these changes. As Ford and the few staff who agreed with her began to reform the organization, the new board members they recruited—professionals at other social service agencies—proved to be natural allies. These women objected to criticisms from the old collective that being more professional and favoring administrative structure equated with being bad feminists. The newcomers argued that times were changing. State governments were now funding programs to address family violence and sexual abuse. To survive, the organization had to become more efficient and formalized. The organization had no choice but to regularize its record-keeping procedures in order to meet contractual obligations and qualify for continued funding.

Ford and her allies also saw a need to make the organization appear more professional to the community. When she arrived and met with local service professionals, she heard that the agency was disorganized and "too radical" in its feminist philosophies. Agencies like the Department of Children and Youth, the Office of Human Resources, Legal Aid, and the police had the power to make many referrals that would greatly expand public access to WRWC's services. WRWC would be a more powerful agent for change once other agencies, such as the police, were persuaded that family violence is serious criminal behavior and were trained to use intervention techniques developed within the battered women's movement. But before WRWC could spread this message, the community of local social service professionals had to be convinced that WRWC was reliable and well run.

Overcoming disorganization was a daunting challenge, in part because of the nature of shelter work at WRWC. Some staff confronted emotional problems in the shelter and on the hotline, and protecting oneself emotionally from the tragic problems of clients was difficult. Furthermore, because the collectivist orientation encouraged staff not to separate their work from their own personal problems, a selective pressure developed that encouraged people to join the WRWC staff *because* they were dealing with emotional problems associated with family violence.

The increase in grant revenues was also causing problems. The organization had grown rapidly before administrative systems had been created that could monitor and support that growth, and the staff was therefore not always trained to effectively perform the tasks required by new programs. Furthermore, many staff members were uncomfortable with their necessary new roles as supervisors of other employees or of volunteers, having been schooled in the democratic ethos of the earlier phase of WRWC. The shelter staff especially found it difficult to adjust to the narrowly defined assignments that evolved as clients' needs became (or were defined by funders to be) more specific. As specialization distanced staff members from the emotional support they were accustomed to receiving from one another, turnover increased. Capable new staff were hard to find and new staff were continually being trained, often making it difficult for outsiders, such as staff at other agencies, to find WRWC staff who knew what was going on.

The Executive Directorship

To combat these problems, Ford created an executive director role that was more separated from the direct services of the organization, more "in charge," and more responsible for basic decision making. Her main responsibilities, she thought, were to maintain the financial security of WRWC and to make sure that the requirements of various grants were met. To find the money to ensure that the staff would be paid every week, she spent most of her time on the phone and at her desk. With funds coming from eight to ten sources, each of which had its own demands and expectations, Ford found that she and the staff were spending a lot of time compiling statistics to meet the reporting requirements. Running a twenty-four-hour-a-day shelter facility was also enormously demanding. A residential facility had to follow a huge number of regulations, many more than would be required of an agency that operated only during the day.

Instead of having various staff members produce the different components of a grant proposal, Ford centralized proposal writing and grant reporting and took control of these functions. Because she was the only person in the agency who understood filling out forms, writing proposals, and the entire financial and administrative picture, Ford devoted increasing amounts of time to completing paperwork and talking on the phone. This pattern of behavior left her isolated from the staff. Whatever peer support the other staff members enjoyed she did not have because she was separated from them on a daily basis and did fundamentally different work.

Ford also faced a lot of stress as she realized that it was impossible for her to complete the tasks required for WRWC to function in a responsible and accountable fashion. The biggest problem was funding sources at the state level. Each government department wanted to be sure its funds were spent on direct service programs rather than on the political agendas of any organization, and agencies such as WRWC filled out forms and submitted reports that proved they were offering a satisfactory amount of direct services. Direct services involved a different approach to WRWC's work from the model followed in previous years, when all functions were merged into one chaotic communal mass, with many staff members working in each of the different programs. Now these activities had to be divided up into discrete programs, someone had to take responsibility for the program, and then it had to be advertised so that people would use it. It took a lot of effort to get these projects off the ground, but once they were launched, people really used them.

The executive group included two other staff members who, like Megan Ford, were responsible for policy decisions and/or administrative tasks. One was a community outreach director whose role was to contact other community agencies, train staff at other organizations, and market WRWC. She was an immediate ally of Ford's partly because she did not work with the other WRWC staff. Often confronting the judgments and expectations of other agencies, the outreach director was also a natural supporter of the professionalization theme at WRWC.

The third member of the executive group was Artis James, the program director. Trained at a prestigious school of social work, James energetically set about making the training programs more clinically sophisticated, information intensive, and aimed at minimizing risk and liability to volunteers, clients, and the organization. Although she played a central role in undermining WRWC's collectivist spirit and in changing the actual daily activities of the staff, her low-key management style softened resentments. She was also especially effective in helping the board understand what was going on at the staff level.

The Governing Board

To create more support for her approach, Ford continued to recruit new board members. As founding board members with their academic-intellectual and activist-feminist perspectives left the board, they were replaced by professionals from agencies with policy-making boards that delegated authority over day-to-day operations to the executive director. In board committee meetings, these new members worked with Megan Ford in reviewing the details of grant proposals, setting up systems for record keeping, rationalizing administrative practices, downplaying lesbian ideology that was incompatible with WRWC's changing feminist culture, and reaching out to wealthy women in the community.

While Megan Ford and Artis James were the most visible agents of change, another transformation involved divestment of responsibility by the founding, collectivist group. For seven years, a tightly knit group of volunteers and low-paid staff had made the shelter the main activity of their lives. When Barbara Armonk left town, it seemed that the glue that bound other long-standing activists to the organization was dissolved. Although other founders remained in town, supporting WRWC fundraisers and events and playing the role of Greek chorus in the local feminist community, they took jobs elsewhere in Wild River, enrolled in the nearby university, and otherwise turned their lives in new directions.

In the earlier phase, these women had been both board members and staff of the organization. With their departure and the emergence of an assertive directorship, a clear demarcation was made between board and staff. The board increasingly was made up of people who held full-time jobs elsewhere. Some had technical skills such as proposal writing and legal and medical expertise that Ford and James could draw upon. Others had personally experienced family violence and believed in the organization. Still others might provide access to influential people (and private donations) in the community. The board, in short, became a group of community members who were strategically selected to serve the needs of the executive directorship.

The Shelter Staff

The shelter staff was not happy with this transformation. They felt that the board was estranged from the day-to-day operations of the organization and did not know enough about the nuts-and-bolts of WRWC to make the kinds of assertive decisions it was making. For instance, new board members were no longer required to participate in the forty-hour training program mandatory for all WRWC volunteers. The staff saw this training as an important opportunity for the board to learn in detail about the nature, incidence, and causes of domestic violence. How could the board make sensible policy decisions without this information? Ford and James answered that they wanted board members with administrative skills and the social access needed for the agency to survive. They were also concerned that if board members took the training and became too close to the staff, they would lose their objectivity and inclination to make hard organizational decisions. Social distance between the board and the staff widened.

wrong — this is how values get passed along

A vague but definite sense of group identity developed gradually among the shelter staff, none of whom had direct interaction with Megan Ford during the course of a typical day. Members of the shelter staff (the direct service manager, the child advocate, the legal advocate, the shelter manager, the volunteer coordinator, and two part-time drug and alcohol counselors) did not necessarily work together, since each was responsible for a different program, but they shared the responsibility of direct contact with clients and an ethos that grew out of that function.

Shelter staff also shared increased pressure caused by the

changes Ford and James introduced. Although the staff liked Artis James and worked well with her, providing each service properly was stressful because people had to do new things and because continuing funding required doing the work well. The shelter was chronically understaffed and its staff overworked: the numbers of clients were steadily increasing, staff often were learning how to do new things, and experienced people had to take time off to train newcomers. One problem fed into and exacerbated the others, creating a circle of frustration and exhaustion that had no end. Frustration gave staff members a measure of shared fellowship, but at the same time they felt disgruntled. They been cut out of many organizational decisions and, as they found their work situation worsening, felt increasingly distant from the executive group and the board.

a sense of solidarity

Despite feeling isolated and stressed by the volume of activity and poor working conditions, shelter staff continued to feel some solidarity with one another because they spent time together in the shelter. Another source of solidarity consisted of their ties to a large volunteer force, a group that had little loyalty to either the board or the executive director. The shelter staff was the main link between WRWC and this cadre of active, committed, informed community people.

neglected bridge

The Volunteers

Even with a growing paid staff, WRWC depended for survival on volunteers who provided much of the basic service. The core operations of WRWC involved running the shelter. The building had to be supervised twenty-four hours a day to meet state regulations and to assure the safety of clients. Within the shelter, a variety of specific services such as counseling, child care, and legal advice had to be provided. Also, the hotline had to be covered so that women calling for emergency help had a trained, sympathetic person to talk to and another person who could go out and pick them up if they needed to come to the shelter.

Since much of this activity was performed by volunteers, the staff felt an urgent need to recruit and maintain the volunteer workforce. Not only did volunteers have to devote many hours to the organization's operations for the agency to survive, but each of those workers also had to complete a forty-hour training course. Casual volunteers, in other words, were not useful. Volunteers had to put in a lot of time, and they had to do so reliably over a period of a year or more. A major frustration was that some people took the training and then put in only a few hours of volunteer work.

However, WRWC survived because most volunteers stayed on the organization's roster and allowed themselves periodically to be on call for women who phoned in, very upset, seeking advice, a caring ear, and often a quick car ride to safety for themselves, their children, and a few belongings. The intensity of these experiences, the opportunities for self-examination inherent in activities at the shelter, and continuing commitment by many women to the values of feminism and mutual aid made volunteering satisfying work.

Volunteering at WRWC could also be emotionally devastating. It was difficult to be awakened from a sound sleep by a woman who had just been beaten or who was terrified that her spouse or lover would hurt her and the children. Driving to a convenience store late at night to pick up a family that might be followed by an angry, violent man was very scary. But more important, volunteers might come to believe that most women in America suffer a measure of abuse simply by virtue of their gender, and this insight might upset their private lives. Volunteers had to come to terms with emotions they had never dealt with before, some realizing that they were in abusive relationships themselves. Volunteering to help others thus became a means for self-transformation that might be traumatizing, demanding support and sympathy from other volunteers and from the WRWC staff.

The volunteers also functioned as a valuable external support group for WRWC. When the agency undertook community fundraising, it was the volunteer force that both organized the event and contributed most of the money.

A Turning Point

In revising the structure of WRWC, the executive director was making a strategic move to control relations among the group. This attempt was neither negative nor aggressive: Megan Ford simply sought to make the organization more "rational" and "efficient" in ways that follow widely recognized rules of good managerial practice. She did not perceive that such moves are (intentionally or not) plays in a game, that their outcome is uncertain, and that organizational life would be very different were other groups to maintain and assert power. A change in power relationships is precisely what happened at WRWC.

The shelter staff continued to be an autonomous group difficult to control in a hierarchical structure. Decision making about program issues continued to occur in open meetings where considerable democracy prevailed. However, the meetings were frustrating to all because they went on at length and produced unsatisfying conclusions, especially for those on the executive side of the organization, who were painfully aware that definite actions must be taken.

At first, the staff tended to direct its anger at the board rather than the executive director because Megan Ford usually attended the meetings. Over the course of her tenure, the board evolved into a separate entity with little connection to the operation of the shelter. Board members were largely uneducated and uninformed about domestic violence work. With the board and staff so separated, the executive director could capitalize on being an intermediary. Especially given her monopoly on knowledge and her control of fiscal affairs, Ford could channel organizational decisions in a way that strengthened her objectives.

Power was diminished for Ford and her allies when individual staff members formed private relationships with board members, socializing them to a perspective different from that of the executive group. This dynamic occurred when a côterie of board members who were holdovers from the founding feminist group began to pressure Ford to participate in direct services. If she wanted to keep in touch with the women WRWC was serving, these board members argued, it was important for her to take her turn being on call for emergencies and answering the hotline. The staff members who shared these views told her so.

Ford retorted that her participation in direct services was impossible because the responsibilities of the director had grown. It was not realistic to expect her to do more than she already was doing. Ford felt that she kept in contact with battered women by attending various conferences and state meetings. Nevertheless, pressure mounted for her to be active in both direct service and

[handwritten margin note: In order to remain current with the ideas & objectives of workers board & director should work with their clients]

[handwritten margin note: Wrong approach - proper delegation would rid this issue]

administrative work, ultimately souring her relationship with the board. After two years, Ford quit.

In the wake of Megan Ford's resignation in 1988, there followed a succession of executive directors who had minimal impact on WRWC. Among these was one woman who lasted two years and another infamously known as "the phantom director" because she lasted a short period of time and no one ever saw her. During this period of turnover in the executive director's office, tension was mounting between the traditional feminists in the community and WRWC over whether the organization should publicly support traditional feminist political positions, such as abortion rights and gay rights. These traditional feminists wanted WRWC to affirm that it was a feminist organization, but the board resisted, hoping to be more successful in securing donations from wealthy, more conservative community residents. This fundraising initiative came about in part because state funding was cut back, and meeting the payroll was increasingly difficult. At this time, Tillie Jones was appointed executive director.

Questions for Discussion

1. What are the key events in the history of WRWC's board and staff?
2. What are the basic issues faced by the incoming executive director? by the board?
3. What strategies might be employed by Tillie Jones to reconcile WRWC's founding mission, with its strong ideological and parochial focus, with an emerging public role in which the organization must appeal to a broad political spectrum and be available to a more diverse clientele than the original collaborative would have served? What is the likely response of the governing board to these strategies?
4. What does this case suggest about setting organizational priorities when stakeholders in an organization sharply disagree and satisfying one group is likely to be perceived as an attack by another group?
5. How might Jones strengthen the role of executive director so that she does not become a lightning rod, taking the blame for conflict between groups?

6. To what degree, if at all, might changes in the organization's structure improve the organization's situation? Does the earlier collectivist philosophy suggest tools for increasing WRWC's ability to secure support from the community? Can some of the cohesion the organization enjoyed in its earlier years be recaptured?

Part B: The Crisis Deepens

With the support of the newly appointed executive director, Tillie Jones, a service auction was organized as a major fundraising event for the Wild River Women for Change. The board of directors decided to hold the auction at the home of a wealthy supporter in hopes that high-income people could be convinced to attend and pay high prices for the services offered. The traditional feminists objected, saying the event represented "classism." They pointed out that fundraisers are social events for the agency as well as moneymakers, and an auction at a rich woman's house would discourage poor people from participating. Most of the clients of WRWC were working class, they said, and none would feel comfortable at an upper-class event. The debate became heated over what should be done and whether WRWC was more worried about the middle class or the working class. In the end, the auction went on, but battle lines were drawn.

Another fundraising event produced a different controversy. WRWC held a walkathon in which members found sponsors to donate money for each mile volunteers walked. The event got underway and as the women marched down Main Street, a group of them began chanting slogans supporting the rights of women. Some of the women chanted, others did not. After the walk was over, Tillie Jones met with the women who had organized the march and told them she was appalled that they had started to chant as they walked through town. She said some of the other women on the walk were embarrassed to be part of such a spectacle. They had no idea that the chants were going to occur and would have taken a different route had they known. The chanters were equally outraged, feeling that basic WRWC values were being sacrificed to sanitize the organization for rich, conservative women. The conflicts over values occasioned by fundraising events signaled a shift in the political stance of WRWC. The conflicts also suggested that fundraising, regardless of principle, had become so important that the essential character of the organization was changed. The breakdown of the old feminist collective seemed complete. WRWC seemed destined to become one of those organizations where a strong executive director selected and manipulated a weak board to support actions that would strengthen the agency regardless of its effects on staff or the mission of the organization.

Concern about the WRWC's values caused some among the feminist founding group to seek out and befriend those on the board and staff who continued to support the traditional feminist values around which WRWC had been founded. At the same time, the staff was becoming critical of Tillie Jones in her role as executive director, and in the summer of 1992, several of the shelter staff met on their own with some members of the board to complain about Jones. This initiative had dramatic consequences. The board decided to respond to the complaints by appointing a committee to interview each staff person. Many members felt that the board had become rather passive and had little knowledge of the actual activities of the shelter. Turnover on the board was high and members often stayed on for only one or two years. The interviews with staff began a process in which board members educated themselves about the organization and its activities.

Despite the mediation efforts of board members, staff dissatisfactions could not be resolved. Late in the fall, four of the shelter staff quit in frustration. In the ensuing crisis, Tillie Jones resigned as executive director and the board rehired the staff who had quit. Until a new director could be hired, the board was in charge of WRWC's day-to-day administration, and members were forced to become more informed about daily operations. This situation also threatened the organization with failure: shortly after Jones left, state regulators threatened to cut off funding due to the chaotic environment of the shelter.

Now, six months later, WRWC is again settled into a routine. At the time the shelter was threatened with closure, an experienced administrator retiring from the state social services department was persuaded to sign a one-year contract as acting executive director. She is patching up relations with state funding agencies, and the shelter staff appears focused on direct service programs. However, the agency lives with a sense of uneasy peace. The essential conflicts remain unresolved because, on the one hand, no one expects the acting executive director to aggressively tackle the internal problems of the organization, while on the other hand the agency is surviving from month to month primarily because the state trusts the acting director enough to continue funding. However, conflicts threaten to break into the open once again as WRWC approaches the time when a new executive director must be found.

Board members continue to feel trauma in the wake of the crisis and the explosive conflicts may not really be resolved. The agency continues to be financially vulnerable and its staff underpaid; an effective fundraising campaign might help reduce these problems but such an effort seems to require that the organization be more neutral politically. The board remains involved in the day-to-day affairs of the shelter, partly because several new board members have direct knowledge of domestic violence issues or occupy positions where they have contact with a client group similar to WRWC's.

Some board members are unsure that WRWC made the right move by dismissing Tillie Jones. By that action, the board appeared to condone the traditional feminists' contention that WRWC had been opportunistic under Jones' leadership and, for the promise of large donations, willing to support right-wing political values and sell out working-class women dominated by and dependent upon men. Social service professionals who have joined the board complain that a strong lesbian contingent in the community's feminist Greek chorus does more to alienate working-class women than would taking a neutral position on the abortion issue. These critics argue that the feminist movement is rooted in the urban upper middle class and that although it idealizes working-class people, the philosophy and style of interaction it promotes is not effective with a poor clientele.

WRWC was organized on the premise that shelters should help women escape abusive relationships. Feminist values helped support that objective by urging battered women to leave violent spouses. Paradoxically, traditional feminists argue, providing shelter alone may be destructive to women if shelters help stabilize violent family relationships, enabling long-term abuse to continue. At WRWC, conflict persists over whether the agency should serve a

What they need to decide first

higher volume of poor and working-class women but with less intensive services, or whether it should place the highest priority on providing services that will help persuade battered women to leave their abusers, thus advancing traditional feminist values. These goals conflict because many victims of family violence seek only a stopgap to resolve an immediate problem and then return to the abusive partner. WRWC's clients live in a subsistence culture in which people tend to be suspicious of government and professional agencies. It is very hard to win their trust and also hard to convince these battered women that they should leave their husbands. Women are likely to use the shelter for emergencies but are reluctant to change their home situation as the shelter-movement philosophy urges.

Members of the WRWC board, in the meantime, continue to maintain that the traditional feminists are ideologues, and that what the agency needs is pragmatism. It needs money so it can provide services. Maintaining ideological purity simply means that the organization will cut itself off from resources that could save the lives of women in need.

Questions for Discussion

1. How would you evaluate the decisions by the WRWC governing board over the course of the agency's history?
2. Do you agree with the current governing board's view that "traditional feminists are ideologues and that what the agency needs is pragmatism"?
3. What should the WRWC governing board do now? What priorities would you propose to the board and why?
4. In appointing a new executive director, which stakeholders would you advise the board to try to accommodate?
5. Comment on the following analysis in view of the history of WRWC: the professional managerial model tends to separate an organization from its community of support. Why turn an agency that grew out of community need and a community effort to work together into a public utility when it could benefit from a local community of concern and serve as a vehicle for nurturing that community?

Suggested Readings

DiMaggio, P., and Powell, W. W. "The Iron Cage Revisited." In C. Milofsky (ed.), *Community Organizations. Studies in Resource Mobilization and Exchange.* New York: Oxford University Press, 1988. Original formulation of the "isomorphism hypothesis," arguing that over time, organizations within an "organizational field" tend to become more similar to each other. Important contribution to "neo-institutional" theory.

Loseke, D. R. *The Battered Women and Shelters: The Social Construction of Wife Abuse.* Albany: State University of New York Press, 1992. Ethnographic study of a battering shelter, explaining why the gap between the shelter staff and the executive described in our case, for example, turns out to be a common pattern in shelters. Suggests that some of the pressures for collectivism existing in shelters arise from the demands of shelter work as well as from the broader ideology of the feminist movement.

Milofsky, C. "Neighborhood-Based Organizations: A Market Analogy." In W. W. Powell (ed.), *The Nonprofit Sector: A Research Handbook.* New Haven: Yale University Press, 1987. Identifies definitional assumptions embedded in much organizational theory and explains why they do not apply to many community organizations. Proposes an alternative set of definitional assumptions that treat organizations as embedded within and subcomponents of the larger communities in which they are located.

Rothschild, J., and Whitt, J. A. *The Cooperative Workplace. Potentials and Dilemmas of Organizational Democracy and Participation.* New York: Cambridge University Press (ASA-Rose monograph series), 1986. Best analysis available of structural experiments that might enable collectivist organizational forms to survive long-term. In context of Weberian theory, suggests why collectivism may be an evolutionary stage beyond bureaucracy. Through case examples and structural arguments suggests how collectivist organizations can resist bureaucratizing tendencies.

Warren, R. L. "The Interorganizational Field as a Focus for Investigation," *Administrative Science Quarterly,* 1967, *S12, 396–419.* Important initial analysis of how social service organizations develop in relationship to the community and to the set of other agencies providing social services. Describes how organizational and community legitimacy are accompanied by many new expectations about services, structure, and funding access that make it difficult for an organization to retain its collectivist traditions.

Chapter Six

Conflicting Managerial Cultures in a Museum

Peter Dobkin Hall

Meeting in emergency session with an outside consultant present, the board of trustees of the Widget Museum was discussing two letters of resignation. One was from the executive director, who cited "recent actions taken by the board's executive committee without staff consultation." The other was from the chair of the board of trustees, who advised members to "make financial stability a higher priority than curatorial concerns" and to pursue "additional de-accession of the widget collection" to provide the necessary funds.

History

The Widget Museum was started by a group of enthusiastic amateurs: local history buffs, widget collectors, and academics with an interest in industrial history. Founded to celebrate the community's historic contribution to the widget industry, the museum is located on one and a half acres that were the site of the nation's pioneer widget assembly plant. The museum consists of four buildings—the office building, the manufactory, the barn, and the boarding house. The land and buildings are owned by the museum, except for the boarding house and a quarter acre surrounding it, which are leased from the Widget Company, a corporate descendant of the original assembly plant.

After a period of intense but unproductive activity under the guidance of volunteers, the organization hired a professional director in 1990. The governing board sank comfortably into inactivity, virtually rubber stamping staff actions and recommendations.

The situation was ideal for the new director, who proved to be an energetic entrepreneur as well as manager. Federal, state, and foundation funders were successfully tapped. Prize-winning exhibitions were mounted. Publications won national awards. The museum's education programs became an integral part of local school curricula. Attendance increased. As the museum's activities took on more variety and excellence, its financial needs increased although its staff remained small, with the executive director and his secretary the only full-time employees. Other staff included a part-time collections curator, a part-time education curator, and two part-time security guards.

Grants underwrote new programs and most of the museum's operating costs (Exhibit 6.1). But as the funding process became more competitive and funders proved less willing to underwrite indirect costs, the executive director concluded that the time had come to systematically cultivate local support, particularly from the business community.

Connecting with the Business Community

From the start, the executive director acknowledged that corporate contributions would require a business-oriented presence on the board. However, being himself a trained manager, the director welcomed that perspective as an antidote to the board's long-standing passivity. It met only quarterly and had delegated most of its agenda to a small and easily mustered executive committee. The executive director hoped that new trustees drawn from the business world would gradually replace the board's deadwood and help mobilize the trustees who remained.

Finding board candidates from corporations in the city was not easy. A number of prominent business people, individuals with demonstrated records of service on other community boards, were informally sounded out about becoming museum trustees. They declined, citing overcommitment to other, usually more prestigious boards. As outlines of the city's nonprofit board hierarchy gradually became apparent, the executive director realized that, as a "stepping stone" board, the museum would have to set its sights considerably lower. Experienced board people were much sought after and, once captured by well-established, high-visibility institutions such as the city hospital, the community foundation, the symphony, the preservation trust, and the historical society, were unlikely to want to invest their limited time on the board of a small, new, and financially insecure museum.

By the time a young executive vice president of a prospering bank came to the executive director's attention, the museum's board had reached the depths of passivity. The chair of the board had stepped down and none of his fellow trustees was willing to take his place. The executive director met informally with the prospective trustee and candidly outlined the museum's difficult situation while also hoping to appeal to his entrepreneurial instincts by speaking enthusiastically of its unrealized promise. The candidate responded with appropriate enthusiasm but set one condition on his joining the board: that he be made chair. Sensing an ally and a kindred spirit, the executive director readily agreed and, with little discussion, the choice was speedily ratified at the museum's next annual meeting.

During the following year, much as the executive director had hoped, the chair proved a catalyst for increasing the business community's interest and participation in the museum. The business presence on the board was increased with the addition of two of the new chair's colleagues. Though neither worked for the chair's firm, both had substantial and profitable ties to it. With the three businessmen voting together on the five-member executive committee, the museum began to move out of the doldrums.

A joint promotional venture was mounted, cosponsored by the chair's bank, a local magazine, and the museum, to present an annual award to an outstanding widget industry executive in the community. The award promised to bring the museum considerable attention and financial support from the region's business sector. It also promoted the interests of the award's business sponsors because, thanks to aggressive marketing, it gave both of these enterprises considerable visibility. The museum's executive director, moreover, was delighted by the venture because the Widget Industrialist of the Year Award complemented the museum's programmatic focus on the historical importance of widget manufacturing. The award winner was to be named by a committee jointly appointed by the three sponsors, and expenses for the ceremony were to be shared by the sponsors.

The Widget Industrialist of the Year Award was a spectacular success. In its second year, nominations came in from throughout the state, the award selection committee included prestigious business people as well as management faculty from the local university, and the award received lavish advance publicity. Nevertheless, there were subtle but unmistakable signs that the tail had begun to wag the dog. Press coverage featured participating businesses but largely ignored the museum. The chair's bank reneged on its commitment to bear its share of the costs of the award ceremony, promising instead to cover any shortfall in the annual budget with a generous contribution. More seriously, during the award selection process, the chair attempted to secure a special exception for his bank when its nominations were submitted one day late.

The Governing Board

Under the chair's leadership, both the executive committee and the board had begun to meet monthly, with the executive committee becoming involved in domains previously delegated to the executive director. Open conflict began to develop between the three business trustees and the executive director and intensified as the board's executive committee shifted its attention from the promotional venture to the museum's purchasing and personnel policies. The museum's accounts were shifted to the chair's bank, of which the other two businessmen were important customers. The change was made to encourage the chair's bank to make a large donation to the museum, although the museum's former bank had offered the same services at the same cost. When the museum was considering a substantial investment in office equipment, the three businessmen urged that it be obtained from the one of the trio who operated an office equipment firm. Having just sold an enormous amount of equipment to the chair's bank, the vendor was willing to make the sale to the museum at cost.

Subsequently, frustrated by the slow pace of a complex negotiation with the Widget Company over its interest in leasing the museum's office building as a Widget education center, the chair took over as the museum's spokesman. His intervention brought the prospect of short-term financial benefits, but the proposed use of the building threatened the museum's future eligibility for historic preservation grant monies. At the same time, the executive committee overruled the executive director's decision to discharge the part-time collections curator, who also managed the museum's rental activities. The curator, though outspokenly hostile to the museum's increasingly professionalized direction, commanded the loyalty of a large group of neighborhood volunteers whose donated labor to a major profit center made them a resource well worth conserving.

The executive committee finally turned its attention to the museum's nationally recognized but unprofitable public programs. In the search for profit centers, temporary exhibitions were suspended in order to free up space in the museum for rental purposes (such as weddings and corporate receptions). Programs serving the schools were suspended and education grant funds diverted to cover the shortfall resulting from the Industrialist of the Year promotion. The committee began exploring the possibility of auctioning off the museum's valuable collection of historic widgets, most of them received as gifts and bequests, and of applying the resulting revenues to the organization's operating funds.

As these developments were unfolding, the executive director began to mobilize the passive nonbusiness trustees to repudiate the actions of the executive committee. Arguing that a purchase of equipment without competitive bids violated the state's Nonstock Corporation Act (Exhibit 6.2) and that the suspension of public programs constituted a broad violation of the museum's commitment to funders and the community, the executive director said the board would either have to repudiate the actions of the executive committee or face serious problems of legal liability. In a meeting of the executive committee notable for its exclusion of the executive director, the committee responded by undertaking an annual review of the executive director's performance, the first such review in his four-year tenure. The committee also requested that the board ratify the executive committee's decisions to terminate one of the museum's public programs and its intention to sell a portion of the museum's collections to pay off the museum's debt of $150,000, on which the interest and a portion of the principal were being paid annually over a ten-year period.

Rationale for the Like-a-Business Approach

The chair and his allies did not believe that they were acting improperly. They had been invited into the museum to make it more businesslike—and they had proceeded to do so. Their central concerns were appropriately fiscal. When they joined up, they found an enterprise whose financial information system was a simple running checkbook balance. The museum did not cost out its activities and was thus incapable of projecting future expenditures. Without this information, it could neither plan pragmatically nor make effective presentations to potential business donors. With the full approval of the executive director, the businessmen had set up a financial management system that not only provided accurate month-by-month information on the museum's cash position but also enabled it to set a realistic budget and to discipline the staff to live within it. Standard business accounting methods were used rather than the fund accounting system favored by many nonprofits, but no one objected to this practice since the new system was such a dramatic improvement over previous practice.

The business trustees had also pragmatically understood that "it takes money to make money." This rationale underlay the museum's transactions with the chair's bank and the computer equipment company owned by his fellow trustee. Trade-offs would lead to contributions from their companies and these, when combined with the high visibility of the Industrialist of the Year Award, would lay the groundwork for approaching other corporate donors. In a written response addressing these transactions, the executive director cited an American Association of Museums ethics handbook that questioned commercial relationships between a museum and its board members. Meanwhile, neither of the attorneys who sat on the board made reference to how this issue was treated in the state's Nonstock Corporation Act.

With the foundation laid for running the museum like a business—through its financial information system and through a series of mutually beneficial relationships with external constituencies—more extensive changes in the museum had to follow. Having accurate information about finances made little difference unless the information was used to make the museum more financially responsible by transforming its programs. Financial stability required zero-based budgeting: each budget line would have to be justified in terms of its potential to yield revenue either through user fees or grant income. Since revenue projections did not appear likely to cover even fixed costs, steps would have to be taken to remedy the situation. The most immediate solutions appeared to lie in cutting programs that yielded no revenue, seeking additional rental income, and converting collections and other idle assets into cash. The treatment of grant funds as unrestricted assets seemed perfectly natural since the accounting system did not reflect the restrictions attached to their use.

Intervention in other aspects of the executive director's domain proceeded from a similar logic. Since the business group's concern was the museum's short-term cash position, its eligibility for historic preservation grants, as a long-term proposition, was not a salient issue when the chair intervened in the negotiation with the Widget Company. Reinstatement of the part-time collections curator who managed rentals was also motivated by an interest in maintaining cash flow.

The conflicts involving the board's chair, its executive committee, and the executive director raised fundamental questions about the Widget Museum's mission, staffing, financial procedures, and board accountability. Ultimately, the board as a whole was forced to engage these issues when the executive director's announcement of his intention to resign was followed by the resignation of the board chair.

The Consultant

As the emergency meeting of the board appeared to be drawing to a close, the consultant was asked to comment. She recommended that the board develop a consensus about what constitutes a board's fiduciary duty of care. She advised members to review carefully the executive director's letter of resignation (Exhibit 6.3) and the board chair's letter of resignation (Exhibit 6.4). The former included word for word the chair's account of "administrative problems" and responded to each item in turn. The consultant also counseled the members to rethink what they as a board might have done over the past two years. She urged a frank exchange of opinions about the actions and philosophies of the former board chair and the former executive director. With these conversations in mind, she assured them, the board would be prepared to develop a plan for dealing with the museum's present situation.

Questions for Discussion

1. Between the chair of the board and the executive director, whose views and actions most fully embrace the fiduciary role of nonprofit trustees? At what point, if any, was the board guilty of a breach of its fiduciary role?
2. Is short-term financial stability or long-term fidelity to mission more important to the future of the museum?
3. To what extent is mission embodied in the museum's budget?
4. What changes in the museum's governance processes would avoid conflicts of this kind?
5. Write a one- to two-page paper outlining actions the board should take and a brief rationale for each.

Exhibit 6.1. Widget Museum Budget
12 Months Ending August 31, 1994.

Revenues

Public Support

State Grants	55,000
Widget City Foundation	27,500
Widget City Education Grant I	3,267
Widget City Education Grant II	6,050
Corporate Contributions	27,500
Memberships	5,500
Donations	2,750
Catalog Sales	1,100
Other	1,100
	$129,767

Investment Income

Interest	4,400
Stock Income	110
	$4,510

Other

Widget Sales	3,300
Rental Income	14,600
	$17,900

Total Revenues	$152,177

Expenses

Educational Programs

Widgets Through Time	4,400
Widgets at Work	4,400
Program #3	4,400
Lecture Series	1,100
Christmas Exhibit	1,100
City Grant I	3,267
City Grant II	6,050
	$24,717

Interest	$12,650

General and Administrative Personnel

Payroll	50,979
Social Security	3,645
Unemployment Taxes	1,100
	$55,724

Other

Insurance	9,350
Utilities	12,248
Telephone	2,750
Office Supplies	1,650
Postage	2,200
Office Expense	1,650

Fundraising (including award)	3,300
Security	1,650
Membership Activities	2,750
Professional Fees	550
Travel	550
Dues and Fees	440
Conservation of Collection	<u>1,100</u>
	$40,188

Total Expenses	$133,279

Exhibit 6.2. Excerpt from Connecticut General Statutes, Title 33, Ch. 600, Nonstock Corporations.

Sec. 33457. Corporate transactions with directors and others

(a)   A contract or transaction between a corporation and a director thereof or a member of his immediate family, or between a corporation and any other corporation, firm or other organization in which a director of the corporation and members of his immediate family have an interest, shall not be voidable, and such director shall not incur any liability, merely because such director is a party thereto or because of such family relationship or interest, if

    (1)   such family relationship or such interest, if it is a substantial interest, is fully disclosed, and the contract or transaction is not unfair as to the corporation and is authorized by

        (i)   directors or other persons who have no substantial interest in such contract or transaction in such a manner as to be effective without the vote, assent or presence of the director concerned or

        (ii)   the written consent of all of the directors who have no substantial interest in such contract or transaction, whether or not such directors constitute a quorum of the board of directors; or

    (2)   such family relationship or such interest, if it is a

substantial interest, is fully disclosed, and the contract or transaction is approved by the affirmative vote of a majority of the voting power of the directors and members entitled to vote thereon; or

(3) the contract or transaction is not with the director or a member of his immediate family and any such interest is not substantial, subject, however, to the provisions of subsection (b) of this section; or

(4) the contract or transaction is fair as to the corporation.

(d) For the purposes of this section:

(3) any contract or transaction between a corporation and a person, corporation, firm or other organization made in the ordinary course of activities at standard prices or on terms not less favorable to the corporation than those offered by the person, corporation, firm or other organization to others shall be prima facie fair. [1959, P.A. 617, S. 39; 1961, P.A. 394, S. 30, 31; P.A. 73–382, S. 8, 12]

Exhibit 6.3. Resignation of Executive Director.

The Widget Museum
John J. Smith
Executive Director

January 18, 1994

Board of Trustees
Widget Museum

To the Board:

I am writing in response to a recent communication from Richard Jones, chair of the board, and will address the memorandum dated January 11, 1994, concerning "administrative problems" point by point. I will conclude with some general comments and observations.

1. "Despite the board's substantial investment in new computer equipment, the director and staff have not learned how to

use it properly for routine museum business such as mailings, budget preparation, etc."

The executive committee and an ad hoc computer committee met on June 25, 1993, to authorize the purchase of a computer system from Computer Depot, Ralph Terry's company. This meeting was held while I was out of town because Mr. Terry anticipated an increase in equipment prices before my return.

For good or for ill, the committee assumed the director's role as purchasing agent for the museum, and the equipment was obtained without consultation with those who would use it. As a result, no agreement was obtained for training the staff or providing manuals. Ralph Terry did come to the museum office on a few occasions to briefly familiarize Mrs. Gates with the basic functions of the system, but this proved inadequate orientation for someone who had no prior knowledge of computers, despite her great enthusiasm for the project.

Although we repeatedly asked Ralph for manuals to accompany the software, we received none. A trustee gave Mrs. Gates some training on label processing, which we can now do in a rudimentary way, and an employee from another board member's office instructed her in very basic bookkeeping procedures. In sum, computer equipment was purchased with no arrangement for training the personnel and with no guarantee of manuals to encourage self-study.

This situation was not the making of the director or the staff. I have spoken with several members of the board about the problem. I have requested assistance from the chair, the supplier, and members of the computer committee. The extent to which the computer is now in use is a measure of the assistance I have received.

2.   "Nominations for the 1993 Industrialist of the Year Award that were submitted by the Bank of Widget City's senior management one day late were returned by the director without consulting the bank's representatives at the museum. This lack of sensitivity on the director's part caused great embarrassment to me."

The deadline for the Widget Industrialist of the Year Award nominations was Friday, October 2, 1993. Some nominations came by regular mail. Some came by express mail. Some were hand delivered. At no time was it ever assumed that nominations from the Bank of Widget City, or anywhere else, were to be given special treatment. To do so would have compromised the integrity of the award, the judges, the administrators of the award procedures, and ultimately of the sponsors themselves. When Richard demanded that I accept the bank's late nominations, I refused. I would do so again.

3.   "The director has implied in conversation that Mr. Terry sold computer equipment to the museum at prices above fair market value and for his own benefit. Mr. Terry actually purchased this equipment for the museum at cost."

Comparative pricing in June of 1993 might have eliminated any questions concerning fair market value once and for all. As it is, the system is in place, the sale is complete, and the matter is closed.

4.   "The director has implied in conversation that the museum's account relationship with the Bank of Widget City is not an 'arm's length' situation and that it was established for my personal benefit and control. All account relationships at the bank are in full compliance with state and federal laws. In fact, all charges on the museum's accounts have been waived as an accommodation; the bank is also a major financial supporter of the museum, having made a $1,000 contribution as a part of the Widget City Community Foundation matching grant."

Where the museum is concerned, we enjoy the right to ask a question or uphold an opinion as long as the expression of that opinion or question does not cause injury to the institution. While an opinion concerning the museum's relationship to the Bank of Widget City, leaked to the *Widget City Herald,* would not be in the best interests of the institution no matter what individual rights justified its expression, questions concerning the museum's business relationships are always relevant to discussion between board members and staff and imply no accusation of personal advantage. As the American Association of Museums Policy Guide, *Museum Trusteeship,* points out (p. 81):

> An all-too-frequent conflict of interest is represented by the board member who sells goods or services to the museum. The situation is difficult to manage at best, for, even if the institution clearly ben-

efits from the arrangement, the appearance of advantage to the trustee may cause embarrassment to both the institution and the trustee. In addition, such an arrangement, once entered into, is difficult to break without hard feelings. In effect, it often limits the museum. Every institution should maintain as much autonomy as possible in selecting and changing suppliers of goods and services, to get the best possible product at the lowest possible price. The museum's ability to demand the highest quality product can be impaired if a trustee is the supplier, for members of the board may find it difficult to exercise a supervisory role over their peers.

Compliance with state and federal banking laws has nothing to do with what is best for the museum. Neither do fee waivers or contributions, which were offered by our last bank, Widget City Trust. It is a simple matter of determining the degree of deviation from standard practice, justifying that deviation, if any, and soliciting board approval. These issues should be brought up, not to embarrass Richard Smith or Ralph Terry, or any other board member, but rather to prevent embarrassment to the institution first and foremost, and secondly to prevent potential embarrassment to Richard and Ralph.

5.   "On December 17, 1987, the executive committee and the board of trustees heard for the first time that approximately $20,000 in tax reimbursements are owed by the museum to the Widget Company.[a]
The tax obligation has been accruing since 1985. This situation is representative of a pattern of last-minute presentations to the board by the director that require quick decisions with incomplete information."
The board of trustees of the Widget Museum was informed of the Widget Company tax problem on at least two documented occasions:

A. At the annual meeting of November 17, 1990: "Mrs. Ireland (treasurer) reported that the tax bill has been received from the

[a]The Widget Company has asked the museum to reimburse the company for taxes paid on the land leased by the museum from the company.

Widget Company for the land around the boarding house. The amount of the bill was felt to be excessive and perhaps inappropriate for a tax-exempt organization. The problem will be investigated." Members now on the board who were present at the 1990 meeting include David Edison, David Sears, and Jean Ireland.

B. In the spring of 1992, I reported to the board that there was a tax problem concerning the land we leased from the Widget Company. Trustee John Conforte was asked to look into the question (museum minutes, April 23, 1992). Members of the present board who were at this meeting include Charles Brown, David Sears, Jean Ireland, Bill Ameche, Karl Boris, Jack Anderson, and Richard Smith, who attended as a guest.

John Conforte suggested consulting with the Widget City municipal attorney, Lillian Ambroglio, and on her advice, we first sought to have the Widget City legislative council authorize a change in the tax status of the Widget Company land so that further taxation would cease. The second part of our plan was to eventually appeal for a rebate of the taxes already paid by the Widget Company. Working with Lucien Thornburg and the municipal attorney, we were eventually successful in our attempt to implement the first stage of our strategy.

6.   "The director has presented a $2,300 'invoice' to the Bank of Widget City for its alleged share (as cosponsor) of the costs of the 1993 Widget Industrialist of the Year Award. No budget was agreed to by the bank ahead of time, and most of the expenses on the invoice relate to the opening of the "Widgets Through Time" exhibit rather than to the award. In any case, the invoice amount is six times greater than the bank's contribution for the award last year."

At a meeting of the public relations committee prior to the announcement of the 1993 Widget Industrialist of the Year competition, Richard Jones (representing the Bank of Widget City), Minott Osborne (representing *Business Digest,* and I (Widget Museum) agreed to the division of the Industrialist of the Year Award expenses as follows. *Business Digest* would pay for the food and beverages. The museum and the Bank of Widget City would divide the remaining expenses equally. No mention of a budget was ever made. None was requested. None was anticipated. We agreed that it was an excellent idea to open "Widgets Through Time" on the same evening as the awards ceremony. The Bank of Widget City, *Business Digest,* and the museum each received one-third of the invitations. When the bill was submitted to the bank, only the invitation items related in any way to "Widgets Through Time," and it did not include rental fees for the space. Last year's bank expense was low because *Business Digest,* celebrating the magazine's first anniversary, paid for the invitations as well as the food and beverages. In the future, commitments made by the bank's representatives should be qualified in advance. And if a budget must be approved by the bank, then it too should be requested in advance.

7.   "The director has interpreted the implementation of standard financial controls by the board, such as check-signing limits, as interference in museum policy and 'lack of trust' in his abilities."

Check-writing controls, requiring two signatures on checks over $1,000, were implemented almost one year ago. I have no problem with that limitation.

8.   "At a luncheon meeting, the Widget Company's chief operating officer (Mr. Minor) said that his organization wanted to lease the museum's small office building for its Widget Education Center. The proposed arrangement would provide cash flow to the museum, take care of our tax liability, and ensure that the property is renovated and occupied by a high-quality tenant for a long period of time. Mr. Minor communicated this to the director, who failed to inform the board in sufficient detail."

When Will Carter of the Water Authority first asked me about renting the old office building, the matter was in no way linked to the tax bill. Consequently, when I told him we needed a fair market rent, he was no longer interested. The Widget Company was at the time considering several other sites and did not anticipate spending more than three or four hundred dollars a month for rent at any location.

A few months ago, Edward Minor contacted me to say that the Widget Company was preparing to sell the boarding house and to discuss the museum's tax liability. The two issues became linked when I invited Robert Sullivan of the Trust for Historic Preservation to my next meeting with officials of the Widget Company. At that meeting, Mr. Sullivan expressed interest in having the trust buy the boarding house. This seemed like an excellent plan. The museum's interest in the property as part of its historic site would be protected by a restrictive covenant in the deed that guaranteed the museum the right of first refusal should the property be resold.

An agreement was in negotiation that would have added the museum's tax bill to the purchase price of the boarding house in return for which the Widget Company would have reduced the tax bill by one-third and would have absorbed finance charges on an eighteen-month delay on the turnover of the purchase price of the boarding house. This arrangement would have allowed us to keep the office building as an income-producing property at the highest rate and would have protected the boarding house by putting it into responsible hands. When I told the board about the preliminary negotiation concerning the tax bill, the matter was quickly taken out of my hands.

Richard's intervention in the Widget Company negotiations destroyed delicate arrangements that would have been brought to the board's attention for discussion or approval. If the board believes that the director is incapable of negotiating agreements concerning the site, making personnel decisions, administering the budget, or managing the museum's collection, then it should replace the director, not assign executive responsibility to its own members.

The AAM policy guide defines the role of the trustee as follows:

The trustees are ultimately responsible for the success of the museum's programs but must remain aloof from the actual execution of the those programs, which is properly the responsibility of the staff under an executive or administrator. By avoiding direct involvement with operational and administrative matters, the trustees maintain the objectivity necessary for effective supervision.

How can policy be distinguished from administration? Policy always covers the general and is concerned with principles while administration is the detailed execution of those principles on a daily basis. It may require great restraint under certain circumstances, but a trustee should avoid imposing his personal administrative, esthetic, political, or social views upon the staff or interfering with the prerogatives at the staff level of operation. The general, structural basic aspects of management are his proper sphere.

A board member will, of course, take an interest in the museum's day-to-day operation, and he may want to confer with the museum director or senior administrative officer on various aspects of institutional management. But he should not instruct the officer to do anything, nor should he criticize any action the executive has taken. If the trustee feels that a problem in management exists, it is his duty to take it to the chair of the board, the appropriate board committee or the entire board. Directives must be issued only by the decision of the board as a collective. If they come from individual trustees, the professional competence of the director is impugned and staff initiative discouraged. [*Museum Trusteeship*, p. 9]

Professional standards should be followed because they relate to the specific conditions that are relevant to museums. Professional standards should be observed because they are based upon hard institutional experience about what works and what does not. Professional standards should be followed because they are the yardstick by which the institution is measured: by funding agencies; by other comparable institutions with whom it is necessary to cooperate on exhibitions, loans, and numerous other museum concerns; and ultimately, by the museum-going public, who can readily distinguish the innovation and excitement that comes from a museum whose staff and trustees work in unison from the occupational servitude and distrust that characterize an institution at war with itself.

My accomplishments as director of this institution leave me satisfied that my work over the years has produced an atmosphere of creativity and innovation. It is a rare privilege to look back on five years of effort and see that it was so worthwhile, so professionally exciting, so personally rewarding.

That is why it is with some regret that I announce my resignation as director of the Widget Museum effective May 15, 1994. Recent actions taken by the executive committee without staff consultation are a critical departure from past practice and undermine the position of director as it is described in the museum's job description. These actions, and others, suggest that the time has come for a different kind of directorship and, more specifically, a different director. A new director will bring you fresh insights and ideas. Hopefully, conflicts will be more easily resolved and a cooperative spirit will prevail.

Sincerely yours,

John J. Smith
Executive Director

Exhibit 6.4. Resignation of Board Chair.

To: Trustees of the Widget Museum
From: Richard P. Jones, Chair
Subject: Resignation from Museum Board
Date: February 25, 1994

Please be advised that, owing to the time commitment required by my recent appointment as chair, president, and CEO of the Bank of Widget City, I am hereby resigning my positions as chair and trustee of the Widget Museum as well as my membership on all museum committees. I plan to continue the corporate fundraising program already underway in an unofficial capacity. We have made great strides in developing controls for the institution through a formal computerized budget process. At the present time the museum's cash position is $92,000 (not including marketable securities), an all-time high for my two-year tenure. However, there are several unresolved financial issues of immediate concern to the board:

1. The $21,000 tax reimbursement liability to the Widget Company, which was incurred prior to my involvement with the museum, remains outstanding. This is a breach of the museum's ground lease agreement with the company and should be remedied as quickly as possible. I have documented elsewhere my support for the company's proposal to rent the office building to the Widget Company in exchange for forgiveness of back taxes.

2. Given the $150,000 loan owed to the Bank of Widget City, which was incurred prior to my involvement with the museum, I recommend that the board make financial stability a higher pri-

ority than curatorial concerns until the debt is substantially repaid; additional de-accession of the widget collection is an obvious source of funds for this purpose. The museum is (or at least should be) making a transition from being a widget collector's repository toward becoming an education-oriented institution devoted to the history of regional business and commerce.

3.   The Widget Industrialist of the Year Award is the museum's most visible connection to the greater Widget City business community and should be continued as a part of its ongoing promotional and fundraising program.

I wish the remaining trustees well in pursuing the financial and administrative course they have chosen.

Suggested Readings

Alderfer, C. P. "The Invisible Director on Corporate Boards." *Harvard Business Review*, 1986, *64*(6), 38–52. Explores the dynamics of inner circles and factions on boards.

Herzlinger, R. E., and Sherman, H. D. "Advantages of Fund Accounting in 'Nonprofits.'" *Harvard Business Review*, 1980, *58*(3), 94–105. Compares and contrasts accounting methods and discusses ways in which organizational mission and goals can be built into financial information systems.

Middleton, M. "Nonprofit Boards of Directors: Beyond the Governance Function." In W. W. Powell (ed.), *The Nonprofit Sector: A Research Handbook*. New Haven, Conn.: Yale University Press, 1987. Explores the ways in which board members span the boundaries between organizations and their social settings, bringing with them the values and viewpoints of the social, professional, and economic groups from which they were recruited.

Moody, L. "State Statutes Governing Directors of Charitable Corporations." *University of San Francisco Law Review*, 1984, *18*(3), 749–761. Examines the statutory aspects of nonprofit board governance, giving particular attention to the shift from traditional trust standards to the newer corporate standards enunciated in recent court cases and in the American Bar Association's Model Nonstock Corporation statute.

Ullberg, A. D., and Ullberg, P. *Museum Trusteeship*. Washington, D.C.: American Association of Museums, 1981. Sets forth this industry's standards for governance structure and process.

Chapter Seven

The Governing Board Faces Rebellion in the Ranks

Candace Widmer

Jane Armstrong hung up her office phone and sighed. This was just what she did not need: a major problem at Community Opportunities Inc. (COI), an agency for the developmentally disabled whose board of directors she chaired.

With a total of 108 full- and part-time employees and an annual budget of $3.1 million, COI provided residential care, day treatment, case management, and educational and advocacy services to the developmentally disabled from all parts of the county. After two years on the board, Armstrong had been proud and pleased to be asked to serve as chair, a position she had assumed two months ago. She believed strongly in her responsibility to serve the community and in the importance of services for the developmentally disabled, in part because her youngest brother had been born with Down's syndrome. Her employer also encouraged its employees, particularly senior executives, to participate in community affairs.

At this point, however, Armstrong felt stretched to the limit by the competing demands on her time. As vice president for public relations at a bank in the throes of a corporate merger she was experiencing unusual pressure at the office; her family was moving into a new house; and her father had recently suffered a minor stroke. Now there appeared to be a full-blown crisis at COI.

The Crisis

This morning's phone call had been from Thomas Walker, a long-time member of the board whose disabled son lived in a COI group home. Yesterday, when Walker had been at the agency to talk with his son's caseworker, the director of residential services had complained to him that COI's executive director was not managing the agency properly and threatened that "either he leaves or I do." Walker had also learned that five of the ten senior staff had recently resigned and that three others were reportedly threatening to resign or at least circulating their résumés (Figure 7.1).

Not all of this information was a surprise to Armstrong. Eric Meyer, COI's executive director, had telephoned late last week to discuss two of the resignations, which he described as good opportunities to replace old-time staff members with younger professionals with better credentials. He had not mentioned dissatisfaction among other staff, but then Meyer usually painted a rosy picture for board members.

Subsequently, Armstrong had received a call from a board member whose son-in-law had been director of advocacy services for the past three years. The board member reported that her son-in-law would undoubtedly be departing soon. He had told her that the executive director was often unavailable due to speaking engagements out of town, that he was unreceptive to suggestions from senior staff members and unwilling to meet with them on a regular basis, and that he seemed to be ignoring potentially serious budgetary shortfalls and numerous staff resignations. These views, when they were made known to the board, would carry special weight. Quite apart from the authenticity of an intrafamily communication, the advocacy director's impeccable credentials and engaging personal style had been identified by the board as setting the standard for upgrading the staff.

But the "old guard" among the staff was apparently equally up in arms. Armstrong had been contacted directly by Brian Pai, a staff member she had known for years. Pai was worried that the board "seemed oblivious to the seriousness of the agency's financial and personnel problems." He felt it was his duty to warn her so that she and the board could act and avoid the embarrassment that would undoubtedly result if the agency's situation were to become public and the board, and she as chair, were caught unawares.

Nonetheless, Armstrong had not been prepared to find in yesterday's mail a petition signed by almost 90 percent of the agency's professional employees (program directors, residence directors, education and counseling staff) stating that they lacked confidence in the executive director and demanding that the board "take action immediately to address the crisis in leadership." Before she was able to reach the vice chair of the board, a fax had come in from him referring her to the morning paper.

At first glance, the news story seemed positive—a human interest piece describing COI's plans to develop additional housing for moderately disabled clients. But she was taken aback by the concluding paragraphs which, citing unidentified sources, questioned the agency's ability to follow through on new initiatives when serious budgetary and staffing problems existed. Armstrong did not know for sure who the unidentified source was, but she thought it might have been a board member, Marc Jacobson, who had repeatedly questioned the wisdom of the agency's continuing expansion and the financial status of the agency as a whole. If Jacobson had gone to the newspaper as she suspected, he must have serious reservations about the agency's financial stability, despite the executive director's reassurances at the last board meeting that COI had no major financial problems.

The Executive Director

Eric Meyer had been executive director of COI for almost six years. From the beginning, Meyer had been a visionary who believed the agency could and should grow, and he had worked with the board and staff to bring this vision to reality. During his tenure, COI had expanded from four group homes to a complex agency with eleven homes and many integrated programs. A successful capital campaign had recently been completed and, until the development director had resigned five months ago, the annual campaign had been doing well also. The director of day treatment services had also resigned recently, and day treatment programs had not proven as financially stable as Meyer had led the board to expect.

Virtually every member of the board considered Meyer masterful at winding his way through the state bureaucratic maze to gain approval and licensing for new programs. He also worked extremely well with local officials and community leaders. He had been able to persuade local banks, including Armstrong's, to make loans, the zoning board to grant variances, and the county commissioners to allocate additional funds—all in record time. He was unquestionably an invaluable asset to an agency such as COI. Also, there was no doubt about Meyer's dedication. He was widely known for his commitment to the rights of the developmentally disabled and his advocacy on their behalf. He was invited by agencies throughout the state to speak at their annual meetings and by national associations to serve on task forces and committees.

Occasionally Armstrong worried that Meyer worked too hard. He often seemed tired, even a bit frantic, and he sometimes took criticism and suggestions very personally, becoming defensive when a board member asked a question or voiced a concern, implying by his response that the board member did not trust him. Armstrong could imagine that his defensiveness might get in his way in dealing with senior staff. Meyer also performed many tasks that might have been delegated. His management style included always meeting personally with representatives of the bank or the state, frequently dropping in at the COI group residences, and often checking or even correcting the work of subordinates. He also did much of the fundraising himself.

Despite having a hand in everything that went on in the agency, Meyer was not a detail man when it came to financial matters. He seemed neither to enjoy that aspect of his job nor to spend much time on it. Although Meyer held the primary responsibility for organizational finances—COI had a bookkeeper but no senior staff member with this responsibility—his financial reports to the board were cursory as well as optimistic. His underlying message seemed to be, this is neither very interesting nor very important and we won't spend much time on it. His passion was advocacy, not budgets (Table 7.1).

With Armstrong's encouragement, the board had finally gotten around to a formal review of Meyer's performance as executive director three months ago. He had not been reviewed for a couple of years, at least not since Armstrong had joined the board. During a brief executive session, most of the concerns expressed had been vague, and there had been many positive comments, particularly regarding his growing national reputation as an advocate.

As part of the performance review, the executive committee had set performance goals, including a balanced budget in 1996. His annual contract had been renewed just a month ago, and he had been granted a sizable bonus at that time.

The Chair's Dilemma

What worried Armstrong most were the staff departures and the calls she had received from board members reporting on conversations with the advocacy director and other well-qualified staff who were threatening to leave if action was not taken. COI had been able to attract such outstanding professionals in spite of a modest salary scale, and the board was particularly proud of this fact. In addition, Armstrong worried that the resignations might spread to the residence staff, without whom the agency simply could not operate. Plus, the petition, signed by so many of the professional staff, could not be ignored.

These issues might prove too complicated to handle in the time Armstrong had available over the next several weeks. Maybe she should resign. Perhaps if she argued that the bank's merger and her father's illness required all of her attention for the immediate future, she could leave without looking blatantly irresponsible. Already she had hinted to the board's vice chair how pressured she was for time, and he seemed prepared to take on as much of a leadership role as she would like. He was the executive director of a small youth agency and, she guessed, would probably welcome the experience of being a key player in a complicated governance problem at a larger agency.

Maybe, though, she should go down to COI and speak informally with some of the staff. She had not been to the administrative offices or any of the residences for awhile, and she might be able to get a better feel for the underlying problems. Alternatively, maybe the staff should be invited to address the board, as several senior staff had apparently suggested to board members. On the other hand, maybe the board should simply let Meyer go about the process of filling staff vacancies. Certainly his past performance suggested that he could rebuild the management team.

In fact, perhaps this crisis could best be handled by Meyer. After all, financial and personnel problems were the executive director's responsibility. The executive committee could express its concern and ask Meyer to report back to the board at appropriate intervals. The personnel committee could also be asked to assume a larger role during this crisis (Exhibit 7.1). On the other hand, it might be best to suggest to Meyer that he resign. The board should not fire him, of course, but they could give him the opportunity to leave gracefully. It was hard to imagine that the staff's confidence in him could be rebuilt when it had deteriorated so dramatically. However, community support for Meyer and COI were closely linked, and losing staff members might be less damaging to the agency than losing Meyer. Furthermore, as a practical matter, for the board to replace Meyer would be a time-consuming task with an uncertain outcome.

Realistically, the board was likely to be criticized no matter what it did. Some staff were already blaming the board for the agency's problems. If COI's conflicts became widely known, as now seemed likely, private gifts and perhaps county funding for the agency might be adversely affected. Then too, Armstrong reflected, her bank would hardly be pleased to have its senior public relations executive associated with a civic controversy.

She picked up her telephone. A reporter from the newspaper had left a message on her voice mail. She must also return the calls of two board members as well as the assistant director of day treatment services, who was apparently particularly upset and the kind of person likely to spread rumors throughout the community if she was not calmed down. COI's next regularly scheduled executive committee meeting was to occur in three days, and the full board was scheduled to meet the following week. What should she do, Armstrong wondered, and what was a board supposed to do in a situation like this?

Questions for Discussion

1. What are the strengths and weaknesses of this agency? What are the primary problems facing COI at this time?
2. What are the choices for board action? Discuss the possible consequences for each. Are ethical issues involved? If so, what are they?
3. What are the best and the worst outcomes that might reasonably be anticipated?

4. What is the appropriate role of the board? How should board members react to staff who "go behind the back" of the executive director to complain to the board? What steps should the board take to address the crisis? What actions should be avoided?
5. Evaluate the behavior of the board and board chair so far. Has it been exemplary, acceptable, inadequate? What criteria should be used to judge their performance? What should Jane Armstrong do now as chair of the board of COI?

Exhibit 7.1. Excerpts from Bylaws.

From Article III:

Section 12: Duties of Directors

A director shall discharge his or her duties as director, including his or her duties as a member of a committee (1) in good faith; (2) with the care an ordinarily prudent person in a like position would exercise under similar circumstances; and (3) in a manner the director reasonably believes to be in the best interests of the corporation.

In discharging his or her duties, a director is entitled to rely on information, opinions, reports, and statements, including financial statements and other financial data, if prepared or presented by

(1) One or more officers or employees of the corporation whom the director reasonably believes to be reliable and competent in the matters presented;
(2) Legal counsel, public accountants, or other persons as to matters the director reasonably believes are within the person's professional or expert competence; or
(3) A committee of the board of which the director is not a member, as to matters within its jurisdiction, if the director reasonably believes the committee merits confidence.

A director is not acting in good faith if the director has knowledge concerning the matter in question that makes reliance as described in the foregoing unwarranted.

Section 13: Committees

The board of directors, by resolution adopted by a majority of the entire board, may from time to time designate from among its

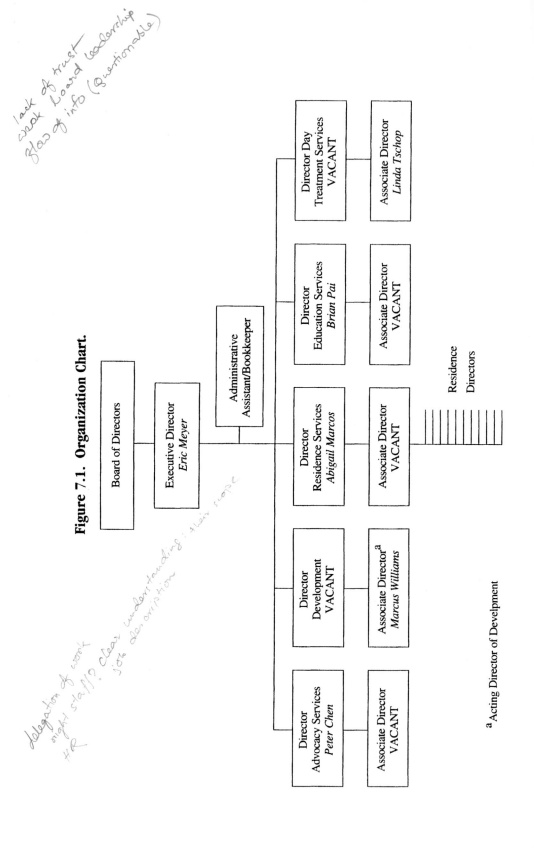

Figure 7.1. Organization Chart.

Board of Directors

Executive Director
Eric Meyer

Administrative
Assistant/Bookkeeper

Director
Advocacy Services
Peter Chen

Associate Director
VACANT

Director
Development
VACANT

Associate Director[a]
Marcus Williams

Director
Residence Services
Abigail Marcos

Associate Director
VACANT

Director
Education Services
Brian Pai

Associate Director
VACANT

Director Day
Treatment Services
VACANT

Associate Director
Linda Tschop

Residence
Directors

[a] Acting Director of Develpment

Handwritten margin notes:
lack of trust
weak board leadership
flow of info (Questionable)

delegation of work
night staff? Clear understanding : their scope
HR   Job description

members an Executive Committee and other committees, and alternate members thereof, as may be deemed desirable, from time to time, each consisting of three or more directors, with such powers and authority (to the extent permitted by law) as may be provided in such resolution. Each such committee shall serve at the pleasure of the board.

From Article IV

Section 1: Number, Qualifications, Election, and Term of Office

(1)   The officers of the corporation shall consist of a president, a secretary, a treasurer, and such other officers, including one or more vice presidents, as the board of directors may from time to time deem advisable. Any officer may be, but is not required to be, a director of the corporation. Any two or more offices may be held by the same person.

Officers of the corporation shall, unless otherwise provided by the board of directors, each have such powers and duties as generally pertain to their respective offices as well as such powers and duties as may be set forth in these bylaws, or may from time to time be specifically conferred or imposed by the board of directors. The president shall act as chair of the board.

Section 7: Executive Director

(2)   The executive director shall be responsible for hiring, discharging, directing, and supervising all employees, subject to approval by the board of directors or its designated committee.

Table 7.1. Revenues/Expenditures.

	1990	1991	1992	1993	1994
Revenues	1,200,000	1,800,000	2,500,000	2,950,000	3,000,000
Expenditures	1,181,750	1,810,900	2,450,380	3,025,000	3,069,000
Excess (Deficit)	18,250	(10,900)	49,620	(75,000)	(69,000)

Suggested Readings

Carver, J. *Boards That Make a Difference.* San Francisco: Jossey-Bass, 1990. Includes recommendations regarding the nature of CEO accountability and the collegial relationship between board members and the CEO. See especially Chapter Six, "Strong Boards Need Strong Executives: The Board Executive Relationship."

Houle, C. O. *Governing Boards.* San Francisco: Jossey-Bass, 1989. Emphasizes the shared responsibility of the board and the executive in Chapter Four, "The Board, Executive, and the Staff." Section 23, "The End of the Relationship," particularly relevant to the case at hand.

"How Should a Board Chairperson Handle a Complaint About the Chief Executive?" *Board Member,* 1994, *3*(6). Newsletter published by the National Center for Nonprofit Boards, Washington, D.C. Brief case study and three responses addressing complaint of long-term staff member to board chair about irresponsible actions of new executive director. Other NCNB publications might be consulted on board-CEO relationships and CEO evaluation.

Kouzes, J. M., and Mico, P. R. "Domain Theory: An Introduction to Organizational Behavior in Human Service Organizations." *Journal of Applied Behavioral Science, 15*(4), 1979, 449–469. Classic paper describing "natural" tensions existing between the policy, management, and service domains of human service organizations that may be contributing to the problems experienced by Community Opportunities Inc.

Waldo, C. N. *A Working Guide for Directors of Not-For-Profit Organizations.* New York: Quorum Books, 1986. In Chapter Three of this useful book, "Interpersonal Relationships Between the Board and the CEO and Staff," the board is advised to be supportive of the CEO "but not blindly so." Ways of facilitating contact between board members and second and third tiers of management are also discussed.

Chapter Eight

Confronting Crisis
When Should the Board Step In?
Ram A. Cnaan

Betsy Shoemaker's face was tight as she closed the door to Ralph Carpenter's office behind her. What could the governing board of New Frontiers Inc. (NFI) do now about the financial crisis that Carpenter, NFI's executive director, had allowed to ruin their dreams? As she contemplated the emergency meeting that was clearly necessary, she thought back over NFI's past.

Mission and Purpose

New Frontiers Inc. had been established some forty years ago to rehabilitate the poor and help them assimilate into the wider society. The founders were concerned local residents and a few social service professionals who followed the adage "give a man a fish and he eats for a day; teach a man to fish and he eats for a lifetime." The basic philosophy of the organization, which had remained intact throughout four decades, was that poor people learn how to be poor; therefore they must undo this learning and be taught how to become active members of society. Poor people, it was argued, were accustomed to failure and degradation, and in order for change to occur, they must develop healthy self-esteem through positive experiences.

Based on this philosophy, New Frontiers contacted poor families in the inner city and offered them the opportunity to join NFI's program. Those who opted into the program were promised uninterrupted services for as long as they wished. They were invited to move, as a family, into houses owned by New Frontiers in one of the city's run-down neighborhoods. These new renters became NFI "partners" and were assisted in making small remodeling changes to accommodate their needs. They were provided with professional and volunteer support and assistance, guidance in household maintenance, vocational training based on their preferences and strengths, counseling in the area of childrearing, and when the time arrived, assistance in securing permanent housing.

In its first twenty years of operation, New Frontiers Inc. received most of its income from wealthy donors in the community, and its board of directors was drawn from the city's "old money." The scope of activity was modest, and no more than twenty families, most from a single neighborhood, were assisted each year. Although private donations continued, public funds gradually became NFI's major source of income. The number of clients increased and so too did the number of neighborhoods in which NFI was active. With these changes, the role and number of volunteers diminished, and professionals became the majority of service providers.

Years of Expansion and Prosperity

Ten years ago, a dynamic psychologist was recruited by the board's personnel committee as the agency's third executive director. Upon accepting the position, Ralph Carpenter announced that he would stay for no more than seven years, believing that no one person should remain in the same managerial position for more than that period of time. Thus, his contract was written for seven years. The board did not offer Carpenter any relocation assistance nor did he ask for it. His initial salary was not considered generous, and a few board members later commented that they got a great director for small change.

Carpenter was a charismatic leader. His unusual ideas were gradually implemented, and the staff came to realize that his vision was ahead of its time. In fact, his pioneering concepts often became the norm in other social service agencies. Board members defined him as an "agenda setter" and appreciated his innovations. Staff members admired his commitment to NFI's partners, his loyalty to the organization, and his genuine interest in new knowledge and ideas.

When Carpenter became the director of the agency, its budget was a modest half a million dollars, and it employed fifteen people. The employees and a few volunteers worked out of a small apartment near the partners' houses. Seven years later, NFI was a new organization. Through many contracts with city, state, and federal governments, New Frontiers had become one of the city's largest social service organizations. It had purchased a spacious new headquarters and established many new departments such as human resources, quality assurance, research, information systems, development, library, property acquisition and management, rehabilitation, and six different units of social services. Each unit was composed of a professional manager, one or two assistants, and at least one secretary. The total number of people employed had grown to about two hundred. The caseload of the agency had expanded dramatically to include some five hundred poor families.

With the assistance of a few board members, Carpenter developed a policy of "minimum rent, maximum ownership." Accordingly, NFI bought houses in decaying neighborhoods of the city and remodeled them to fit the needs of the partners to whom they were rented. In this fashion, New Frontiers Inc. became both its own landlord and tenant. Although the agency owned the houses, the mortgage was paid through government subsidy of the rent paid by NFI partners. This practice, which enabled the organization to own a significant stock of houses and apartments, was hailed by government officials. At about this time, housing activities were spun off as a subsidiary within the NFI corporate structure.

Carpenter did not want the organization to continue to be dependent upon the city as its major source of income. Delays in city payments had already forced NFI to negotiate short-term bank loans to pay salaries. Problems with slow reimbursement were aggravated because one of the city's commissioners of social services did not like Carpenter. As a result, this commissioner instructed his subordinates to delay payments for as long as legally allowed and, by enforcing the fine print of eligibility requirements, succeeded in reducing the number of referrals to New Frontiers. With the blessing of the board, Carpenter continued the agency's expansion by opening subsidiaries of NFI in two adjacent counties and in two neighboring states. Each new subsidiary was able to con-tract with the state in which it was located but oversight continued to be carried out by the NFI board. The directors of these satellite organizations, along with four managers of large units in the head-quarters, became the executive committee of the organization, with Ralph Carpenter serving as CEO.

In this environment, NFI was fortunate in its chief financial officer, Mrs. Holt. An experienced bookkeeper whose clientele had included small businesses such as mom and pop gift shops and one-store greeting card franchises, she had decided to spend the latter half of her professional career "doing some good," as she put it. Although her skill in transferring funds among accounts to pro-vide cash for current needs was perhaps not explicitly understood by Carpenter, his expansionary vision was supported by her ability to make the most of NFI's minimal cash reserves. Auditors from government agencies were not always savvy enough to follow Holt's explanations, but her deft management of accounts was universally admired and she was unfailingly courteous in her answers and explanations.

As the years went by, the reputation of the organization grew in professional circles and in the community-at-large. Through the efforts of NFI's development department, the organization's model for preventing and coping with homelessness was featured in the media. Carpenter actively avoided personal exposure, claiming that the staff who assisted the partners should be featured. His real interest was in understanding what was effective in the organiza-tion's work, and he persuaded the board to establish a research unit that presented its findings at numerous national conferences.

The Board

The board was composed of members of wealthy and distinguished families who had been recruited by the founding director to assume their civic responsibility to combat poverty. Board mem-bers included partners in large and prestigious law firms, bank executives, or executives and owners of large businesses—all men—and the wives of men like them. Recruitment of new members occurred primarily through personal acquaintance. In the years after Carpenter's arrival, the board grew in size to reflect the organization's expansion and its widening scope of activities. A few of the new members came from outside the city's elite, but the old members continued to set the tone for the group. The board met ten times a year and attendance was high. Members often commented that their organization was fast becoming a model for the nation and that the philosophy of the organization, if utilized nationally, might solve many social ills.

Members of the board's finance committee observed Holt with a mixture of respect and bemusement, chuckling wryly about being in the poorhouse long ago if their wives had developed Holt's financial legerdemain in capitalizing on "float" (the time lag between issuance of a check and deposit of the check in a bank, which makes it possible to write checks against funds that are not presently in an account). They were comfortable with her managerial style, which was similar to the one they themselves employed in their own companies and law firms. That is, Holt advocated computers for her staff but never used one herself, sent her staff to professional seminars to learn the latest techniques but was herself satisfied to use a hand-held calculator, and ran her department much as she had done when NFI was smaller. In recent years, the locally based accounting firm performing the independent audit for the board's finance committee had noted errors in certain finance department procedures but had described them as "consistent with a period of growth and a very slim margin of excess revenues." The annual review of the audit was something of a chore for committee members, who complained that fund accounting and government funding mechanisms were impenetrable.

Carpenter encouraged board members to visit NFI's new sites and to meet with as many staff members and partners as they wished. However, very few board members took advantage of this invitation. They trusted Carpenter completely, and his reports and the reports of his staff satisfied them. Board members boasted about their affiliation with this successful organization but were not required to provide much actual labor. For example, at one board meeting Carpenter reviewed a satellite program, indicating many problems in its operation. The board listened attentively and concluded by expressing confidence in Carpenter's judgment; they asked him to do his best and report back in three months. The board supported the direction taken by Carpenter

de facto

since they trusted him implicitly. During this period, Carpenter, already an ex officio member of the board, was elected to a regular three-year term identical to that of other volunteer board members.

Five years after Carpenter arrived, the chair of the board, a seventy-year-old shipyard owner, stepped down from his position after more than fifteen years. The board deliberated about who would be the new chair and included Carpenter in their many discussions. Finally, Gloria Shoemaker, the wife of Reginald Shoemaker III, CEO of the high-profile First Equitable Bank, was elected chair. It was said that Shoemaker's parents were once poor and managed to reach prosperity; she was therefore a great believer in the ability to transform every poor person into an independent and contributing member of society. She truly believed that poverty is a result of social forces and that people who lived in poverty for too long lost their social skills and gave up hope.

Gloria Shoemaker had more energy and time to devote to New Frontiers Inc. than did the previous chair. As a result of her vigor and commitment, she was in personal or telephone contact with Carpenter almost daily. The board was thus informed of every major activity and plan of its chief administrator.

At the End of Seven Years

In accordance with his promise, Carpenter notified the board after six and a half years of service that he intended to leave the organization in six months. No one knew for sure if he acted out of true conviction or if he needed to save face by keeping his word. However, the board as a whole and Gloria Shoemaker in particular were not willing to listen to such an idea.

Board members pressured Carpenter to withdraw his resignation and to continue as executive director. He was offered an attractive package that included a sizable increase in salary and additional financial benefits if he would sign another five-year contract. He ultimately agreed to stay for an unspecified period but waived most of the financial benefits. He opted for a modest raise, which brought his annual salary to about $50,000, supplemented by health coverage and a pension. A clause in the new contract provided that at any time and for any reason the board could ask him to step down with three months' advance notice and that he could resign on the same basis.

Even after Carpenter's salary was increased under the new contract, it remained lower than that of certain other key executives. When approached by some board members to explain this unusual practice, he noted that as a divorced man (his wife had left him three years earlier) living alone (his two children were enrolled at college) his needs were few; furthermore, in order to attract qualified executives it was necessary to pay them competitive wages, and he preferred that funds be allocated to that purpose.

As a result of these events, no new search took place at the end of Carpenter's seven-year tenure, and he seemed destined to stay at NFI indefinitely. In the meeting in which he accepted the new contract, he also explained his plan for the organization over the next several years. The board unanimously approved his course of action.

The New Course of Action

Ralph Carpenter's plan amounted to making New Frontiers Inc. into the McDonald's of social service agencies and playing a major national role in the eradication of poverty. The idea was to synthesize the key practical elements of NFI's practices into a set of guidelines. By adhering to these detailed guidelines, social service agencies across the country would have the opportunity to become franchises of NFI. This vision held that a poor family anywhere in the United States could become a partner of its local NFI and receive services identical to those provided by NFI in its home city. A person entering a McDonald's restaurant in any city or neighborhood sees the same menu as at other franchises and can expect identical food. Similarly, poor families would be able to enter any franchise of New Frontiers and receive exactly the same set of services.

Shortly after Carpenter's new contract had been signed, a detailed plan for expansion was brought to the board for discussion. It was expected that in the first few years the program would cost a few hundred thousand dollars, but by the fourth year it would start paying for itself through training charges, accreditation and licensing fees, royalties, and special consulting fees. As

chief financial officer, Holt reviewed the current annual budget of
$16.5 million and reported that over the past six years the organization had accumulated a surplus of more than half a million dollars, which could help fund the proposed expansion. The board
enthusiastically supported the new venture. In fact, one board
member resigned in order to become an employee of NFI and take
charge of the team that synthesized the principles of service, and
another member worked pro bono with the team before resigning
at a later time. Gloria Shoemaker requested periodic reports on
team progress, and members of the team frequently reported to
the board. Board members who were lawyers developed guidelines
for drafting contracts with prospective franchisees.

In the meantime, the agency had continued to grow (Table 8.1).
In NFI's home city, the unfriendly commissioner of social services
had resigned, and new contracts had been obtained by headquarters as well as by subsidiaries in adjacent areas. The organization
had been approached by the city's health department to develop
services for drug and alcohol rehabilitation; this program evolved
into a new unit that quickly grew into a small empire. However, the
swift recruitment of large numbers of drug and alcohol counselors
made it impossible to orient them effectively into NFI's mission
and philosophy.

NFI was constantly hiring new workers not only because of its
expansion but also because, like other social service agencies, it
experienced high turnover among its low-wage, lower-level employees. Furthermore, workers who chose to persist for a significant
period of time found too few opportunities for upward mobility
and eventually became frustrated and left the agency. To counteract this situation, Carpenter established an in-house training unit
that developed special programs for new and veteran employees.
In addition, a staff committee was formed to study new ways to
increase opportunities for upward mobility. The committee developed a plan for in-house recruitment for supervisory positions, and
courses were developed to train interested workers in acquiring
relevant skills.

Three years after Carpenter's second contract was signed, the
organization seemed to be at the dawn of a new era of national
prominence. Most internal problems seemed under control, and
those that still haunted the organization appeared manageable. In

his annual report to the board, Carpenter stated that many challenges and risks lay ahead but they could be overcome by the organization's increased size and financial stability. He noted that because no single funder was the major source of income for the organization, a delay of payment by one funder would not cause more than a 10 percent loss of income. The board unanimously approved the annual budget and commended Carpenter's superb leadership. There were calls for a significant salary increase, which Carpenter declined.

The Crisis

One Tuesday morning at ten o'clock, shortly after the above-mentioned annual board meeting, Carpenter called Gloria Shoemaker, requesting an "urgent" meeting. Shoemaker later recalled that although she and the executive director communicated daily, he had never before asked for an urgent meeting, yet she did not sense any urgency in his voice. They agreed to meet later that afternoon in his office at NFI headquarters.

When Shoemaker entered the building, she could not see any sign of crisis. She noted with satisfaction that, in comparison to the past when NFI headquarters resembled a Third World village, in the new building the organization looked like the finest of corporations. The receptionist was as cordial and friendly as always and so were the few employees she met on her way to the fourth floor where Carpenter's office was located. The secretary received her with a smile and her usual greeting and asked if she wanted coffee. Upon entering Carpenter's neatly furnished executive office (which was modest compared to others in the building but envied by many executives from other social service agencies), she realized she had never before seen a look of confusion or worry on his face.

After a few minutes of polite chit-chat, Carpenter got to the point. Just after lunch the day before, he had received a phone call from NFI's account manager at First City Bank notifying him that the organization was $3 million in debt and would not have the resources to pay its upcoming biweekly salaries. Carpenter said he had no idea how NFI had reached such a state. Until yesterday, he had assumed, based on what he was told by the chief financial officer, Holt, that NFI was in a sound financial position.

The staff's executive committee was having an emergency meeting later that afternoon, and Carpenter asked Gloria Shoemaker to join them. Because Shoemaker had other obligations, she could not attend the meeting but asked Carpenter to call her that evening and report what he had learned over the course of the day.

Shoemaker left the building concerned and bewildered. She was the first to admit that she was unfamiliar with financial management. Over dinner she discussed the news with her husband and he agreed that an emergency board meeting should be convened. Around eight o'clock, Carpenter telephoned to say that the bank's revelation was a shock to everyone on the staff and that no one had seen it coming. Furthermore, Holt was as puzzled as the rest of them and in the staff executive committee meeting had said angrily that if a deficit existed, First City Bank should have called her sooner. Carpenter said that since he was not an accountant, he would like the board's permission to hire a nationally known accounting firm to go over the books and to assist in negotiating a delay of payments to the bank until after the picture became more clear. Shoemaker gave him tentative approval for both activities but added that she would have to assemble the board for an emergency meeting and get them involved.

That evening, Shoemaker attempted to reach as many board members as she could. They reacted with disbelief, saying that the bank must have made a mistake and that she should not be alarmed or worried—the organization had been solidly managed for years. When she finished her round of calls at about ten o'clock, Carpenter phoned. He apologized for calling so late, remarking that her line had been busy earlier. He had arranged for a meeting with First City Bank's CEO for the next morning and wondered if Shoemaker would like to join him. Shoemaker was ambivalent; she feared that acceptance might seem distrusting of Carpenter but declining might mean the neglect of NFI's interests. She told Carpenter that if it was his preference she would join him, and they agreed to meet at the agency and drive together to the bank.

The next morning, when they arrived at the office of Mr. Albright, the CEO of First City Bank, they were shown in immediately and treated warmly. Carpenter had met Albright in previous negotiations, and Shoemaker knew Albright through her husband. After some conversation about the bank's long-term relationship with New Frontiers and its support of the agency, Albright informed them that the bank's accountants had taken quite some time to realize that New Frontiers Inc. was in such financial disarray. When asked to explain, he noted that Holt had opened over fifty accounts under NFI's name, each for a different source of payment or program. It was quite common for Holt to move money from one account to another in order to cover short-term debts and then to transfer the money to yet another account. In fact, Albright noted, there were days when Holt ordered over a hundred such transactions, and the bank was regularly unable to assess all of the NFI accounts combined.

Because of the agency's good credit history and Holt's successful management, all her orders were routinely obeyed. Only recently had one of the bank's accountants realized that too many NFI accounts were in the red. A thorough investigation revealed the magnitude of the situation. As Albright continued his explanation, it became clear to Carpenter and Shoemaker that every two weeks, on or shortly after pay day, Holt transferred money from several other accounts into the salary account to cover the biweekly payroll. Albright concluded by saying that in the absence of a major deposit, he did not see how NFI would be able to pay salaries in ten days. Shoemaker informed Albright of the board's planned meeting on Monday and asked to meet with him again on the following Tuesday. Albright agreed and assured her that the bank would be willing to work with the board on a financial recovery plan.

The days before the Monday meeting were full of telephone and face-to-face discussions among board members as well as between staff and board members. The cloud hanging over New Frontiers Inc. made board members more interested in the staff, and staff members were prepared to protect their interests. Carpenter himself was only sporadically involved in these discussions since he was working with Holt and the finance staff to try to understand how it was possible to drift so swiftly from royalty to ruins.

A number of suggestions emerged from these conversations. The two former board members now on staff suggested that, on a temporary basis, the board assign a board member to meet every two weeks with the three senior staff members of each NFI unit. They feared that the drug and alcohol rehabilitation unit was "another smoking gun" from the standpoint of both excess personnel and shaky finances. The chair of the board's finance committee, the retired CEO of a publishing company, reviewed the board's liability insurance and concluded it was inadequate to cover the present crisis. Two lawyers on the board recommended terminating Carpenter immediately and asking the retired CEO of a local hospital, a person known to many board members, to take the helm until a search for a permanent CEO for NFI could be completed. The youngest and newest members of the board, both women in their mid-thirties, had sounded out a mutual friend who was on the fast track at the city's premier investment banking firm; this investment banker would be willing to join the board to assure that her services in developing a financial bail-out would be pro bono.

Longtime board members, including Gloria Shoemaker, felt that resolution of the crisis should be left to the senior management staff and that Ralph Carpenter should not be terminated. Several felt that Holt should also be allowed to remain on staff but that a new chief financial officer ought to be recruited immediately and brought in "over her." No one had any clear idea about how the $3 million debt might be repaid unless the new building were sold, in which case NFI would probably have to discontinue some of its programs and lay off up to half the staff. Several members wondered if a legal suit against the local accounting firm would be a feasible way of securing some of the funds required to pay the debt. The former board chair said that he would have no part of guaranteeing NFI's debt personally even if such an option were suggested by the bank.

On the day of the emergency board meeting, Shoemaker met with Carpenter and asked him to summarize the bad news for the board, explain what went wrong, and suggest ways to restructure the situation. Carpenter willingly accepted the task. He began by reminding the board that his contract allowed them to terminate his tenure at NFI at any given time. He then made the urgency of the situation clear and expressed his concern that even if it was possible to salvage New Frontiers Inc., the organization would suffer a major setback in its new course of action, the franchising program. As to the reasons for the unexpected crisis, he could not provide the board with specific information. In general, he accepted the hindsight hypothesis of mid-level as well as senior managers that the organization had grown too quickly for many of its units to keep up the pace. In retrospect, it appeared self-evident that although Holt's wizardry had worked well in the management of a few accounts, she had gradually lost control when NFI increased in size and she had begun moving money from one account to another without putting in place the proper checks and balances.

As to the future, Carpenter said that the national consulting firm was already analyzing the agency's books and procedures. He then turned the meeting over to the head of the consulting team, who made a succinct report:

- The board should act immediately to terminate the employment of any person not essential to service provision. This step would enable the agency to live within its income, thus reducing the deficit to less than $3 million. Such an action might result in long-term and irreversible damage to the staff's pride and the agency's reputation, but that risk would have to be taken.
- Albright of First City Bank must be persuaded to open a new line of credit while the consulting team was working with the staff to develop a financial recovery program. For such a credit line to be secured, board members might be required to cosign with the agency, thus guaranteeing the agency's debts.
- The NFI headquarters building had a market value approaching $3 million. However, even with a smaller staff, moving expenses were estimated at $150,000, and leases and remodeling on new quarters would require up-front monies of approximately $100,000.
- Sale of the housing stock owned by NFI was not a viable option because the real estate had depreciated in value. Furthermore, such sales would result in severely reduced revenues for the agency.

After the consultant concluded his report, Carpenter assured the board that for the immediate future he had arranged deposits from a few of NFI's many sources of income and that these deposits would cover the upcoming payroll. This was only a short-term solution, however. Carpenter reminded the board that he was a psychologist and a manager but not an accountant or fiscal expert. He also asserted his willingness to work with the board to implement its decisions.

It was a retired shipyard owner, the former chair, who eventually asked Carpenter if the board could discuss the situation alone. Carpenter understood the tacit message and left the room. Now, for the first time in almost ten years, the board of New Frontiers Inc. was faced with the need to proactively discuss urgent matters.

Questions for Discussion

1. Should the board have asked Carpenter to leave the meeting, or should they have shown more trust in him by including him in the discussion?
2. Despite Carpenter's loyal and successful tenure and in view of his lack of management skills, should the board take advantage of his contract and terminate his employment?
3. What role should the board assume in the face of this financial crisis? Should handling the crisis be left to the executive staff of NFI? Should board members use their considerable personal influence to accomplish their goals? Should they, if asked, take personal responsibility for NFI's debts?

Table 8.1. Operating Summary.

	199-	199-	199-	Current Year
Total Revenues	7,589,618	9,331,954	11,972,121	
Total Expenditures	7,376,139	9,348,436	11,835,825	16,426,000 est.
	213,479	(16,482)	136,296	
Total Clients Served	2,734	2,651	2,534	3,100 est.

4. Should the board restructure its work and have a board member oversee each unit to make sure that it operates according to expected standards? If so, for how long?
5. Faced with a new challenge, to what extent should the board alter its traditional composition and its socially elite norms and atmosphere? Should it open its gates to new members who are experienced in dealing with financial crises? If so, how should the new members be encouraged to quickly become actively involved in solving the present crisis?

Suggested Readings

Alderfer, C. P. "The Invisible Director on Corporate Boards." *Harvard Business Review,* 1986, *64*(6), 38–52. Stimulating analysis of submission of individual board members to group norms. Explains perpetuation of destructive board practices and board members' inability to observe problems and emerging crises.

Carver, J. *Boards That Make a Difference: A New Design for Leadership in Nonprofit and Public Organizations.* San Francisco: Jossey-Bass, 1990. Useful and popularly received distinction between "ends" as the proper focus for the board in contrast to "means" for the staff. Author's perspective on board's relationship to "the complexity and details of staff operations" in Chapter Five, "Setting Limits: Standards of Excellence and Prudence."

Chait, R. P., Holland, T. P., and Taylor, B. E. *The Effective Board of Trustees.* Phoenix, Ariz.: Oryx Press, 1993. Proposes six dimensions of board effectiveness: contextual, educational, interpersonal, analytical, political, and strategic.

Clark, M. L. "The Board of Directors as a Small Dynamic Group." *Administration and Policy in Mental Health,* 1988, *16*(2). Undercited overview of boardroom dynamics. Suggests that certain behaviors in governing boards are predictable, including member roles, leader issues, problem behaviors, and developmental stages.

Janis, I. L. "Groupthink: The Desperate Drive for Consensus at Any Cost." In J. S. Ott (ed.), *Classic Readings in Organizational Behavior.* Belmont, Calif.: Wadsworth, 1989. Seminal article on the pressures toward conformity in groups. Implies flaws in the conventional wisdom that boards work best when they operate by consensus.

Oster, S. "Nonprofit Organizations as Franchise Operations." *Nonprofit Management and Leadership,* 1992, *2*(3), 223–238. Describes variations on franchising arrangements such as the one New Frontiers Inc. planned to develop.

Chapter Nine

Outgrowing the Governing Board

A Conundrum → a riddle/question

Judith R. Saidel

The founding executive director of Windham Programs, a provider of services to developmentally disabled youth, glanced anxiously at his watch. Tom Mills knew that tonight's board of directors meeting was going to be different from the usual three-hour, easygoing monthly session. Earlier in the week, he had met with Julia Morris, the hard-working president of Windham's board of directors, for their customary preview of the upcoming board meeting.

Mills had spoken about the management team's urgent concern that substantial governance changes were necessary, given the dramatic growth in agency revenues over the last ten years and the equally dramatic shift in revenue mix. Originally a ten-thousand-dollar, parent-run camp, Windham was now a multiservice agency with a $5 million annual budget. In several long conversations, the management team had considered a number of alternative recommendations, including significant changes in board membership, a limit on years of service, and establishing a new Windham Advisory Group.

Morris, whose son was in Windham's elementary program, had responded in the thoughtful and solicitous way that had endeared her to other board members and the executive staff. She questioned why the usual procedure of nominating new board members to fill vacancies would not be adequate to address the management team's anxieties. "Especially," she emphasized, "given the extraordinary level of dedication of our board members. Don't forget—most of us are parents of Windham children who have our hands full at home and still manage to show up each month, sit patiently through very long meetings, volunteer for the garage and bake sales, and support all our other fundraising efforts" (Exhibit 9.1).

Mills appreciated the value of parent board members. Himself the father of a Windham young adult, he had experienced personally the rewards of channeling his energy and emotions into work on behalf of others like his son. He had seen many parents, at first bewildered by the mystery of their children's disabilities, grow into informed and articulate advocates. Many such parents had served faithfully on the Windham board year after year and had developed great loyalty to Mills and his leadership. They usually left the board only because of burnout or a job transfer from the area.

Still, he had watched as the business of the board became more and more complicated and fewer members participated in discussions or raised questions. If Mike D'Aleo, an administrator in the State Department of Social Services, missed a meeting, the entire evening often went by without a single probing question or comment from a board member. D'Aleo was one of the few members with a grasp of the new policy environments in which Windham Programs was operating. After these meetings, Mills often took the time to thank D'Aleo for questioning program modifications required under new government contracts or for expressing caution about the potential loss of valued program features or participants.

Windham's Growth

Ten years ago, after several years of operation, Windham Programs' budget of $200,000 was financed in part by fundraising events run by volunteers. Fundraisers included a weekly bingo game, a football lottery, a concert by a well-known violinist, garage and bake sales, and a "Run for Windham" race through the neighborhood surrounding the camp. Another source of revenue was fees paid by counties when parents of preschoolers undertook the complicated process of filing the requisite petitions in county family courts. In addition, several counties included modest appropriations for the agency in their annual budgets. Two part-time volunteers with financial expertise shared the role of treasurer and kept the organization's books.

Five years ago, when parents and camp staff decided to open a school in space donated by the executive director's church, they were able to secure tuition reimbursement for youngsters aged five to seventeen through local school districts and the State Education Department (SED). Tuition was determined through a complicated rate-setting formula developed by SED. School districts paid the per pupil cost as set in individual jurisdictions and SED subsidized the "excess cost" of educating the special needs students.

Windham's budget very quickly jumped to over a million dollars, and staff reports at board meetings began to focus on the complexities of public agency procedures and decision making. These reports frequently provoked expressions of aggravation and disbelief by board members because of the unfamiliar and seemingly inappropriate requirements imposed on the agency by government bureaucrats. Reports resulting from SED's annual financial and program audits were so complicated that the executive director gave only a brief description of the SED auditors' main conclusions at board meetings.

After the school was several years old, and after intense soul searching late into the evening at several meetings, the board voted to purchase a large home in a residential neighborhood, and Windham opened its first community residence. Moving into residential services meant that the agency was now in the policy orbit of another large state bureaucracy, the Office of Mental Retardation and Developmental Disabilities (OMRDD). Tensions developed early when OMRDD tried to insist that 50 percent of the residents come from a state-run developmental center that was closing under court order. Windham Programs successfully resisted the pressure and protected most of the residential slots for its own families, but not without a significant expenditure of staff and parent energy and a board member letter-writing campaign targeted at key OMRDD administrators and state legislators in a position to influence policy.

The addition of revenues from OMRDD again increased Windham's budget substantially, prompting the agency to hire its first professional business administrator and to establish a finance committee at the board level. The committee was chaired by the board treasurer, who was knowledgeable but not expert in finance, and included two other board members, neither of whom had any financial background. In this circumstance, the committee chair recruited two nonboard members for the committee, each of whom was selected especially for his knowledge of balance sheets and complicated financial statements. Meetings of the committee were attended by the three members of the management team and were usually devoted to reviewing agency budgets. The committee was also responsible for receiving the annual audit and accompanying management letter that, in accordance with a requirement of OMRDD and SED, were prepared by an independent accounting firm.

Given the membership profile of the finance committee, meaningful oversight of the organization's financial affairs was performed by the two nonboard members and to a lesser degree by the committee chair. When the committee chair made her report at the board meeting, most members nodded in tacit agreement. They hoped the finance committee understood the complexities of the various budgets, financial statements, and audits.

The Management Team

Recently, Mills and the other two members of the management team—the business administrator and the residential services director—had been talking about what, if anything, to do about recruiting different types of people to join the board. "Too much is at stake for us to continue as we are now," the business administrator had argued in a management team meeting. "We need advisors who understand our finances. Just the other day, the regional administrator at SED asked me if we distribute the independent auditor's report and management letter to board members. I didn't quite understand where she was coming from because last month she went out of her way to praise us for the number of parents still on our board. Anyway, I don't think most board members would understand those reports, do you?"

The residential services director responded, "Maybe we should develop financial reports that our board members can understand

and then devote a meeting to board training on financial reports and requirements. At the same time, we must identify potential new board members who will ask us the tough questions, like D'Aleo does. We're so close to daily operational hassles that we may not think about the values trade-offs and broader implications of what we're doing."

Mills added, "Let's not forget the importance of advisors who understand government policy-making and can help us influence it. Also, they must be able to raise substantial private contributions. We have always wanted to do things government won't pay for, and we certainly need help getting through the inevitable periods of cash flow pressure."

All three members of the management team were painfully aware of the agency's growing dependence on government grants and contracts and agreed that the agency needed board members or other advisors who could tap significant foundation, corporate, and individual philanthropy to bring some balance to the agency's revenue picture. It seemed clear to them that Windham Programs had moved rather quickly from a private to a quasi-public agency.

In fact, Mills had written about this evolution in the agency's resource base in a paper for a graduate course he had taken to comply with SED's requirement that he earn a professional degree in administration. In pondering the implications of this change, he had speculated, "Maybe we'll have to bite the bullet, revise the bylaws, and limit board members to two three-year terms" (Exhibit 9.2). Yet, how to make a smooth transition from the current board to a new governance structure was a puzzle, and how to approach the issue diplomatically was very much on Mills's mind as he headed for the conference room where board members were beginning to gather.

He would introduce the three-year term idea along with a suggestion that Windham require a certain minimum percentage of board members to be parents. This provision, which could be added to the bylaws, addressed his own hesitancy about diluting parent involvement at the board level. In addition, the provision might allay the concerns of current members about the possibility of an abrupt change from long-standing board practices.

He also intended to initiate discussion about creating an advisory group that would incorporate individuals with needed talents into the agency's governance structure. Under this scenario, Windham would retain its largely parent-led board and establish a Windham advisory group to counsel the organization's management team (Figure 9.1). Linkage to the board would be accomplished through the management team and two board members who would attend advisory group meetings.

Mills had in mind that the chair of the governing board would be an ex officio member of the advisory group, and the chair of the board's finance committee would be invited to attend advisory group meetings. Mills's father, a longtime community resident with ties to many of his influential peers, would be very helpful in recruiting bankers, investment specialists, attorneys, corporate leaders, and individuals connected to wealthy philanthropic circles in the community to serve as founding members of the advisory group. Still, when the management team had discussed this option, the reactions of the other administrators had struck a responsive chord with Mills. "How will the board members feel?" the residential services director had questioned. "Will they feel bypassed and undervalued?" The business administrator added his concern that advisory group members would agree to serve only out of personal loyalty to the elder Mr. Mills. "Will they continue to support Windham Programs when your father is no longer involved?" he asked.

"Perhaps we should go the same route as the Clayton Center," the business administrator continued. "They changed their board membership radically and have added the very kinds of persons we're interested in recruiting. They didn't think it was necessary to start a whole new advisory group." "Yes," said Mills, "and look at what's happened there. Parent and consumer influence has largely disappeared from board proceedings. The organization is now run more like a corporation and the board disposes of business in short bimonthly meetings in a kind of pro forma way. Clayton Center could be any business enterprise. Very few of the board members remember why the organization was established in the first place."

The management team meeting had concluded with no consensus about which direction to pursue. Reflecting this evening on his earlier discussion with Julia Morris, Mills realized that no clear alternative had been agreed upon with her. "Well," he thought as he opened the door to the conference room, "I wonder which option the board will prefer."

Questions for Discussion

1. From your perspective, what are the three most important issues raised in this case?
2. If you were Julia Morris, what would you have said or done in reaction to Mills's statement that he was going to recommend changes in the board's governance structure? If you were Tom Mills, how would you have handled the governance issues prior to the board meeting?
3. Evaluate the alternatives Mills is suggesting; what other alternatives might he consider?
4. What are the interests of the State Education Department and the Office of Mental Retardation and Developmental Disabilities in this situation? How might they be different from those of Windham Programs' board and staff?
5. If you agree with the management team's view that the current board is not qualified to meet its responsibilities given the agency's growth and changes in its revenue mix, explain why. If you believe the current board is qualified, explain why.

Exhibit 9.1. 1994–1995 Board of Directors, Windham Programs.

Position	Name	Occupation
President	Julia Morris*	Homemaker
Vice President	Michael D'Aleo*	Administrator, State Department of Social Services
Secretary	Sarah Maxon*	Homemaker
Treasurer	Joan Sears*	Consultant; Ph.D. student
Executive Director	Thomas Mills*	
Delegates[†]	Lawrence Moran*	Small business owner
	Benjamin Blake	English professor
	Anne Simon*	Homemaker
	Gerald Pendleton*	Small business owner
	Allen DeFleur*	Community college computer instructor
	Edgar Graham	Corporate accountant
	Louise Spitzer*	Homemaker
	Donald Little*	Employee assistance

	program, state agency
Noreen Harris'	Temp service secretary
Leanne Brown*	Homemaker

*Indicates parent of individual served by Windham Programs.

'All except three of the delegates serve as committee chairs.

Exhibit 9.2. Excerpts from Bylaws.

Article V: Directors

1. *Management of the Corporation.* The corporation shall be managed by the board of directors, which shall consist of not less than three directors. Each director shall be at least nineteen years of age.

2. *Election and Term of Directors.* At each annual meeting of members, the membership shall elect directors to hold office until the next annual meeting. Each director shall hold office until the expiration of the term for which he was elected and until his successor has been elected and shall have qualified, or until his prior resignation or removal.

3. *Increase or Decrease in Number of Directors.* The number of directors may be increased or decreased by vote of the members or by a vote of a majority of all of the directors. No decrease in number of directors shall shorten the term of any incumbent director.

13. *Executive and Other Committees.* The board, by resolution adopted by a majority of the entire board, may designate from among its members an executive committee and from the general membership of the corporation other committees, each consisting of three or more members. Each such committee shall serve at the pleasure of the board.

Figure 9.1. Board of Directors Organization Chart.

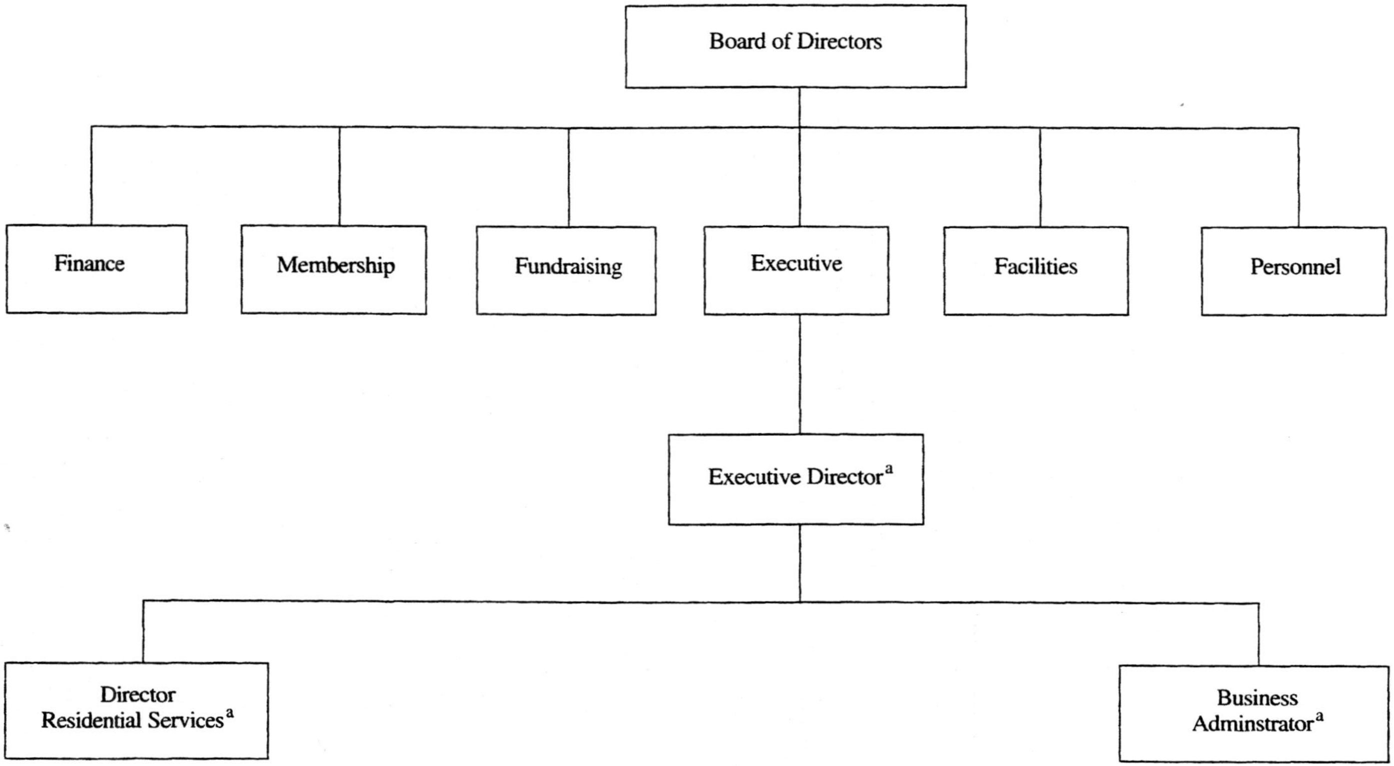

Board of Directors

Finance

Membership

Fundraising

Executive

Facilities

Personnel

Executive Director[a]

Director Residential Services[a]

Business Administrator[a]

[a] Member of management team

Suggested Readings

Fletcher, K. B. "Effective Boards: How Executive Directors Define and Develop Them." *Nonprofit Management and Leadership,* 1992, *2,* 283–293. Reports research examining ways in which highly rated executive directors work actively with their boards in recruitment, financial management, fundraising, long-range planning, and leadership development. Particularly valuable for practitioners.

Grønbjerg, K. A. *Understanding Nonprofit Funding: Managing Revenues in Social Services and Community Development Organizations.* San Francisco: Jossey-Bass, 1993. Based in part on case studies, offers a richly detailed analysis of fiscal patterns and associated management tasks. Chapters One, Eight, and Eleven of particular relevance to this case.

Harlan, S. L., and Saidel, J. R. "Board Members' Influence on the Government-Nonprofit Relationship." *Nonprofit Management and Leadership,* 1994, *5,* 173–196. Examines whether, how, and under what conditions nonprofit boards of directors influence the government–voluntary sector relationship. Finds many boards playing multiple roles, simultaneously enhancing interdependence and maintaining the boundary between state government and nonprofits. Based on random sample of four hundred nonprofit organizations.

Kramer, R. M. "Voluntary Agencies and the Contract Culture: Dream or Nightmare?" *Social Service Review,* 1994, *68,* 33–60. Analysis of rationale and incentives for purchase-of-service contracting. Examines processes, transaction costs, and strategies involved. Explores consequences of contracting for service delivery system, governmental and voluntary organizations, as well as implications for policy and future research. Insightful overview pulling together major research during past ten years.

Smith, S. R., and Lipsky, M. *Nonprofits for Hire: The Welfare State in the Age of Contracting.* Cambridge, Mass.: Harvard University Press, 1993. Examines implications of contracting for the governance of nonprofit organizations. Chapter Four particularly relevant to this case. Book as whole valuable for understanding the context and consequences of government and voluntary sector relations.

Stone, M. M. "Competing Contexts: The Evolution of a Nonprofit Organization's Governance System in Multiple Environments." *Public Administration Review,* forthcoming. Uses in-depth historical case study of one organization to examine consequences for governance of substantial changes in the relationship between government and nonprofit organizations from the early 1950s until 1990. Implications for governance structures and the distribution of responsibilities between board and executive staff of particular interest.

Chapter Ten

Using Community Networks to Diversify the Board

J. Allen Whitt
Gwen Moore

Montrose City Community Theater (MCCT) is an amateur theatrical troupe that stages four productions each year. All members of the troupe are unpaid nonprofessionals who rehearse in the evenings and on weekends. Sources of revenue to support the theater's budget include ticket sales, an annual fund drive directed toward the general public, and a sizable annual grant from a family foundation in Montrose City.

Today, over a brown bag lunch, members of the nominating committee of the governing board of MCCT have taken their seats around a small conference table. Those present include Marge Withers, chair of the nominating committee, and three other committee members: Richard Moran, Cindy Balcom, and Frank Kenyon. Also in attendance is Ken Althorp, MCCT's part-time executive director.

> *Withers:* Our executive director has requested this meeting, and I'm glad you were all able to make it on such short notice. Ken, why don't you take over.
>
> *Althorp:* When Marge came to me in her role as nominating committee chair and said you were going to nominate Harriet Miller, the wealthy grande dame, and

Susan Kadish, a member of the MCCT troupe, I just felt I had to speak up. . . .

Frank Kenyon
(interrupting): My wife has known Harriet for years and says she's now thinking about the legacy that she personally would like to leave in this town. So I think we have a good chance of getting some endowment money from her, or the promise of it. Another thing: she has that big old house and all those beautifully manicured grounds, and my wife says she's looking for a way to get back in the social swim now that her husband has died. She's known by everyone, of course, being about the bluest of the bluebloods around here.

Althorp: Well, I can see how she might be a good candidate, but I'm worried because she can't give us any ties to other organizations in the community, and that's one of our problems. Being quite a bit older than many community leaders, she isn't personally acquainted with the younger, more active movers and shakers who are on other boards and could bring us skills, like maybe being a lawyer or investment manager.

Richard Moran
(murmuring): What do we need with an investment manager since we have no endowment?

Althorp
(nodding at Moran): It's been wonderful for me, as director of our plays, to have so many of you on the board who are also amateur actors and members of the MCCT troupe. But the royalties we have to pay to get rights to any musical or drama that people will come out to see are horrendously high,

and one reason our attendance is going down is that we can't afford the kinds of plays that people like. And the stage riggings are a disgrace. I was really concerned last year when we had that accident during the dress rehearsal for *Peter Pan,* and I shudder to think of the kind of personal injury insurance we should be carrying. Of course, the riggings and the roof and the seating can be repaired, but when I had an estimate done six months ago, it turned out to be somewhere in the neighborhood of $125,000—that's three times our annual budget!

Cindy Balcom (nodding vigorously): I agree with Ken. I'm sorry I didn't speak up at our last committee meeting, but frankly I didn't want to rock the boat. You know I'm on the board of the Fine Arts Museum, and we had a consultant last year who told us that the community networks a board member can give an organization access to are more important than what the person does for a living or what he or she is expert in.

Althorp: We need to be more tied in to other community groups through members who are well connected to movers and shakers. Recruiting members who are on several boards and who are active and in the middle of things would be of great benefit to MCCT in raising our visibility and facilitating fundraising. I'm afraid if we nominate Harriet and Susan we'll remain to some extent out of the action here.

Kenyon: Harriet's in the swim—she's lived in this community all her life. She's well connected to other wealthy families in the community. Isn't she just what we need to increase our profile?

Moran: And Susan would be a dedicated board member. She performs in nearly all our productions and has been a reliable cast member for at least a decade. Since her children are grown and she works part time in her family's computer business, she would have time to attend all of our meetings.

Balcom: I agree with Ken. The consultant told us that having board members with good network positions is crucial. She explained that people who sit on more than one board know a wide range of active people, know what goes on in several organizations, can convey information from one organization to another, can share their expertise and skills with more than one organization, and may be a source of financial support to both organizations. They also get to know and interact with members of other boards and may be able to influence other organizations in the community. They can introduce members of one board to members of another and develop a wider range of information than members of a single board. The boards whose members are most fully tied into the heart of a community network are likely to have success in raising funds, getting strategic information, and attaining good governing expertise.

Althorp: Cindy and I are obviously on the same wavelength. To follow through on the idea that we need board members with good network ties to other organizations, I offer for the committee's consideration

Helen Bloome, Michael Harpe, and Sarah Jones. Each is prominent in Montrose City and is experienced as a board member. Each is knowledgeable about the organizational life of the community and can help us forge ties to other key organizations and leaders.

Moran: I've heard of Sarah Jones but not the others. Tell us more about them and what they can do for MCCT.

Althorp: Actually, the consultant to the Fine Arts Museum that Cindy was talking about made a presentation at that nonprofit governance workshop I attended last year. So I've done a little network analysis myself to show where MCCT stands in the community and to see how adding specific board members might elevate our profile. To begin, I had to identify community organizations and their board members. Since there are many nonprofit organizations here, I picked those funded by the United Way as most prominent and mainstream. I contacted the executive director of each and got a list of their current board members. We wouldn't want to leave out the major business powers here, so I also got lists of the boards of directors of the three national corporations headquartered in Montrose City. Here's the result [Exhibit 10.1].

Althorp (as members are reading through the list): We're looking for people who are on more than one board.

Moran: Cindy, you're the only one of us on another board. *(He chuckles.)* Guess we're not too well connected!

Althorp
(after a short pause): I calculated how near the center of the organizational network each one of these organizations was. It's quite easy with a computer program.[1]

Anyway, this second page [Exhibit 10.2] shows us where we stand in the community organization network. The higher the score, the more "central" is the organization in the overall network of organizations since high centrality means that the organization is on the average "close to" each of the other organizations. We can easily see where we stand in this network: the most central organization is the Interfaith Partnership for the Homeless, and the least central is, sadly, MCCT.

Balcom: I'm afraid this confirms our suspicions that MCCT is pretty marginal among mainstream organizations. We're practically out of the loop. How can we improve our standing?

Althorp: Let's now see how specific choices of board members would affect MCCT's centrality. If Harriet Miller or Susan Kadish were invited to join the board, its overall centrality would be unchanged. Harriet or Susan adds nothing to MCCT's centrality because neither is on any other boards and therefore does not create linkages between boards. By contrast, Helen Bloome is already on two

---

1.   In his computer analysis, Althorp used UCINET IV, a software program designed to calculate centrality and other network characteristics. UCINET IV is available from Analytic Technologies, 6616 Christie Road, Columbia, S.C. 29209–2047. At this writing, the student version costs about $20.

boards, Rivex Corporation and Central Hospital. As an African American physician, she also has valuable connections and expertise for MCCT. What would her presence contribute to the overall centrality of MCCT? On this page [Exhibit 10.3], I've analyzed our position if she were on our board.

Moran: We move from tenth place to sixth place in centrality. Not bad at all. I'm beginning to see the value of well-placed board members in tying MCCT into the community.

Althorp: If we instead invite Harriet Miller, Susan Kadish, or another person with no other board connections, of course, centrality would not have changed at all, and a person with a single other board connection would strengthen centrality only a little. Helen Bloome, on the other hand, would bring in two connections and a big jump in our centrality score. MCCT would have a lower average distance between itself and the other nine organizations in the local network.

Notice what happens if, instead of Helen Bloome, MCCT recruits Michael Harpe [Exhibit 10.4]. Even though he's on the board of two other organizations, the same number as Helen Bloome, Harpe boosts centrality more than Bloome. With Harpe, MCCT's centrality goes up to third place instead of sixth. Harpe has a more positive impact because he's connected to the Interfaith Partnership for the Homeless and the Food Pantry, which have greater total centralities than Bloome's organizations. So he gives a higher level of centrality to our organization. In practical terms, when picking a board member in order to increase centrality, it's not simply the number of other organizations to which the person is tied, but the centrality of those organizations that's important.

Withers: Tell me more about Michael Harpe.

Althorp: He's a partner in Smythe, Wiley, and Harpe, the law firm of choice for many of our socially prominent citizens. His specialty is trusts and estates. In addition, he's on two boards of social service agencies and is active in the Democratic party. I understand he has the ear of the mayor and several members of the city council. But another candidate on the list could raise centrality even more than Bloome or Harpe. Sarah Jones is on three other boards—Interfaith Partnership for the Homeless, Rivex Corporation, and Memorial Hospital. And as you can see in this handout [Exhibit 10.5], adding her to the board would elevate the centrality of MCCT from last place to second place.

Balcom: Sarah and I are both members of the Spofford Club so I know her a little. She's lived here for about ten years and is quite active in the community. She's in some sort of management position in Pisa Credit Card's accounting department and might be able to give us financial advice. I think she'd be a good catch for us.

Kenyon: Okay, I can see that networking is important. But MCCT needs other things as well. For example, we have very little connection to ethnic minority organizations, even those in the arts. I would like to nominate John Wu to the board. We teach together at Montrose City High School and he impresses me as an energetic young man. He's interested in the arts and told me last week that he's one of the founders of the Chinese-American theater that apparently started up last year. He's also involved with a group that wants to set up an Asian museum. I guess he's not on any of the boards of organizations supported by the United Way, since he isn't on the list Ken handed out. Still, I think he would be a valuable addition to our board.

Althorp: Frank, the consultant stressed the importance of broadening connections to other organizations that have no board member links to central organizations. If we recruit a member from a less central organization, he or she can bring in information and people from groups not closely linked to mainstream organizations and centers of influence. Without looking at the names of all of the board members of the Chinese-American Theater, we don't know if any are on other important nonprofit or corporate boards, but as far as I know none are. John Wu would link MCCT to Asian-American organizations.

Withers: It's nearly one o'clock and we must bring the meeting to a close. We have six candidates: Harriet Miller, Helen Bloome, Michael Harpe, Sarah Jones, Susan Kadish, and John Wu. Each of you should write on a piece of paper the three names you want the committee to propose to the board.

Questions for Discussion

1. How would you weigh the relative importance of increasing centrality and creating ties to less central organizations against the personal characteristics of potential board members such as ethnicity, race, wealth, and occupation?
2. What other information about potential board members, other than that cited above, would you want to have before inviting them to join the board?
3. What other information about MCCT and the members of its board would you want to have before making a decision about nominating new candidates for the board?
4. Based on the information in this case, which candidate do you think best meets MCCT's needs? Which candidate least meets its needs? Why?
5. Which three potential board members would you vote for and why?

Exhibit 10.1. Analysis of Board Candidates.

Montrose City Nonprofit Organizations, Local Corporations, and their Board Members[a]

Board Member	Organization
Harpe	Homeless
Herman	Homeless
Jones	Homeless
Tucker	Homeless
Balcom	Youth Ballet
Wells	Youth Ballet
Able	Family Services
Fischer	Family Services
Meyer	Family Services
Perkins	Family Services
Smith	Family Services

[a]*Note:* This hypothetical example includes only a few organizations with small boards.

Bloome	Rivex Corporation
Jones	Rivex Corporation
Klein	Rivex Corporation
Baltzell	U-Build, Inc.
Ellison	U-Build, Inc.
Goldman	U-Build, Inc.
Powell	U-Build, Inc.
Sweet	U-Build, Inc.
Powell	A-1 Furniture
Tucker	A-1 Furniture
White	A-1 Furniture
Brown	Memorial Hospital
Jones	Memorial Hospital
Kelly	Memorial Hospital
Smith	Memorial Hospital
Bloome	Central Hospital
Herman	Central Hospital
Moore	Central Hospital
Ellison	Food Pantry
Harpe	Food Pantry
Wells	Food Pantry
Miller	"Blueblood" family; no boards
Kadish	No boards
Balcom	MCCT
Kenyon	MCCT
Moran	MCCT
Withers	MCCT

Exhibit 10.2. Centrality Scores for Montrose City Organizations.

1	Homeless	64.29
2	Food Pantry	56.25
3	Rivex Corporation	47.37
4	Memorial Hospital	47.37
5	A-1 Furniture	45.00
6	Central Hospital	42.86
7	U-Build, Inc.	40.91
8	Youth Ballet	40.91
9	Family Services	33.33
10	MCCT	30.00

Exhibit 10.3. Centrality Scores as a Result of Adding Bloome.

1	Homeless	69.23
2	Rivex Corporation	60.00
3	Food Pantry	56.25
4	Central Hospital	52.94
5	Memorial Hospital	52.94
6	MCCT	50.00
7	A-1 Furniture	47.37
8	Youth Ballet	45.00
9	U-Build, Inc.	40.91
10	Family Services	36.00

Exhibit 10.4. Centrality Scores as a Result of Adding Harpe.

1	Homeless	75.00
2	Food Pantry	60.00
3	MCCT	56.25
4	Rivex Corporation	52.94
5	Memorial Hospital	52.94
6	A-1 Furniture	50.00
7	Central Hospital	47.37
8	U-Build, Inc.	42.86
9	Youth Ballet	40.91
10	Family Services	36.00

Exhibit 10.5. Centrality Scores as a Result of Adding Jones.

1	Homeless	75.00
2	MCCT	60.00
3	Rivex Corporation	60.00
4	Memorial Hospital	60.00
5	Food Pantry	56.25
6	A-1 Furniture	50.00
7	Central Hospital	47.37
8	Youth Ballet	47.37
9	U-Build, Inc.	40.91
10	Family Services	39.13

Suggested Readings

Granovetter, M. S. "The Strength of Weak Ties." *American Journal of Sociology,* 1973, *78,* 1360–1380. Classic paper arguing critical role of acquaintances and other "weak ties" in bridging fragmented groups and integrating social systems.

Powell, W. W. "Neither Market Forms Nor Hierarchy: Network Forms of Organization." In B. M. Staw and L. L. Cummings (eds.), *Research in Organizational Behavior.* Vol. 12. Greenwich, Conn.: JAI Press, 1990. Discusses networks as a pattern of economic organization.

Wasserman, S., and Faust, K. *Social Network Analysis: Methods and Applications.* New York: Cambridge University Press, 1994. Comprehensive presentation of social network methodology.

Whitt, J. A., and Mizruchi, M. "The Local Inner Circle." *Journal of Political and Military Sociology,* 1986, *14,* 115–125. Investigation of local corporate directors' participation in governance of nonprofit and other organizations and their degree of attitude similarity.

Woodward, K., and Doreian, P. "Utilizing and Understanding Community Networks: A Report of Three Case Studies Having 583 Participants." *Journal of Social Service Research,* 1994, *18*(3/4), 1–41. An application of network principles to the governance issue of interagency cooperation among social service agencies.

Part Three

Interpreting Mission and Accountability

Although the governing board of a charitable nonprofit is legally accountable to the state that charters the organization, board members rarely think of themselves as performing a civic act and as accountable to the public interest. The concept of a "public interest" that transcends special interests—including stakeholder interests—lies at the core of democratic theories of government. These theories, as interpreted in the founding of the earliest American colleges, established the precedent of an autonomous governing board with full authority over a charitable organization but accountable to the state *pro publico bono* (Wood, 1985).

One method for identifying to whom and to what an organization is accountable involves looking at the organization from two perspectives: from the inside out and from the outside in (Aykac and Gordy, 1993). During this process, each stakeholder group (internal, external, or mixed) will tend to defend its view as being in the public interest, and sometimes resolution among the contending groups will not occur. In these instances, according to the political and structural theories of governance discussed in the Introduction, the governing board (itself a stakeholder) makes or oversees trade-offs that result in a synthesis of stakeholder interests. However, a negotiated settlement, although providing an acceptable allocation of accountability, may not be synonymous with the public interest, and that possibility is a subtext of the cases in this section.

Concepts of accountability and the public interest are at the center of Davis's "Dissolution or Survival: The University of Bridgeport and the Unification Church." Basing his case on a series of real events, Davis develops the persona of a fictional trustee who, in the midst of clamoring stakeholders, is advised that he must act in the "best interests" of the university. The trustee's situation and that of the university are exacerbated by the university's location in an economically battered industrial city and by the identity of the party willing to come to the university's rescue: the Unification Church, popularly known as the "Moonies" and widely perceived as a cult. The reader must decide which values—academic, moral, economic, civic—are worth risking when the motives and values of the rescuer appear ambiguous.

In "Mission Versus Revenue: The California Hospital Medical Center" by Lammers and Beaudin, the mission statement commits the hospital to forgo competing with other city hospitals for prestige and patients and to focus instead on serving the surrounding impoverished neighborhoods. Whether the hospital can break even using this strategy is uncertain, as is the willingness of the board of the hospital's corporate parent to underwrite this mission in the weakest member financially of its chain of subsidiary hospitals. This case illustrates some of the complex issues linking health care for poor populations with the public interest, a topic also raised by Gray, Chauncey, and Wood in the first case in this book.

In "Strategic Planning at AIDS Project Los Angeles," Beaudin, Senak, and Goodstein show that therapeutic advances have changed the services required by people with AIDS. Only a decade ago, AIDS organizations offered short-term care for the dying, but now they are called upon to provide long-term services for the chronically ill. At AIDS Project Los Angeles (APLA), an organization as ideologically driven as the women's shelter described by Milofsky and Morrison in Part Two, stakeholder views are strongly held and clash with the administrative practices and professionalism associated with organizations as large and elaborately structured as APLA has become. In anticipation of diminished resources and increasing numbers of clients, the APLA governing board has initiated a planning process in a rapidly expanding organization with a variety of stakeholders who claim to know the right path for the organization's future development. Whether the public interest requires more than the resolution of stakeholder conflict, or perhaps a different approach altogether, is a question implicit in the narrative.

References

Aykac, A., and Gordy, M. "The Emerging Corporatism: Business Executives as Social Managers." In B. Sutton (ed.), *The Legitimate Corporation: Essential Readings in Business Ethics and Corporate Governance.* Cambridge, Mass.: Basil Blackwell, 1993.
Wood, M. M. *Trusteeship in the Private College.* Baltimore: Johns Hopkins University Press, 1985.

Chapter Eleven

Dissolution or Survival
The University of Bridgeport and the Unification Church
Glenn Scott Davis

Hoping to avoid newspaper and television reporters as well as faculty, student, and alumni demonstrators, Stuart Russo (a fictional trustee) arrived well in advance of the University of Bridgeport (UB) board of trustees meeting. The controversial proposal before today's meeting offered the only hope for averting what Russo and every other trustee dreaded—closure of the university. At the meeting, Russo would be voting on whether to accept loans from the Professors World Peace Academy, an organization founded, funded, and controlled by Sun Myung Moon, leader of the Unification Church, and feared by critics as the head of a dangerous cult. If the governing board accepted the $50 million in loans offered by the Academy, the university would stay open. In exchange, the board of trustees would be contractually obligated to grant the Academy the power to select a majority of the board's members. The loan agreement specified that the Academy's loans would be secured by a mortgage on the university's eighty-six-acre seaside campus, making the Academy the institution's major creditor.

Note. This case draws on the author's master's thesis at Wesleyan University and is based on materials taken from the public record. The author is active in the Coalition of Concerned Citizens, which opposes control of the University of Bridgeport's board of trustees by the Professors World Peace Academy.

While Russo waited for the other trustees to arrive, he thought about how much Bridgeport and the university had changed since his undergraduate years in the early 1960s. UB had started as a small junior college in the 1920s and had grown into a university during the post–World War II years with the support of local industrialists and philanthropists. Enrollment boomed and by 1970 exceeded nine thousand students. The future seemed bright. But twenty years later, Bridgeport, a thriving industrial city during its heyday, had become known as the city that had declared bankruptcy and as the home of a failing university in the midst of controversy.

Time was running out and Russo, normally decisive, had not yet decided how he would vote. It was not so much the loans that bothered him. Like the other trustees, he wanted to keep the university open. Because he was a UB alumnus and native Bridgeporter, the institution meant a great deal to him. The loans would solve the university's short-term crisis, but Russo was troubled by provisions in the contract that gave the Academy control of the board. He was also concerned about the connection between the Academy and Sun Myung Moon and the effect that relationship would have on the reputation of the university.

A University in Trouble

Russo had worked his way up to the position of CEO of a locally owned manufacturing firm and had served on other nonprofit boards in the city. His leadership abilities, fundraising experience, and connections in the business world earned him an invitation to serve on the university's board of trustees. Hardly naïve when he joined the board, Russo knew that UB faced hard times. The signs were evident. Raising funds from the alumni had become increasingly difficult. For the past two decades, UB had struggled with declining enrollments, escalating tuition, stiffer competition, and the negative image of Bridgeport. Then there were the never-ending conflicts between the faculty and administration, who could never agree on the mission of the university or how it could best be managed. Some faculty favored a professional curriculum, others the liberal arts, while the administration wanted to market those programs that would attract the most students. Every third year, the university and the Association of American University Professors engaged in contract negotiations. Faculty strikes had occurred in the past, and the threat of a strike always loomed at contract time.

Russo reviewed the university's current status:

• An independent auditing firm was uncertain about the university's capacity to continue operating but noted that the university's management believed the Academy's loan would assure continued operation. Given the uncertainties about the university's future, the auditor declined to express an opinion on the financial statements.

• On annual budgets of $50 to $60 million, the university had experienced a deficit during each of the past five years. The accumulated deficits put the university in default of covenants on bank loans. Debts to the banks were over $18 million, and some $3.5 million was owed to trade creditors. The trustees had used a significant portion of the restricted endowment to cover general operating expenses without the permission of donors or the state courts.

• From a peak of over 9,000 in 1970, student enrollment had dropped to 4,150, including a loss of 1,000 in the past academic year. Sixty-eight of the university's faculty of 160 had been on strike for over two years.

• In December 1991, the university was placed on probation by its regional accrediting body, the New England Association of Schools and Colleges, because of the association's uncertainty that the institution could continue to meet its standards. Probation was the association's last step before suspending accreditation.

In 1990, a major investment firm had expressed interest in bailing out UB with a thirty-four-million-dollar bond package. The proposal proved unfeasible because of the university's severe credit problems. All the trustees, Russo among them, agreed that survival would depend on UB's ability to attract an outside creditor willing and able to invest in UB in spite of its deteriorating financial condition. In August 1990, just a few weeks before the faculty strike began, the university president reported to the board that she had been approached by a professor of religion from Bard College who represented a group of investors. These investors, the president reported, were interested in presenting a proposal for UB to affiliate with an international network of universities. Only later did the trustees learn that the religion professor represented the Academy and that the Academy was funded and founded by Sun Myung Moon and the Unification Church.

The Board's First Vote on the Academy's Proposal

In March 1991, a group of UB trustees traveled to Washington, D.C., to tour the headquarters of Sun Myung Moon's American operation: the *Washington Times* newspaper; the Universal Ballet Company, the Atlantic Video Production Company, the *World & I* magazine, and the American Freedom Coalition. During the visit, the trustees were told that funds for an Academy-UB affiliation came from the Unification Church and that Sun Myung Moon had lined up Japanese investors.

A few months later, in early October, the university president announced that UB might close within a year if it could not raise millions of dollars, restructure its debt, or obtain significant financial support from an outside investor or creditor. In the same month, the board of trustees began discussing whether to pursue an agreement with the Academy. Bridgeport's one-time mayor, formerly UB's board chair, denounced any agreement involving Moon's organization. The dean of UB's law school, its most prestigious academic unit, declared that consideration of an affiliation with the Academy was an act of desperation deserving of no further consideration—the law school wanted no part of it. Some trustees attempted to end further consideration of an affiliation with the Academy, but they were outvoted. Russo abstained from this vote, in which the trustees agreed to consider the Academy's proposal. Russo was unhappy with himself, troubled over his own indecision.

Differing Perspectives on the Academy

When Academy representatives approached the board of trustees, they emphasized the programs and mission of their academy. A nonprofit organization granted Section 501(c)(3) status by the United States Internal Revenue Service, the Academy was established as a worldwide association of scholars interested in promoting international peace. Academy representatives encouraged UB trustees to consider the benefits of an affiliation with them. UB would join a network of universities dedicated to educating students from around the world for the twenty-first century, and enrollment would increase as the Academy recruited international students. The Academy's publicly proclaimed objective was to educate youth from around the world to understand the requirements of a global community. A worldwide university system was to facilitate the exchange of knowledge by students and professors from all nations and cultures. A guiding principle was that professors would exemplify moral conviction and a clear sense of values.

Among the trustees opposed to an affiliation with the Academy was a woman who for years had devoted her energy and resources to the development and promotion of UB's arts programs. She looked into the Academy's activities, and when a board meeting was scheduled at which Academy representatives were to present their proposals, she wrote to her fellow trustees summarizing her findings.

Her letter asserted that Sun Myung Moon would seek to control the University of Bridgeport through intermediaries in the Academy. Having examined the relationship between Moon and the *Washington Times,* she expressed alarm that academic freedom would be threatened at UB if it was under Academy control and questioned whether, in practice, the Academy was truly independent of the Unification Church. Reverend Moon's stated goal was the establishment of a worldwide theocracy of which a new messiah, Moon himself, would be the head and in which the separation of church and state would be abolished. As part of the strategy to create this theocracy, Moon planned to gain control and/or influence over a variety of institutions, including universities. His effort to gain influence in the academic world centered on the activities of the Academy, which, this trustee contended, was promoting an underlying political and religious agenda antithetical to the goals of a university. The Academy was just one of the hundreds of nonprofit and for-profit organizations controlled by Moon and funded with hundreds of millions of dollars from unknown sources in Japan. She asked the other trustees to reject affiliation with the Academy.

In late October, after hearing the views of faculty, students, and alumni, Russo and the other trustees voted unanimously against pursuing any agreement with the Academy. Afterward, the board chair said in a televised statement that the Academy's offer was not in the best interests of the university and that UB was not going to have anything to do with the Academy.

The dean of the law school, although pleased with the rejection of the Academy's offer, announced that if the university could not guarantee a solution to the public relations nightmare, financial crisis, and accreditation problems, he might seek a new home for the law school.

In early November, the university president resigned and the provost took over as president. Three weeks later, the trustees sought permission from the state court to spend additional endowment funds. The court granted the university permission to spend its endowment funds for operating expenses but refused to grant retroactive permission for funds the board had already spent without donor or court approval. Russo felt the trustees were vulnerable to legal action by the state attorney general's office and possibly by donors on the ground that the governing board had violated its duty in failing to hold restricted endowment funds in trust for the particular purposes for which they were donated. The board's expenditure of these restricted funds had kept the university's doors open during the previous year, but the funds were now significantly depleted.

The day after the court decision on the endowment funds, Russo cast a reluctant yea vote when the board decided to cut thirty-one majors in the arts and sciences, including English, psychology, history, biology, music, and cinema. Programs in business, engineering, chiropractic, dental hygiene, and fashion merchandising were among those retained. The academic reputation of UB continued to plummet. When the positions of striking professors were filled by new hires whom the strikers angrily referred to as "scabs," UB became the first American university to employ permanent replacements for striking faculty.

Pursuing Survival

Through the late fall and winter of 1991–1992, several means of survival were considered by the board. One possibility was to merge with other educational institutions. Merger talks had opened with neighboring Sacred Heart University, but the law school's faculty and advisory board refused to consider this option, believing that Sacred Heart was not the appropriate institution for the law school. In defiance of the UB board of trustees, the law school dean and the advisory board opened affiliation negotiations with Quinnipiac College in Hamden, Connecticut.

In an unprecedented move, the law school declared independence from the University of Bridgeport and merged with Quinnipiac College, in spite of claims by the UB board and administration that the law school, which had come to the university from another institution several years before, was legally subject to the authority of UB's board. To avoiding ongoing negative publicity, the UB trustees very soon terminated their claims to authority over the law school and agreed to lease space to Quinnipiac College for the operation of the law school on the UB campus. The lease arrangement was to be continued until 1995, by which time Quinnipiac would have completed construction of a permanent facility on its Hamden campus.

In addition to merger, another possible means of survival was the transformation of the university into a real estate entity, whereby UB's academic programs would be taken over by other higher education institutions in the area and operated in leased facilities on the UB campus. The trustees, however, determined that the income from such an arrangement would be insufficient to meet the university's debt obligations.

A proposal from J. C. Bradford, a Nashville securities firm, offered some hope for survival by proposing the sale of bonds to finance the university's recovery. In early February, the university's vice president for finance reported to the trustees that in view of the law school's transfer to Quinnipiac College and the enrollment figures projected for the fall, the issuance of bonds proposed in the Bradford Plan was unwarranted. The trustees rejected the Bradford Plan even though the Bradford investors were willing to close the deal. Russo wondered if the full board of trustees had given enough consideration to the details of the Bradford Plan, but he, like other board members, relied on the opinions and findings of the board leadership and university staff. The Bradford Plan was dead and with it any hope of preventing the university's closure. Two weeks later, on February 13, 1992, with no other proposals or options on the table, the board passed a resolution to close the university the following August.

Reaction in Bridgeport to the announced closure was immediate. Small business people, store owners, resident homeowners, landlords, and residents in the South End of Bridgeport, the neighborhood bordering the UB campus, feared the worst. Stories spread that abandoned UB dormitories would be turned into giant crack houses and become refuges for violent criminals and drug dealers. Banks faced the loss of a major institutional customer while businesses faced the loss of trade by UB and its students. City and state officials, recognizing that UB had exhausted all of the alternatives to closure, grew nervous over the prospect of a political nightmare—an empty eighty-six-acre campus in Bridgeport. The governor privately expressed interest in pursuing the possibility of moving some state offices and facilities to the campus but the public was unaware of this option. Increasingly, the phrase "Any alternative is better than an empty campus" was heard around the city. Russo's phone was ringing off the hook. "What can you do to keep UB open? Something must be done!"

Renewal of the Academy's Offer

Three weeks after the announcement that UB would close, the board chair received a letter from the Academy. The letter renewed the Academy's offer and assured the trustees that the professors' group was firmly committed to the tradition of academic freedom and nonsectarianism. The new overture promised that should UB and the Academy enter into an agreement, the Academy would respect the independence of the university. The letter reassured the trustees that much of the concern on campus and in the community about the relationship of the Academy to Sun Myung Moon was based on secondhand information and misunderstanding. In fact, the letter stated that the Academy was proud of its association with Reverend Moon and appreciated the energy and vision he provided. An affiliation of UB with the Academy would be good for UB, the Academy, and the city of Bridgeport.

The board voted to reconsider the offer and the board chair forwarded the Academy's latest offer to a New York law firm requesting a legal opinion that would advise the trustees of their fiduciary duties in light of the proposal. Their opinion noted the belief of the board that the possibility of alternatives other than the Academy had been exhausted and stated that the Academy's offer was the only option that addressed all of the university's basic problems. The legal opinion advised the trustees that they were *obligated* to try in good faith to come to an agreement with the Academy.

Russo thought about all he had read in recent weeks in the newspapers. Professors on strike opposed an Academy affiliation, as they had done from the beginning. Some nonstriking faculty were condemning the affiliation with the Academy because it would endanger the independence and credibility of the university. Other nonstriking faculty had been overheard saying that an agreement with the Academy would at least save their jobs. Students were divided. Some were outraged, while others were relatively unconcerned, and many planned to transfer to other schools regardless of the board's decision about the Academy affiliation. Echoing in Russo's mind was a newspaper editorial admonishing trustees that they couldn't sell their seats because they didn't own them; they held them in trust.

For weeks, Russo had been receiving mail from parents telling troubling stories about how their sons or daughters were recruited into the Unification Church and what had happened to them after joining. The emotional letters warned of deceptive recruiting practices and expressed fears that the Unification Church would use the university as a recruiting center. The parents described the "Moonies" as a dangerous cult. Religious and community figures whom Russo respected urged him to vote against any agreement between UB and the Academy. A coalition of community leaders, students, alumni, former faculty members, and donors circulated an open letter to the trustees detailing the ways in which affiliation with the Academy would threaten the basic purposes and goals of the university. This group threatened a lawsuit, claiming that any agreement giving away control of the board in exchange for loans would amount to an illegal conflict of interest and an illegal abdication of the board's powers to select its own membership.

At the same time, Russo was experiencing intense pressure from fellow board members, friends, and colleagues in the business community to support an Academy agreement to keep the university open. Powerful and influential bankers and business people in Bridgeport were nervous about the prospect of local banks not recovering the millions owed to them by the university in the event of the school's closure. They were quite willing to live with the Academy if it meant keeping UB's doors open.

Mulling over the idea of closure, Russo read the university's charter, in which provision was made for the dissolution of the corporation (Exhibit 11.1). Unfamiliar with the law of nonprofit corporations, he sought the advice of his attorney, who advised him that he was required by Connecticut law to perform his duties in "good faith" and in a manner that he "reasonably" believed to be in the "best interests" of the university. The law required that he perform his duties as a trustee with "such care as an ordinarily prudent person in a like position would use under similar circumstances" (Exhibit 11.2).

Good faith? Reasonable belief? Prudent care? The words raced through Russo's mind. "What if these parents are right and the Unification Church uses the school for its own purposes?" he asked his attorney. "Suppose some kids get hurt? On the other hand, if I vote against a viable deal to keep the school open, will I be violating my fiduciary duty?" The attorney questioned the legal opinion from the New York law firm. He was not convinced, as the opinion asserted, that Russo had any legal obligation to pursue a deal with the Academy if he thought it was not in the best interests of the university. Russo asked if anything about the proposed agreement with the Academy was illegal. The lawyer admitted that he did not know the answer, and in the little time remaining before Russo would have to make his decision, a thorough review of the case law was not possible. The lawyer did express doubts that persons bringing a lawsuit challenging a UB-Academy agreement would be granted standing in a court of law. "Ultimately," the attorney told Russo, "all you can do is use your best judgment to decide what you believe to be in the best interests of the university."

Russo faced a dilemma, and he could not figure out which alternative was in the university's best interests. "Stu," a fellow trustee called from down the hall, "the meeting is starting."

[handwritten annotations:] what's in the mission * the actual intention of the academy through reliable source * other possible resource and negotiating and contacting

Questions for Discussion

1. What does the board need to know? How can it get the information it needs? *by adding its external & internal stakeholders*
2. How could a decision by the board to reject a financially viable alternative to closure of the university be justified as being in the best interests of the institution?
3. How could a decision to accept the Academy's offer be justified as being in the best interests of the university considering all the controversy and objections to the Unification Church?
4. In making this difficult decision, to whom does the board owe its duty of loyalty? Is Russo's duty of loyalty identical to that of the board as a whole?
5. Is there anything inappropriate or unethical about an agreement in which the university's major creditor is granted the power to select 60 percent of the seats on the board of trustees? Does this arrangement constitute a conflict of interest?
6. What would you do if you were in Russo's shoes?

[handwritten margin notes:] Board as a unit not its individual have the authority to gov — Diversifying Community network — Resource development — Accountability — similar other org's history

Exhibit 11.1. Excerpts from "An Act Concerning the Incorporation of the University of Bridgeport" (Senate Bill No. 222).

Section 6. In the event of the dissolution of the corporation, any surplus remaining shall be conveyed, transferred and delivered to such other institution of learning in Fairfield County as shall then be serving in a similar capacity; and, if there is more than one, then to that one specifically designated by the board of trustees, and if there is none such, then to the state of Connecticut.

Approved, May 8, 1947.

Exhibit 11.2. Excerpts from the General Statutes of Connecticut, Revision of 1958, Revised to January 1, 1993. Volume 10.

Part V (d) Section 33–447. Board of directors. (a) Subject to any provisions pertaining thereto contained in the certificate of incorporation, the activities, property and affairs of a corporation shall be managed by its board of directors . . . (d) A director shall perform his duties as a director, including his duties as a member of any committee of the board upon which he may serve, in good faith, in a manner he reasonably believes to be in the best interests of the corporation and with such care as an ordinarily prudent person in a like position would use under similar circumstances. In performing his duties, a director shall be entitled to rely on information, opinions, reports or statements, including financial statements and other financial data, prepared or presented by (1) one or more officers or employees of the corporation whom the director reasonably believes to be reliable and competent in the matters presented, (2) counsel, public accountants or other persons as to matters which the director reasonably believes to be within such person's professional or expert competence, or (3) a committee of the board upon which he does not serve, duly designated in accordance with a provision of the certificate of incorporation or the bylaws, as to matters within its designated authority, which committee the director reasonably believes to merit confidence, but he shall not be considered to be acting in good faith if he has knowledge concerning the matter in question that causes such reliance to be unwarranted. A person who performs his duties in accordance with this subsection shall be presumed to have no liability by reason of being or having been a director of the corporation.

Suggested Readings

Ben-Ner, A., and Van Hoomissen, T. "The Governance of Nonprofit Organizations: Law and Public Policy." *Nonprofit Management and Leadership*, 1994, *4*(4), 393–414. Suggests that contemporary governing
boards may not support the interests of an organization's important
constituencies. Proposes a legal and policy framework for empowering stakeholders such as donors, clients, and students.

Haskell, P. J. "The University as Trustee." *Georgia Law Review*, 1982, *17*(1),
1–32. Challenges traditional concepts of the standards of conduct,
liability, and accountability of university trustees. Proposes that the
fiduciary standard associated with the law of trusts replace the business standard currently applied to university governing boards.

Ingram, R. T., and Associates. *Governing Independent Colleges and Universities.* San Francisco: Jossey-Bass, 1993. Comprehensive handbook for
higher education trustees sponsored by the Association of Governing Boards of Universities and Colleges. See especially Chapter Six
on board responsibilities.

Middleton, M. "Nonprofit Boards of Directors: Beyond the Governance
Function." In W. W. Powell (ed.), *The Nonprofit Sector: A Research
Handbook.* New Haven, Conn.: Yale University Press, 1987. Places
governance issues in the context of various formal and informal networks from which trustees come to their trusteeship and with which
boards must interact in the larger community.

Chapter Twelve

Mission Versus Revenue

The California Hospital Medical Center

John C. Lammers
Christy L. Beaudin

As director of social work at California Hospital Medical Center, Ernilyn Navarro had been asked to make a presentation to the board of directors of the hospital about one of the activities of her department: the Health Ministry program. Although she had worked for the hospital for eight years, she had never made a presentation to the board, and now the board chair himself had requested her presentation.

Many good things had been said about the Health Ministry over the past eighteen months, but Navarro believed its future was in jeopardy. The program was not self-supporting; it was difficult to measure the bottom line or identify its outcomes. Navarro believed that California Hospital must reach out to the surrounding neighborhoods, where many residents were impoverished and Spanish-speaking, but some hospital personnel just did not buy into activities that occurred outside the hospital walls. The recent passage of Proposition 187 denying nonemergency health care to illegal immigrants was yet another concern. Her greatest apprehension, however, was the corporate policy of the hospital chain of which California Hospital was a member. In recent months, the

---

Note: This case is based on actual events that have been altered slightly for teaching purposes.

corporate office had undertaken to "re-engineer" the chain and all the hospitals in it. As a result, all programs that were not consistent with the corporate mission of the system, or that did not return revenues to the system, were under consideration for elimination to save expenses. Navarro knew that several members of the California Hospital board also served on other boards overseeing the whole chain and that those other boards were trying to eliminate nonrevenue-generating programs throughout the system. She had heard that the corporate office was more concerned with maintaining national prominence in the area of acute care services than in serving the primary care needs of local neighborhoods. Now, Navarro was wondering how the California Hospital board would vote on the Health Ministry program.

Background on California Hospital

California Hospital was established in 1887 and in 1921 became an affiliate of the Lutheran Hospital Society of Southern California. Today, it is a 344-bed facility with almost fifteen hundred employees in a city of over 3.4 million. The medical staff includes 470 physicians. Each month at the hospital, the emergency room treats over two thousand patients, and more than five hundred women give birth. A cancer center provides care to some fourteen thousand patients annually. During the 1992 riots following the trial of the police officers who were videotaped beating Rodney King, the hospital emergency room treated more patients than any other downtown facility.

In 1988, partly to solve financial concerns, the Lutheran Hospital Society merged with another group of hospitals to form UniHealth America, a charitable nonprofit corporation. California Hospital thus became one of a nine-member hospital chain with associated insurance and related health maintenance organizations. At that time, construction on California Hospital's new seventy-five-million-dollar physical plant had just been completed, and its board was prepared to carry on the hospital's traditional mission, which involved local service in the context of national prominence. The tie to the University of Southern California, the availability of the latest equipment and services, and even membership in the UniHealth system as one of its larger facilities—all this spoke of regional and national prominence. But with Good Samaritan, Cedars Sinai, and UCLA hospitals only short distances away, continued competition on tertiary turf (highly specialized, expensive care) seemed risky. However, the alternative of seeking an increased market share in secondary care (short stays) and primary care (emergency and outpatient) in the hospital's immediate locale was financially problematic because those services simply do not pay well.

The decision to focus on surrounding neighborhoods was difficult for the California Hospital board of directors. Changing strategic direction meant local visibility but regional and certainly national obscurity—no wealthy, international heart, transplant, or surgical patients. As a result, cash flow everywhere in the hospital would be tight, with no slack created by highly remunerative services. Even so, as a key administrator later observed, "The strategic choice to serve this community and not the nation or the region was the only choice we could make. If we had not made that choice, we would simply not be having this conversation today. The hospital would be gone."

Redrafting the mission statement of the hospital was the exercise that brought board members along (Exhibit 12.1). Having been hampered by the old, unworkable vision of regional and national prominence as well as the financial instability of the late 1980s, they wanted a clear policy most of all. To their surprise, once the hospital focused on the needs and concerns of the immediate neighborhood, it found allies in unlikely places. The board chair of its nearest competitor assisted in obtaining favorable rates for state reimbursements for maternity charges. Later, the hospital received special allotments from the state as a "disproportionate provider" of services to the poor. As a provider of uncompensated care (resulting from incomplete payment or no payment from patients, government, or insurers), California Hospital found itself at the forefront in Southern California in the private sponsorship of a public mission.

However, despite this history of growth, savvy management, and merger, California Hospital's leadership soon ran afoul of a paradox faced by most inner city hospitals: as affluent populations moved to outlying neighborhoods and towns, hospitals like California were left with massive physical plants, highly paid staffs, and expensive technologies to serve less affluent, even poverty-stricken, uninsured, and underinsured inner city populations. In the year ending September 30, 1991, the hospital's expenses exceeded its revenues considerably (Table 12.1). In that year, only its membership in the UniHealth system saved it from closure. The logical concern that system control might thwart the hospital's mission was replaced with gratitude for the system's wealth that rescued the ailing institution.

Unfortunately, the obstacles to California Hospital's permanent financial recovery lay outside the UniHealth system in the federal government's efforts to control Medicare costs by making fixed payments for classifications of services, regardless of the actual costs to a hospital. With the government leading the cost-cutting drive, insurance companies and large employers followed with "managed care," a bundle of methods for serving large groups of patients on a contractual basis. In this environment, only hospitals offering the most highly reimbursed medical procedures and with the wealthiest patients find it easy to remain solvent.

Nonetheless, when California Hospital's present CEO took over in 1991, he understood and agreed with the strategic change and later said:

> The board made a commitment to a community approach. If there is a winner or survivor in the future, we will survive but not as tertiary care providers. If universal coverage becomes effective, I can't see anything that would change our direction. The need is there. It will take our local competition several hits on the head before they see that tertiary care is not happening. If others get into the primary and secondary care business, then there will be competition. Our success in the last three or four years came from having to serve the community. If we stick with that mission, our success will come true. We serve South Central and Central L.A. The basic issue is: we are what we are.

The Hospital Board and Its Governance Environment

In joining a larger system, California Hospital's board of directors had given over some of its authority to other governing bodies (Figure 12.1). Although the hospital retained its independence as a separate nonprofit corporation with its own 501(c)(3) tax-exempt status and self-perpetuating governing board, the UniHealth Corporation owned the hospital's physical plant and equipment and paid its staff. Furthermore, UniHealth had created a fourteen-member MedCenters Board of Governors to review and coordinate the activities of the nine hospitals in the system. Two of California Hospital's fourteen directors were governors. Second, UniHealth had created a Medical Advisory Board to advise on the clinical direction of the system (which included outpatient centers, mental health programs, and two HMOs); two members of California Hospital's board were members of the Medical Advisory Board. Third, overseeing the chain as a whole was the UniHealth system board; large expenditures and major capital programs were undertaken only with the UniHealth system board's approval. None of California Hospital's board members were also members of the Unihealth system board. Consequently, although California Hospital's board of directors remained active, it approved programs and expenditures with the oversight of the board of governors, the UniHealth administration, and the Unihealth system board.

There were other costs of belonging to a system as well. The hospital's CEO pointed out that "UniHealth is large and moves slowly. The needs of the individual hospital and the corporation need to be balanced. Our goals may be different from those of the corporation."

Indeed, as in every corporation of considerable size, the distance between the central office and the branches was fraught with tension. UniHealth's corporate offices were located in suburban Burbank, a thirty-minute freeway ride and several communities and cultures away from California Hospital in downtown Los Angeles. California Hospital's needs were considered in the context of a system that included newer, more profitable members. As a California Hospital board member observed, "There was a shift from local autonomy to the 'we versus they' phenomenon. Now, it is Big Brother we have to deal with. The reality is that we are dependent upon UniHealth to get rid of our large debt." However, the continuing willingness of the UniHealth system board to bail out its weakest financial member remained a question, and California Hospital's directors were not optimistic on that score. The system's board might reasonably choose to hoard system surpluses in the expectation that managed care would continue to threaten the bottom line in even the more prosperous of its affiliates.

Another governance issue to which certain hospital staff were sensitive concerned the composition of the hospital's board of directors. How could the hospital function effectively as a community-based institution, they asked, when members of the community it served were not on the board? The eighteen members of the California Hospital board were almost exclusively white, male, and professional, as were the fourteen members of the system's board. Only one member of each board had a Spanish surname like so many of the hospital's patients. To bring the hospital leadership closer to its local clientele, a President's Council of neighborhood residents met twice annually with the hospital CEO and several hospital board members. The council provided a forum for reviewing health needs and services and for airing other mutual concerns. However, at both the hospital and system levels, board members were more likely to be knowledgeable about insurance regulations than about the needs of a local population.

Ernilyn Navarro's Presentation

Standing at the head of the long, oval boardroom table, Navarro began with a brief historical summary of the Health Ministry program. It had grown out of a program in Chicago that was based on observations of the medical care system in China. In the Chinese system, village and regional health care providers are involved intensively in education, immunization, and health screening. This approach reduces overall costs and makes better use of scarce and costly technologies, facilities, and highly trained professionals. Originally designed to serve senior citizens, the program had serendipitously become a key to reaching African American and Hispanic populations in South Central Los Angeles.

The Health Ministry had begun as the Parish Nurse program—following the Chicago model—with outreach to local churches. When secular organizations wanted to become involved, the program was broadened in scope and was renamed the Health Ministry. Outreach now included six regular sites at churches, as well as ad hoc health screenings at schools, clinics, and local senior centers and residential facilities. The program was started with a grant from the Good Hope Foundation to support community health outreach activities. For the current year, it was being supported by the hospital on an experimental basis, but before the next fiscal year a decision would be made about whether to make it a permanent service of the hospital.

Initially, a single parish nurse was hired and sent to Chicago for training. The parish nurse has four roles: to serve as a health educator to congregations; to serve as a health counselor to individuals, providing advice about whether to seek care for medical problems; to teach volunteers to assist congregations; and to organize community support groups around health problems of common interest to parishes. The parish nurse is a cross between a grassroots organizer and a direct caregiver. She works with volunteers, congregations, and others to empower them to meet their health needs.

The Health Ministry presently employs five nurses part-time. Using the list of ministers maintained by the hospital's Pastoral Care program, they contact local churches. The Health Ministry is sold as an adjunct to what the churches already do. Churches traditionally have spiritual and social ministries, Navarro explained; the Health Ministry allows them to extend healing to the physical aspect of their parishioners' lives. Selling the program is not difficult.

An example of the Health Ministry in action is the weekly visit one nurse makes to St. Thomas's Church, five miles away. The church has ten thousand members, most of whom are Central Americans who are uninsured or underinsured for health services and medical care. The hospital pays the nurse and supplies the equipment; the church supplies the office space. Parishioners are seen for a variety of ailments but mostly for preventive care. These patients wind up in our emergency room anyway, Navarro continued, wishing more of the directors would meet her eye. Through the Health Ministry, they are given education about access, their eligibility for services or coverage, and preventive practices.

The parish nurse provides articles for the church bulletin on seasonal topics such as dehydration in babies during the summer or immunization for seniors during the fall. The nurse also helps arrange health fairs to provide information and screening and makes common cause with other organizations in the same business, such as the American Cancer Society (which provides prostate cancer screening) and the American Diabetes Association.

The program is tough to staff, Navarro continued. The churches want a real hospital nurse, but like other hospital personnel, nurses are trained to value and believe in in-patient care, or at least in care that happens within the walls of the hospital. The staff need to be reeducated to value activities such as health screening and helping out at health fairs. Recruiting volunteers is also difficult because ideally the nurse should be bilingual and such persons are rare. Furthermore, the program requires that nurses work in downtown areas and central residential neighborhoods, where crime and poverty are high.

The Health Ministry is a way of marketing the hospital, Navarro assured the board. The program is expanding (Table 12.2). Plans include another Catholic church, a Lutheran church, and a Baptist church. The fit with the neighborhood seems good. The average California Hospital patient will not go to large, flashy institutions, which intimidate them. They would rather go to a clinic environment, and that is just what the Health Ministry provides.

Navarro went on to ask rhetorically, How can we document the returns to the hospital? The nurses can count the number of parishioners seen or contacted or the number of health fairs planned and held. Projecting in dollars how the hospital will benefit is difficult at this point, but in the long run the program will seem very inexpensive. Why? Because the population we work with will not read ads in the newspapers or respond to TV and radio. We need to get out in the community and build trust so that when people need help, they will come to California Hospital. Navarro then added the punch line recommended by the hospital's CEO: If health reform ever turns the underinsured and uninsured into consumers of health services, they will be at California Hospital's door.

Her presentation finished, Ernilyn Navarro resumed her seat.

The Health Ministry and California Hospital's Strategic Objectives

A member of the board of governors who sat on California Hospital's board then spoke up. After complimenting Navarro politely, he turned to the rest of the California Hospital board members.

The real issue, he said, is not whether some folks in local churches are being helped by this charitable program. Instead, the real issue is whether public health and primary care should be the core mission of the UniHealth system. As the system has embarked upon its effort to re-engineer and streamline the system's hospitals, a guiding principle has been the goal of operating in the black. The real issue is to make moves that will generate revenues, bring national prominence to the system, and focus on programs and services like obstetrics-gynecology, the well-respected emergency room, and other profitable programs. Nor is it sufficient to be self-sustaining. Programs that survive must generate the revenues needed for survival, growth, and reinvestment. Unless the Health Ministry program could demonstrate such revenues, he would recommend that it be eliminated. Frankly, he concluded, I would rather hear about contracting with a multispecialty medical group that could attract more paying patients.

The boardroom was silent for some moments, and then California Hospital's CEO began to speak. Every hospital in the United States, he said, is trying to position itself for developments in health reform. Although it is difficult to show a return on the Health Ministry today, the program is consistent with this hospital's mission, and it does serve a strategic purpose. "We simply can't sit back and wait," he continued, scanning the directors' impassive faces. Certainly the state of California is not waiting. This year has seen passage of the toughest law yet requiring nonprofit hospitals to provide "community benefits" to retain charitable status (Exhibit 12.2). In pursuing its present mission, the CEO pointed out, California Hospital was leading the way in satisfying the state's expectations.

> As we all know [he continued], our clientele in this part of South Central are the transitional immigrants who have always come to Los Angeles first, legals and illegals. Our services are like none they have ever experienced in their lives. The churches in our area are crying out for support.
>
> We are in this area to break even. The cost of the Health Ministry is minimal. It's only 1.7 FTEs[1] right now, though it is growing.

---

1.   One full-time equivalent (FTE) is calculated at approximately $55,000 per year.

For the future, much will depend upon reimbursement patterns. We in the administration look to the board to assist us in making sense of the overall strategic objective of California Hospital, which is "To remain financially viable providing quality services to those who need it in a way that is culturally sensitive."

Folding his hands on the papers before him, the CEO concluded that on large budget items the hospital administration must adhere to the mandates of the UniHealth corporate office. But with a small program like the Health Ministry, which would not normally merit the attention of the corporate office, he felt the California Hospital board might want to take a more independent position. "As members of the California board," he said, "you are faced with a tough decision. Will you continue to support the needs of this community or will you support mandates of the corporate office that do not serve the best interests of this community? With your vote on the Health Ministry program, that is the choice you will be making."

Questions for Discussion

1. Why has the CEO chosen to make a high-profile issue of the Health Ministry?
2. As a board member of California Hospital, what do you believe is the right thing to do? What opportunities and constraints are associated with your view? How will you actually vote in the board meeting?
3. If you are member both of the California Hospital board and the Unihealth System Board of Governors, can you advocate for fiscal conservatism while at the same time supporting local outreach programs like the Health Ministry?
4. Assume you are a trustee of the UniHealth system board and a motion before the board calls for the closure of California Hospital. What would your response be based on this case? To whom is a member of the UniHealth system board accountable?
5. Based on this case, how should the health needs of the inner city be provided for?
6. The U.S. hospital "business" is much different from other non-profit "industries" in its complexity and extent of corporatization.

Note that corporatization—the merging of hospitals and related entities into larger systems—is a response to threats to survival. With that response, however, traditional missions or local needs may fall by the wayside. Can you identify this trend in other types of charitable nonprofits? Are there areas in which corporatization could aid in the survival of nonprofits without threatening traditional or local missions?

Exhibit 12.1. California Hospital Medical Center Mission Statement.

California Hospital Medical Center has been a member of the downtown Los Angeles community since 1887 and is committed to improving the health status and increasing access to care for the multiethnic population of Central and South Central Los Angeles, while maintaining its presence in the communities it has traditionally served. As an affiliate of the nonprofit UniHealth system, California Hospital Medical Center utilizes both UniHealth and community resources to create a network of care providing a broad range of basic services and areas of specialization that reflect the particular needs of the community. To achieve financial viability, the hospital works with its physicians, payors, and employees in the creation of a climate of mutual opportunity and shared destiny encouraging innovative, cost-effective approaches to the process of continuous quality improvement.

- California Hospital Medical Center exists to serve the health care needs of both downtown and South Central Los Angeles.
- We are committed not only to improving the health of those communities but to increasing the access of care.
- Our emphasis is on primary care services as exemplified by our family practice, obstetrical services, ambulatory clinics, and large Emergency Department.
- We are committed to working cooperatively with employees, physicians, and the health planners through which patients access care.
- We are committed to the process of Continuous Quality Improvement.

Table 12.1. Revenues and Expenses,
California Hospital, 1991 and 1993.ᵃ

Revenues	1991	1993
Net patient service revenues	$82,926	(not available)
Investment and other income	$3,736	(not available)
Total Revenues	$86,662	$100,000
Costs and Expenses	$110,410	$97,400
Excess of expenses over revenues	($23,748)	$2,600

ᵃFigures in thousands.

Sources: 1991 data taken from financial audit by Ernst and Young dated January 3, 1992. This simplified report contains neither losses associated with certain subsidiaries nor much other detailed information. 1992 data taken from personal communication, Steven Adams, Chief Financial Officer, UniHealth.

Figure 12.1. The Relationship of California
Hospital to UniHealth.

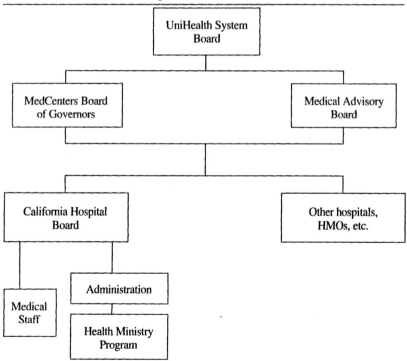

Table 12.2. Summary of Health Ministry Activities.

Category	Number
Total regular service sites:	6 churches
Total personnel involved:	5 part-time nurses, one coordinator, one manager
Annual budget:	$96,000[a]
Persons served:	240 per month at 6 regular sites[b] and 80–150 people at occasional health screenings

[a]Prorated from expenditures for the last quarter of 1994; will increase as additional sites are developed.

[b]Based on a report of 8–12 walk-in patients per site per week at a developed site (10 patients x 4 weeks x 6 sites).

Exhibit 12.2. New California Community Benefit Requirements.

Under a new California law, every not-for-profit in the state must:

By July 1, 1995:	Reaffirm or revise its mission statement to reflect the public interest.
By January 1, 1996:	Complete a community needs assessment.
By April 1, 1996:	Adopt a community benefits plan and update the plan on an annual basis.
By January 1, 1996:	Submit copies of the plan for each fiscal year starting on or after January 1, 1996.

In turn, the California Statewide Office of Health Planning and Development must:

By January 1, 1996:	Make all submitted community benefit plans available to the public.
By October 1, 1997:	File a report with the state legislature regarding hospital compliance with the

new law and recommendations for improving the law or provisions of community benefits[a] themselves.

---

[a]Community benefits include charity care, bad debt, Medicare and Medicaid shortfalls, financial support of public health programs, donations of time, money, or services, and community health and education programs.

Suggested Readings

Bryson, J. *Strategic Planning for Public and Nonprofit Organizations: A Guide to Strengthening and Sustaining Organizational Achievement.* San Francisco: Jossey-Bass, 1988. Useful guide to governance activities as they relate to strategic planning and choice. See Chapter Three for a schematic diagram of steps to follow in planning.

Hale, J. A., and Hunter, M. M. From *HMO Movement to Managed Care Industry: The future of HMO's in a Volatile Healthcare Market.* Excelsior, Mich.: Interstudy, 1988. Short collection of charts and tables showing regional and national trends in managed care. A source of up-to-date information for anyone making decisions about hospitals and health organizations.

Hammer, M., and Champy, J. *Re-engineering the Corporation.* New York: HarperCollins, 1993. Has inspired large profit-making and nonprofit hospitals alike to reduce programs and budgets, sometimes creating fear among employees whose positions may be eliminated as a result of "re-engineering." See Chapter Two.

Umbdenstock, R. J., and Hageman, W. M. (eds). *Critical Readings for Hospital Trustees.* Chicago: American Hospital Association, 1991. Essential reading list for first-time and continuing trustees in the areas of the board's role and function, relations with the CEO, relations with the medical staff, and health care payment and policy issues. See especially Chapter Two on critical areas for effective governance.

Williams, S. J., and Torrens, P. R. (eds). *Introduction to Health Services.* (4th ed.) Albany, N.Y.: Delmar, 1993. Provides readers with basic information about the history, structure, and finance of hospitals and other health organizations. See Chapter Six on hospitals, Chapter Eleven on finance, and Chapter Thirteen on managed care.

Strategic Planning at AIDS Project Los Angeles

Christy L. Beaudin
Mark Senak
Ronald C. Goodstein

In early 1993, the board of directors of AIDS Project Los Angeles (APLA) began the process of developing a long-term strategic plan to address the increasingly diverse needs of persons with human immunodeficiency virus (pwHIV) and persons with acquired immune deficiency syndrome (PWAs). Assisting the board in this undertaking was the executive management team (EMT) and the Planning Department. The agency had no previous experience with strategic planning, a circumstance not uncommon among AIDS service organizations (ASOs). As a first step toward developing a three-to-five-year strategic plan, a consultant from Washington, D.C., was hired to advise the board regarding APLA's capacity to begin the planning process. After an initial assessment, the consultant suggested that APLA was not ready to begin planning and should better understand the current and future needs of its clients. Simultaneously, the board was also undertaking a search for a new executive director because its incumbent chief executive officer would be leaving in December 1993.

At that time, the APLA board, administration, and employees were divided in their views and preferences about the strategic direction the organization should take. Some wanted to reclaim the personal, client-oriented practices of the past; for instance, eliminating the voice mail system would enable clients to phone and talk directly with a human voice. Administration was wrestling with balancing the differing needs of employees and clients. Employees felt they needed more human and financial resources to serve clients. Clients, however, felt that too much money was being spent on administrative overhead and staff and not enough money was being expended on direct services. Some thought that in addition to providing social services APLA should create social opportunities for persons with HIV/AIDS by building a gym or starting a club. Board members, however, had the enormous responsibility of generating enough funds through private and public sources to sustain all programs over the long term or, alternately, of restructuring and downsizing.

The thought of reducing the availability of services was troubling. Over the past several years, the demand for social services by diverse groups of people at risk or already infected with HIV had increased. However, many in the AIDS community were weary of APLA's annual galas for the wealthy set, each bigger than the last. Also, the apparent decrease in public interest in the epidemic threatened agencies like APLA that relied on private contributions. The potential problem of "donor fatigue" was compounded by the death from AIDS of many original supporters who volunteered time or donated money to ASOs.

The Needs Assessment

In the summer of 1993, the board again retained outside help, this time hiring a group of consultants to conduct a wide-ranging needs assessment in line with the recommendation of the organization's newly formed Planning Department. The assessment would focus on client needs and provide data to help identify possible strategic directions for future programs and services. According to the board chair, "We decided to hire a consulting firm to assess what APLA does well, what it thinks it does well, and what we know doesn't work." The board and the EMT wanted a plan that reflected their concern about human dignity and quality of life not only for people with AIDS but also for those in the earliest stages of HIV disease.

Several evaluation research activities—a client phone survey, client focus groups, one-on-one employee interviews, employee focus groups, and a mail survey of thirty HIV/AIDS community agencies—were completed concurrently during the period July-September, 1993. Also during this period, a survey assessed the need for education programs on prevention and early intervention. Market research was conducted, and a survey of employees was undertaken to clarify job-related duties and responsibilities in the context of a salary and wage analysis. Board retreats were also held with a strategic planning focus.

According to clients participating in the needs assessment, APLA had done above average to excellent work overall in providing client services. Clients gave high ratings for staff friendliness, a caring attitude, and meeting clients' personal needs. Departments receiving positive marks included Insurance/Public Benefits, Necessities of Life, Dental Services, Publications (provided by both the Materials Development Department and the Communications Division), and Treatment Education (Figure 13.1). Programs receiving mixed marks were Legal Services, Case Management, Intake, and Mental Health. Clients registered dissatisfaction with lack of easy access to programs, waiting time for callbacks, and consistency of staff responses to questions. In summary, client dissatisfaction with APLA appeared to be program specific, rather than agency based.

Incongruence also appeared to exist between what the agency overall and certain departments felt they provided and what clients and community agencies felt was delivered. The lack of consensus between APLA providers and consumers stemmed from misunderstandings about eligibility criteria for certain APLA programs, differing perceptions about what constituted timely service delivery, unhelpful attitudes of some staff, and waiting lists for services. The voice mail phone system exacerbated the problem. Many felt that voice mail disabled them and added to their personal stress when trying to solve a problem. Both clients and staff from community agencies wanted to talk to a human voice. Although it was natural for bureaucratization and professionalization to emerge as APLA developed and matured, the organization's constituents yearned for the personal touch of the early years. Paradoxically, these same people expected APLA to be strong and take care of all people with HIV/AIDS who needed help.

The needs assessment also identified several employee concerns that affected the organization as a whole, and the board and the EMT feared that these attitudes might contribute to tensions during the strategic planning process. Most significantly, staff believed that care of clients was hampered by territoriality, staff turnover, and competition and infighting over resources. While employees felt "We are here to serve people with AIDS," they questioned the strategies used by the organization to adapt services to meet client needs. They reported that APLA adequately provided for the basic needs of PWAs but that breakdowns occurred in providing a continuum of care that was informative, accessible, and consistently delivered. Given employees' desire to be humane, they were distressed by the bureaucratization of internal operations and by interdepartmental relationships that could lead to competition instead of cooperation. Staff often became "protectionists" to maintain their own programs and self-interests.

At the same time, staff noted the need for professionalization. Some felt that co-workers were placed in positions for which they had not received adequate training. Communication styles and poor information systems led to duplication in efforts. Growth in the number and types of APLA employees and departments mirrored the growth and specialization of the organization, but employees reported that competition for resources together with their lack of knowledge about what other departments provided led to compromised teamwork and lack of clear responsibility in problem solving for clients.

Employees were concerned about attrition among their ranks. Reasons for leaving APLA included burnout, noncompetitive salaries, inadequate wages and benefit packages, the desire to work in a small, grassroots organization, and infighting among staff and departments. Although the attrition rate for staff was decreasing over time, the permanence of AIDS led to the same frustration and anger among staff at APLA as at other organizations providing HIV/AIDS services. Furthermore, although APLA employees appreciated their organization's ability to raise money, they also felt entitled to direct the board and management in decisions about how and where the money was allocated.

Issues raised by employees constituted internal obstacles to the strategic planning process. External obstacles included changes in the disease, in the resources available to combat it, and in the organizations serving its victims. As the board began to reevaluate APLA's present mission (Exhibit 13.1), these external factors came forcibly to its attention:

- Most AIDS organizations had been founded in response to a crisis that many believed would be resolved before the end of its first decade. Instead, the numbers of pwHIV and PWAs had grown. Many ASOs had evolved from traditional, voluntary grassroots organizations into more formalized organizations touched by the influences of bureaucratization and professionalization.
- HIV had changed from a disease affecting a single population at risk to one affecting multiple populations including women, children, injecting drug users, and specific ethnic groups (for example, Hispanics and African Americans). The ASO consumer required redefinition.
- Extended life expectancy for pwHIV and PWAs had created the need for expanded chronic, long-term health and social services. The availability of chemotherapeutic regimens in the late 1980s and the development of community-based support services had contributed to AIDS becoming more a life-threatening disease than an immediately fatal one.
- The continuum of care required by PWAs was no longer concentrated in end stage and palliative support services. Programs addressing psychosocial needs were required to provide financial and legal assistance, public benefits and insurance counseling, food, housing, social support, and mental health treatment as well as education on prevention, early intervention, and treatment.
- Changes in the virus itself had contributed to an increased rate of reinfection by variant strains of HIV among PWAs, thus increasing the need for education about early intervention and prevention.
- The number of underinsured PWAs had increased. In both the public and private sectors, coverage and benefit levels had decreased because of cost-cutting measures. The result was more out-of-pocket expenses for medical care and less disposable money for the consumer to pay for the basic necessities of life.
- Economic conditions had contributed to unemployment of PWAs, resulting in loss of income and of disability and health care benefits. These conditions contributed to homelessness.

- A growing proportion of pwHIV were found among the chronically mentally ill, the chronically homeless, and newly released prisoners. By virtue of having AIDS, these individuals were provided assistance through HIV/AIDS care while otherwise they would have had no source of coordinated health and social services. As a result, ASOs had to contend with a broader range of social problems than those originally presented by the epidemic.

- Given the greater demand for AIDS-related social services by a broader spectrum of individuals for longer periods of time, public interest and consequently donor interest in the epidemic were decreasing. This development was especially threatening to agencies largely reliant on private contributions rather than government support.

- HIV and AIDS were no longer urban phenomena. In the future, the increasing incidence and prevalence of the disease in suburban and rural areas would affect the outreach efforts of ASOs and complicate resource allocation and equitable geographic access to health and social services.

In sum, client needs had shifted over time from primarily crisis response services (that is, education and palliative care) to long-term personal support services. A broad range of services was now required by pwHIV/PWAs, reflecting a wide variety of health and psychosocial issues.

The Organization

In 1993, APLA was the largest among a diversified group of some two hundred nonprofit and government organizations responsible for providing HIV/AIDS services to the 8.5 million residents of Los Angeles County who live in a geographic area covering four thousand square miles. Founded in 1981 by members of Los Angeles' gay community, APLA initially operated out of a founder's apartment with one telephone hotline staffed entirely by volunteers, who provided information (what little was available) to concerned callers. In 1983, APLA became a formal nonprofit organization and a prototype for other Los Angeles ASOs. Once a grassroots organization, by 1993 APLA had become the second largest ASO in the country and remained a cultural identifier of the LA gay community.

APLA had $19 million in revenue in 1993 and, with a paid staff of 214, had become more professionalized and more bureaucratic than in its early days. In 1993, it moved from rented 55,000-square-foot premises to an immense, ten-million-dollar, three-story, 127,000-square-foot building for which a Hollywood magnate donated a million dollars to provide the 10 percent required to obtain a mortgage. Formerly a movie and sound studio, the new home of APLA became symbolic of the institutionalization of AIDS for those who had believed that the disease would be cured before the end of the century.

In addition to providing a full range of social and support services to over four thousand clients annually in Los Angeles County, APLA in 1993 also maintained a large public policy department at its main location and three full-time lobbyists in Sacramento. APLA's preeminence as a service provider to PWAs was supported by a client who stated, "You get HIV and the first thing you hear about is APLA" (Exhibit 13.2).

Clients

As of 1992, the cumulative total of AIDS cases in the United States was 253,448. Of these cases, 88 percent were male, 52 percent Caucasian, and 57 percent gay/bisexual. In Los Angeles County, the cumulative total was 17,120, of which 96 percent were male, 70 percent Caucasian, and 79 percent gay/bisexual. The APLA client profile was similar in 1993—mostly gay (75 percent) and male (94 percent) but slightly more diverse in ethnic distribution (Table 13.1). Caucasians represented the majority, but the APLA caseload had continued to shift and included increasing numbers of African Americans and of Hispanics whose first language was Spanish.

Clients and consumers of APLA services, programs, and products included individuals, their significant others/family, and the community at large, including schools, business and industry, media sources, public officials, research organizations, health care professionals, civic organizations, pharmaceutical companies, government organizations, and community agencies. Although APLA required a physician-certified AIDS diagnosis to register, the roster of registered clients actually included individuals who were pwHIV symptomatic and asymptomatic, those who were certified but did not use APLA services, and those who were certified and did use APLA services. Some clients confessed to collusion with physicians to certify an AIDS diagnosis in order to become eligible for APLA services they would not actually need until a later time. Clients with an AIDS diagnosis fell into two categories: those with a case manager and those without. The advantage of having a case manager was one-stop shopping, in which the client had a central point of contact rather than being transferred from department to department or leaving messages on faceless voice mail and awaiting a callback from staff. However, this convenience was available to only 7 percent of clients.

Many registered APLA clients viewed their disease as a continuum reflecting the clinical manifestations they were experiencing. Sometimes they were HIV positive but asymptomatic while at other times they had AIDS or were HIV positive and symptomatic. Most clients waited about eight months from time of diagnosis to register. A redefinition of AIDS by the Centers for Disease Control in 1992 increased the numbers of the newly diagnosed in LA, and by July 1993, APLA had registered 1,916 new clients, increasing the client base to 3,298. Most clients were between twenty-five and forty-four, an age category in which AIDS is the third leading cause of death among men.

Resources

Revenue and Expenses

APLA's fundraising track record was impressive, and since its founding, the organization had raised more than $77 million. Gay bars and discos were the sites of early fundraising efforts. The organization sponsored the world's first AIDS Walk in 1985. With Rock Hudson's disclosure of his AIDS, Elizabeth Taylor led a campaign in the entertainment community and promoted what is now the annual "Commitment to Life" event, which by 1993 raised some $3 million annually.

The primary individual donor base for APLA during the early

years was gay white men. Over time, the major source of revenue, which for some years had been derived from individual and corporate contributions and grants from funding organizations such as United Way, shifted to a base cemented in fundraising events (Table 13.2). For fiscal year 1992, over 50 percent of the $17 million in total revenue resulted from fundraising efforts, which had increased in number from three in 1985 to seventeen by 1993. The biggest fundraising events in 1992 included Commitment to Life VI ($3.7 million gross revenue), AIDS Walk Los Angeles ($3.1 million gross), and the AIDS Danceathon ($1 million gross).

By 1992, the number of foundation and corporate contributors had grown. Conde Nast Publications, the Hearst Foundation, and the MCA Corporation each had given more than $100,000. Buddies for Life (individual donors giving more than $100,000 a year) included many celebrities and many hundreds of lesser known individual donors. Another source of APLA revenue was government grants. The Ryan White Comprehensive AIDS Resources Emergency Act of 1990 was one source of such funds, but it was to be up for legislative renewal in 1995. Ryan White funds had helped support case management and dental care, and how those programs would be supported if Ryan White funds were not available beyond 1995 was unclear. Another concern was the increased competition for funding among HIV/AIDS providers in Los Angeles. As the population of pwHIV and PWAs swelled, so did the ranks of organizations created to meet their needs. To work successfully in an environment of scarce funds, APLA would have to pursue two somewhat conflicting strategies: (1) cooperation and collaboration with other organizations and (2) unique positioning in relation to other LA AIDS organizations.

Employees

In 1993, APLA had eight divisions: Community Support Services, Client Services, Education and Training, Human Support Services, Communications, Planning, Public Policy, and Development. Of its 214 employees, the largest percentage (89 employees) worked in Client Services. Other estimated employee numbers available were Community Support (29), Education and Training (24), Development (15), Human Support Services (29), Chief Financial

Officer (5), Public Policy (8), Communications (7), Planning (3), Chief Operating Officer (1), and CEO (4). Of the $13.2 million operating expenses in 1992, 63 percent was spent on client services, 13 percent on education and training, 13 percent on development, 6 percent on public policy, and 5 percent on administration (the latter representing the sum of costs from throughout the organization).

Volunteers

The 1980s witnessed an explosion in the number of volunteer workers, who compensated for the lack of government and private funding to pay staff to provide AIDS-related services. Still dependent on volunteer labor in 1993, APLA maintained a volunteer pool of more than two thousand people, and the number of hours they volunteered increased each year. Since 1990, the agency had annually trained more than a thousand new volunteers, who provided 151,148 documented volunteer hours from July 1992 to June 1993. In 1992 and 1993, the service areas with the highest utilization of volunteer services were special events (51,096 hours per year), the Buddy Program (22,285 hours per year), the Hotline (15,862 hours per year), Necessities of Life (14,106 hours per year), and Office Services (13,481 hours per year).

Leadership

The first board of directors, formed in January 1983, secured Section 501(c)(3) status for APLA. For the next five years, the elected chairs of the board reflected the organization's grassroots origins. In 1988, when the organization experienced the first financial stresses resulting from its growth, a business leader was brought in as chair, and the board began to turn away from micromanagement of day-to-day operations. However, with no strategic plan in place, the board had little to do beyond fundraising. In early 1990, it began to focus on governance and what its responsibilities might be in the future. By 1992–1993, the Hollywood influence on the board was apparent in the corporate base of its membership and in the view of some members that governance required commitments beyond check writing.

By 1993, the board had grown to twenty-seven directors, all volunteers. Members included representatives from the gay community, LA's business and civic leadership, and APLA constituencies (that is, the executive director, one client, and one employee). The board was 74 percent male, 59 percent gay/lesbian, 19 percent HIV positive, and 78 percent Caucasian. Vocationally, executives from the entertainment industry (movie and television) constituted the largest percentage of members. The remainder consisted largely of upper-level managers from nonprofit consulting, clergy, law, medicine, retail, and banking. The board's primary tasks were fundraising, policy development and implementation, strategic planning, and the hiring, firing, and oversight of the CEO.

The board had five officers and six working committees, one of which was the Planning Committee. Initially involved in reviewing programs, the committee ventured into the realm of strategic planning in 1993 by initiating the needs assessment. This assessment was one of APLA's first organized efforts to deal with the uncertainty of HIV/AIDS as a disease and with the certainty of finite resources with which to address the growing numbers and needs of clients.

As APLA's range of service delivery expanded, so did its need for expertise to build and maintain programs. Because the organization had become more "industry oriented" and bureaucratic, some board members—especially those who were themselves executives—felt that APLA leaders and managers should be as skilled as those found in the private sector. Opportunities for mobility and levels of compensation should be competitive enough to attract experienced professionals, they believed, and in 1992 APLA's CEO was paid $143,400, in comparison to five-figure salaries for his executive counterparts at other HIV/AIDS agencies. The board members' attitudes were not shared by many APLA clients and by organizations in the HIV/AIDS community dedicated to the ideals of AIDS care as a grassroots phenomenon. They did not believe that the "corporatization" of AIDS, together with the skills and expertise necessary to manage a large organization, implied the need for more highly educated and higher-paid professionals in upper management.

In December 1993, the formidable fundraiser who had been hired as CEO of APLA for a two-year period completed his contract and left the agency. In response to the preferences of the EMT and other employees, the board focused on identifying a successor with the leadership and management skills required to take the agency "down a more client-driven road."

While the executive search was taking place, the planning process was to be continued. The issues of resources and leadership were to be examined in the context of AIDS statistics, which would influence priority setting for new programs, maintenance of old programs, or termination of current programs (Exhibit 13.3). However, by the end of 1993, the board and the EMT had been challenged in taking even their first steps toward the development of a concrete strategic plan. The plan was theoretically being developed by the board with the assistance of the EMT, but on a practical basis it had to be at least minimally acceptable to clients and other APLA constituencies. However, balancing the needs of the clients, working with employees to implement change, and meeting the expectations of the community were not proving to be an easy task.

Questions for Discussion

1. What approaches might you employ to organize the strategic planning process? Who would be involved? What would they be expected to do?
2. What are the critical issues to be considered during the planning process?
3. What mechanisms would you recommend for monitoring the outcome(s) of the strategic planning process?
4. What should be APLA's response to the changing face of AIDS? Develop the outline of a plan for APLA of no more than five pages.
5. How might environmental trends threaten future opportunities?

Exhibit 13.1. The AIDS Project Los Angeles Mission Statement.

The purpose of AIDS Project Los Angeles is to support and maintain the best possible quality of life for persons in Los Angeles County with AIDS and AIDS-related illness and their loved ones by providing and promoting public and privately-funded vital human

Figure 13.1. APLA Organizational Chart (as of July 1993).

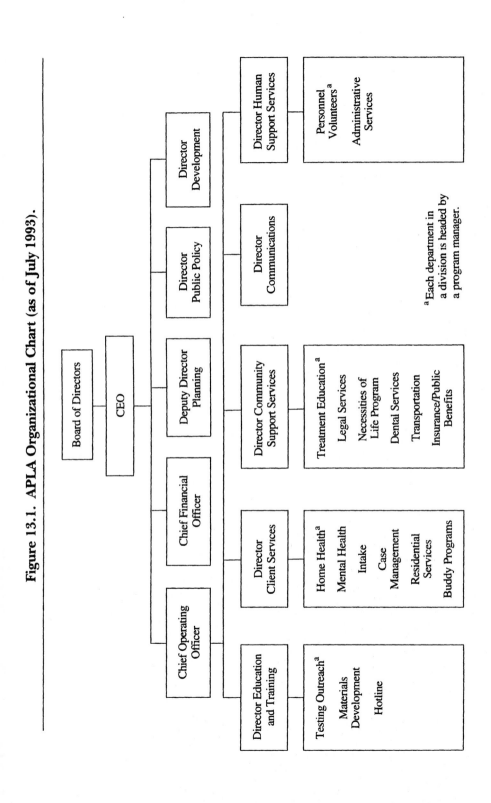

Board of Directors

CEO

Chief Operating Officer | Chief Financial Officer | Deputy Director Planning | Director Public Policy | Director Development

Director Education and Training | Director Client Services | Director Community Support Services | Director Communications | Director Human Support Services

Testing Outreach[a]
Materials Development
Hotline

Home Health[a]
Mental Health
Intake
Case Management
Residential Services
Buddy Programs

Treatment Education[a]
Legal Services
Necessities of Life Program
Dental Services
Transportation
Insurance/Public Benefits

Personnel Volunteers[a]
Administrative Services

[a] Each department in a division is headed by a program manager.

services for them; to reduce the overall incidence of Human Immunodeficiency Virus (HIV) infection by providing risk-reduction education and information to persons primarily affected by and at risk for AIDS, and the general public; to reduce the levels of fear and discrimination directed toward persons affected by AIDS, and to enhance and preserve the dignity and self-respect of those persons by providing and promoting the critically needed education to the public, health providers, educators, business and religious leaders, the media, public officials, and other opinion leaders; and to ensure the ongoing support for all these services by involving, educating, and cooperating with a wide range of organizations and individuals in AIDS-related service provision, and by supporting effort at all levels of the public and private sectors to secure adequate development and finance of AIDS research, education, and human service programs.

Source: AIDS Project Los Angeles 1993 Annual Report.

Exhibit 13.2. APLA Programs by Division as of June 30, 1993.

Human Support Services.   Was the physical backbone of the agency with wide ranging responsibilities. It oversaw the physical plant, ensured sound employment policies, and attended to the needs of employees. It also recruited and trained over a thousand volunteers annually.

Client Services.   Provided guidance and support for clients through a variety of programs. The Intake Program assessed an incoming client's needs and referred the person to various services within the agency, supporting him/her with the Client Line, Client Contact, and Phone Buddy programs, in which clients received emotional support and acute case management by telephone. Case Management provided staff who served as resources and advocates for clients in the APLA system at large. For registered clients, Mental Health provided counseling, hospital visitation, addictive behavior counseling, and support groups; in 1993, nearly eight hundred support group sessions were conducted, serving some 1,450 persons. The Buddy Program provided services to about five hundred people over the course of the year. The Home Health Department provided some forty-nine thousand hours of attendant care to persons in their homes during the course of the year at a cost of about $613,000. Residential Services provided housing through an eight-unit apartment facility, a fourteen-bed facility, and more broadly through Section 8 Housing, which each year provided government-subsidized housing to about 650 persons who would otherwise have been homeless.

Community Support Services. Operated several programs open to PWAs who were not registered with APLA as clients but required direct support. The Necessities of Life Program, a food pantry, provided a supplement of grocery items to those who earned under $700 per month, serving over a thousand people monthly. In 1993, this program experienced an increase in utilization of 32 percent. The Dental Clinic was Southern California's only HIV-dedicated dental facility. The clinic served nearly three thousand people annually. The Transportation Program provided taxi vouchers and volunteer drivers to the hundreds of clients needing assistance in meeting their medical appointments. Legal Services assisted individuals with wills, powers of attorney, and discrimination problems. Insurance/Public Benefits assisted those needing help in securing benefits such as Supplemental Social Security Income and provided advocacy for public and private insurance coverage. Treatment Education kept track of the results of clinical trials and provided community education regarding the most current chemotherapeutic interventions.

Education and Training. Educated the public and "high risk" populations about HIV/AIDS. Two of this division's programs, the Speakers Bureau and the Hotline, had a very high profile and were staffed by volunteers. The Speakers Bureau reached over twenty-five thousand individuals through presentations and health fairs. The APLA/Southern California HIV/AIDS Hotline answered some ninety-three thousand calls from persons needing information about testing, risk education, treatment and referrals, or emotional support. The HIV Testing Outreach Program, a statewide project, provided materials to clients participating in state-funded testing and promoted outreach activities to encourage more HIV testing. The Materials Development Program produced educational materials for APLA prevention and client programs. Some eight hundred self-care manuals were distributed annually to APLA clients free of charge.

Communications.   Focused the attention of the media and the public on APLA and was also responsible for issues of public policy. This division produced a wide variety of publications to inform staff, volunteers, donors, and clients about issues that directly affected them. Four publications were produced, as well as a countywide directory of services available for people with HIV.

Planning.   Examined the epidemic from many perspectives. It provided information vital to grant applications, assisted the media in story development, and provided the board of directors and management with information about emerging trends that influenced client needs and agency services.

Public Policy.   Was responsible for APLA's participation on a national level with AIDS Action Council in Washington, D.C., its representation in the state capital, Sacramento, and its relations with gay, lesbian, and HIV/AIDS coalitions. The division promoted health care education and groups that lobbied for prevention education, funding for health services, and protection of the rights of those affected by HIV. Locally, the division coordinated testimony before the LA City Council in August 1985 that resulted in the ban on discrimination against people with AIDS. It created the "Neighborhood Network," an avenue for LA residents to mobilize and voice concerns about public policy issues. In 1993, the division sponsored a candlelight march of some five thousand participants.

Development.   Raised money; 80 percent of the funds raised came from sources other than government. This division created all the direct mail appeals and planned special events such as the Commitment to Life dinner, which in 1993 honored David Geffen and Barbra Streisand and raised $3.6 million in one evening.

Exhibit 13.3. AIDS Statistics Affecting the Strategic Planning Process.

Age.   The age category twenty-five to forty-four continues to cumulatively increase and contributes the largest number of PWAs.

Gender.   Ninety percent of AIDS cases are men; 10 percent are women, primarily Latinas and African Americans.

Ethnicity.   Among new diagnoses in 1993, the largest percentage was Caucasian. However, Hispanics have experienced the greatest intrapopulation increase. The LA County profile of new PWA

Table 13.1. Comparison of 1992 Cumulative AIDS Cases in Los Angeles County, California, the United States, and APLA.

Category	Los Angeles		California		U.S.		APLA	
	Number	%	Number	%	Number	%	Number	%
Male	16,433	96	45,619	96	223,971	88	3,521	94
Female	687	4	2,017	4	29,477	12	215	6
Latino	3,628	21	7,152	15	42,199	17	896	24
African American	2,853	17	6,289	13	75,997	30	602	16
Anglo	10,220	60	33,153	70	132,625	52	2,057	55
Asian/Pacific Islander	271	2	756	2	1,610	<1	42	1
Native American	28	<1	121	<1	448	<1	39	1
Gay/Bisexual	13,350	79	36,592	77	142,626	57	2593	69
IDUs[a]	882	5	3,110	7	57,412	23	167	5
Gay/Bisexual IDUs	1,181	7	3,955	8	15,899	6	191	5

[a]Injectable drug users.

Table 13.2. AIDS Project Los Angeles
Financial Statements for Fiscal Years 1985–1992.[a]
(000s omitted)

	1985	1986	1987	1988	1989	1990	1991	1992
Total Revenue	3,342	5,157	6,650	8,899	10,029	10,487	11,336	17,057
Direct public support[b]	2,391	2,431	3,827	5,726	6,515	3,371	4,026	5,691
Indirect public support[c]		62	90	67				
Government grants[d]	1,419	2,429	2,507	3,079	3,247	2,753	2,855	3,052
Fundraising[e]	1,834	1,134	1,435	1,122	1,172	5,448	5,775	10,277
Net Assets[f]	639	1,537	1,257	1,042	1,887	3,200	4,396	8,240
Functional Expenses[g]	2,826	4,486	6,946	8,818	9,185	9,175	10,139	13,213
Total Liabilities & Fund Balances (end of year)	910	1,942	2,832	3,073	3,726	5,359	7,869	22,124

[a]Note: Figures rounded to nearest thousand; all data derived from IRS Form 990 as filed; APLA fiscal year is July 1–June 30.
[b]Individual or corporate financial contributions and gifts.
[c]Money received from other funding organizations such as the United Way.
[d]Monies received from local, state, or federal government entities.
[e]Special events and activities that generate gross revenue, direct expenses, and net income, which is included in the organization's total revenue.
[f]Fund balances at the end of the fiscal year.
[g]Employee salaries and wages, professional fundraising fees, legal fees, supplies, telephone, postage and shipping, equipment purchase and rental, office lease/rent, printing and publications, travel and depreciation.

cases is Caucasian (43 percent), Hispanic (33 percent), African American (22 percent), and Asian (2 percent). The new APLA profile differs as follows: Caucasian (56 percent), Hispanic (26 percent), African American (17 percent), and Asian (1 percent).

Risk. The highest risk category for transmission continues to be gays. However, the categories of injectable drug users and gay injectable drug users have experienced increases since 1985.

Diagnosis. The Centers for Disease Control redefinition of AIDS in 1992 created a sharp increase in the numbers of newly diagnosed cases in LA. In 1992, the number of new cases reported monthly ranged from 196 to 344. When the revised definition was implemented in January 1993, 1,609 new cases were reported in Los Angeles; by the end of the third quarter of 1993, 4,000 new cases had been diagnosed.

Suggested Readings

Drucker, P. F. *How to Assess Your Nonprofit Organization, User Guide.* San Francisco: Jossey-Bass, 1993. Suggests asking five questions: (1) What is our business (mission)? (2) Who is our customer? (3) What does the customer consider value? (4) What have been our results? and (5) What is our plan? Workbooks for board members available with *User Guide.*

Merton, R. K. *Social Theory and Social Structure.* London: The Free Press of Glencoe, 1957. Revised edition of Merton's examination of the history and systematics of social theory, theories of the middle range, and the codification of sociological theory. See Chapters Six and Seven on structure of bureaucracy and Chapters Eight and Nine on role of reference groups.

Nutt, P. D. *Planning Methods for Health and Related Organizations.* New York: Wiley, 1984. Source book useful in teaching planning and management practice in health administration, public administration, business policy, and strategic planning. Overview of planning approaches and methods in Chapters One through Three.

Powell, W. W. (ed). *The Nonprofit Sector: A Research Handbook.* New Haven, Conn.: Yale University Press, 1987. Reviews and assesses scholarly works on nonprofit sector. See Chapter Eight on board functions and behavior; Chapter Nine on determining organizational effectiveness; and Chapter Eleven on organizational change due to internal and external processes.

Shortell, S. M., and Kaluzny, A. D. *Health Care Management: A Text in Organization Theory and Behavior.* (2nd ed.) Albany, N.Y.: Delmar, 1988. Provides an open systems theory and contingency perspective on the management of health care organizations. Examines motivation, leadership, social structure of work groups, operating technical systems, organization design, organization-environment relations, and strategic management. See especially Parts One through Five.

White, D. D., and Bednar, D. A. *Organizational Behavior: Understanding and Managing People at Work.* (2nd ed.) Needham Heights, Mass.: Allyn & Bacon, 1991. Textbook providing overview for developing and more effectively using resources to meet the challenges of organizational performance and managing people. See especially Chapter Five on productivity and motivation; Chapter Twelve on leadership; Chapter Seven on individual and group decision making; and Chapter Fourteen on quality of work life and work design.

Index

grants to, 62–71; grant requests by, 72, 73–81
Internal Revenue Code Section 501(c)(3), 16; criteria for, 32; hospital criteria for, 33

J

Janis, I. L., 164

K

Kaluzny, A. D., 240
Kozes, J. M., 148
Kramer, R. M., 10, 174

L

Lammers, J. C., 11, 190, 206
Leadership: of AIDS Project Los Angeles, 230–232; in political model of governance, 4–5. *See also* Board chair; Executive director; Governance; Governing Board
Lipsky, M., 61, 174
Local Association for Retarded Citizens (LARC). *See* Agency for retarded citizens
Loseke, D. R., 117
Luckman, T., 2

M

Management: change from collective to hierarchical, 100–105; conflict over style of, 118, 123–124, 128–137; crisis in financial, 157–162; versus governance, 3. *See also* Governance
March, J. G., 4
Marmor, T. R., 37
Merton, R. K., 240
Mets, L., 3
Mico, P. R., 148
Middleton, M., 9, 138, 205
Milofsky, C., 10, 11, 82, 95, 99, 117
Mintzberg, H., 8
Mission, 7–8; agency for retarded citizens, 52–53; anti-poverty organization, 149–150; community

foundation, 62, 72; versus hospital revenue, 206–219
Mission statement: AIDS Project Los Angeles, 232, 234; California Hospital Medical Center, 216; Community foundation, 72; Connecticut Department of Mental Retardation, 44, 59
Mitchell, S. M., 4
Mitroff, I. I., 3
Mizruchi, M., 188
Montrose City Community Theater (MCCT). *See* Community theater
Moody, L., 138
"Moonies." *See* Unification Church
Moon, S. M., 193, 196, 197
Moore, G., 11, 97, 176
Morrison, N., 11, 95, 99
Museum, 125–128; and business community, 119–121; conflict over management of, 118, 123–124, 128–137; consultant for, 124–125; governing board of, 121–122; history of, 118–119

N

Nason, J. W., 4
Networks, 9; centrality of organizations in, 180n, 181, 185–187; for diversifying board, 176–184; readings on, 188
Neubauer, F. F., 3, 6
New Frontiers Inc. (NFI). *See* Anti-poverty organization
Nohria, N., 9
Nonprofits: franchising of, 9, 164; industries of, 7; public policy regarding, 15–16; resource dependence of, 15–17; small, 82
Nonstock Corporation Act (Connecticut), 122, 127–128
Nutt, P. D., 240

O

Organizational change, 2
Organizational culture, 8

Printed in the United States
32839LVS00002B/223-231

9 780787 901394